The New Wine
Companion

D1471369

By the same authors
Wine Regions of the World

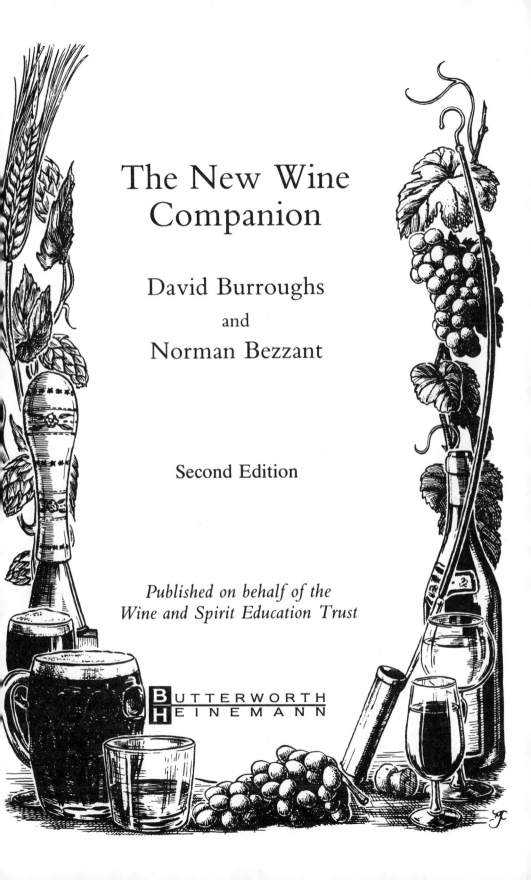

The New Wine Companion

David Burroughs

and

Norman Bezzant

Second Edition

*Published on behalf of the
Wine and Spirit Education Trust*

BUTTERWORTH
HEINEMANN

Butterworth-Heinemann Ltd
Linacre House, Jordan Hill, Oxford OX2 8DP

ℛ A member of the Reed Elsevier plc group

OXFORD   LONDON   BOSTON
MUNICH   NEW DELHI   SINGAPORE   SYDNEY
TOKYO   TORONTO   WELLINGTON

First published as *The Wine Trade Student's Companion*
and *The Wine Companion* by William Collins Sons and
Co Ltd 1975
First published by Butterworth-Heinemann Ltd 1980
Reprinted 1982, 1984, 1985, 1987
Second edition 1988
Reprinted 1993, 1994

British Library Cataloguing in Publication Data
Burroughs, David
    The new wine companion – 2nd ed.
    1. Alcoholic drinks
    I. Title   II. Bezzant, Norman   III. Wine
    and Spirit Education Trust
    641.2'1

ISBN 0 7506 1274 6

Maps by Reginald Piggot
Drawings by Virginia Smith and Martin Cottan
'Gin Lane' etching reproduced by permission of the Mary
Evans Picture Library

Printed in England by Clays Ltd, St Ives plc

Contents

Chapter 1   THE ORIGINS AND THE ROLE OF NATURE   1
Definition of wine – History of wine-making – Wine and Christianity – The English wine trade begins – Early influence of spirits – Era of Victorian Reform – Levels of production – Wine-producing areas of the world

Chapter 2   THE VINE AND THE GROWER   19
Importance of natural conditions – Microclimates and topography – Climate and soil – Vine types and propagation – How grapes become sweet – Pruning and training – Pests and diseases – Methods of grafting – The annual vineyard cycle – Ripening and harvest

Chapter 3   THE MAKING OF WINE   34
The grape – Wine yeasts and wild yeasts – Fermentation – Wine-making for red wines – Maturation, racking, and fining – Wine-making for white and rosé wines – Varying maturation periods for different wines

Chapter 4   LIGHT WINES   47
French wines – Appellation Contrôlée – Bordeaux: districts, wines, and the 1855 Classification – Burgundy, Rhône, and Loire – Alsace – German wines, districts, and wine law – Wines of Italy, Spain, and other European countries – Wines of other important world districts

List of Maps

Introduction
to the Second Edition

By Jeremy J. B. Bennett
Chairman of Trustees: Wine & Spirit Education Trust
Chairman of Council: Academy of Wine Service

David Burroughs and the Wine and Spirit Education Trust are synonymous, both dedicated to improving the knowledge of wine by the quality of instruction and the basic tools of learning.

This book is just one item, now completely revised and updated, which takes you on a tour of the vineyards of the world. It introduces you to all aspects of the manufacture of alcoholic beverages and is ideal for those who wish to make a career in the licensed trade.

David helped to form the WSET eighteen years ago after a career in the Army. He was in at the start and his natural administrative skill and instructional ability quickly developed in the Trust, providing it with an enviable reputation which has now become worldwide. In addition, the Trust advises the Academy of Wine Service, an organization set up in 1987 to instruct wine waiters and provide them with professional qualifications. This is an increasingly important requirement for the catering industry.

The authors write on 'The Social Aspects of Alcohol'. The Trustees consider that all students should have a clear understanding of the potential dangers of consuming alcohol so that they can make their own judgements. Sensible drinking is not a danger and can provide great aesthetic pleasure – but students must understand the problems. The chapter is thoughtfully written and addressed to 'everyone'.

This foreword would not be complete without mentioning Norman Bezzant. He is a 'wordsmith' of the old school producing clear and concise narrative which has been thoroughly researched and revised. The two authors have produced an extremely well-structured book full of information, up-to-date and in a style that is easy to read. It will give you pleasure in reading it and the pleasure of appreciating wine all your life.

Authors' Preface

To understand and appreciate wines, spirits, liqueurs, and beers, the reader needs to know something of each of the three stages in their lives: firstly, their origins and the sources of their ingredients; secondly, their refinement into bottles bearing any one of a thousand different labels; and thirdly, their selection for various purposes and their care in the home.

But that is not all: in a rapidly changing world, up-to-date information is a necessity, and recent changes in the world of wines and spirits are quite dramatic. To clarify the present situation, we have reviewed the whole field. This book examines the history and geography of wines, spirits, and beers, with short descriptions of life in the vineyard, the winery, the distillery, and the brewery. More immediately, there is a wealth of advice to the consumer on tasting, selecting, storing, and serving wines and spirits.

Many who read this book will do so as Trade students. To them, we recommend that they should first read through the whole book quickly, including the appendixes and glossary, but without attempting to memorize any matter and taking no notice of the footnote questions. This will give a general view of the field and show where detailed information can be found. The student should then study each page carefully, and attempt to answer the questions at the foot of each right-hand page; if he finds that he is unable to answer any question, he should search for the reference in the text he has just read. It should, however, be stressed that the appendixes and glossary contain much vital information not appearing anywhere else in the book, and in fact the answers to some questions will be found in them, or in the figures or maps appearing in the text.

The answers to the questions are given at the foot of the following page. If the student finds that he has given a wrong answer, he should again check it in the text. These running questions are also an admirable aid to revision before examinations, in which case the student may read straight through the footnotes only. Having done all this, he will be capable of passing the Certificate examination of the Trust and, if he has assimilated *all* the information, he will be well on his way to the Higher Certificate standard; but for this he will require a more detailed knowledge of the wine regions of the world, which may be found in the companion volume of that name.

1
The Origins and the Role of Nature

DEFINITION OF WINE

'Wine is the alcoholic beverage obtained from the fermentation of the juice of freshly gathered grapes, the fermentation taking place in the district of origin according to local tradition and practice.' This definition gives an excellent starting-point to the story of wine. Very many varieties have been perfected over the centuries, and without doubt wines with new characteristics are yet to be discovered, but to be classed as wines they must all obey the precepts of this definition.

The phrases 'district of origin' and 'local tradition and practice' instantly beg the question 'Where and when did it all start?' And

If you have not yet read the Authors' Preface on page xiii, you should do so now: it will help you to use the book to your best advantage.

1 Why will I find the answer to this question at the foot of the next page?
2 If the answer to a question cannot be found in the preceding text where else could it be found?

although this is a romantic story, it does not begin with 'Once upon a time' quite so much as with 'Here beginneth . . . '. For the art and skill of the wine-maker predate the written record, and it was archaeologists who discovered evidence of wine-making some twelve thousand years ago. When, later, Noah is recorded as landing with his ark on the slopes of Mount Ararat, he planted a vineyard, and was to be reproved by Jehovah for his drunkenness.

Was it such an accident that already man knew the secret of wine production, and its benefits? It will be shown in this book that in the grape, Nature herself provided a most remarkable set of prepacked ingredients in a form exceeding in ingenuity all the skills of the modern food manufacturer. It only remained for man to open the package and mix the ingredients.

THE HISTORY OF WINE-MAKING

And there, under Mount Ararat, on the southern slopes of the Caucasus Mountains, flanked by the Caspian and Black Seas, the cultivation of the vine first flourished. The making of wine originated in this area, centred on Shiraz in ancient Persia, and here the poet Omar Khayyam posed the whimsical question: 'I often wonder what the vintners buy, one half as precious as the stuff they sell . . . '.

From the Persians the craft spread southwest to Assyria, south to Babylon, and northwest to the shores of the Black Sea. The Assyrians made much of the innovation. The Babylonian king, Nebuchadnezzar, became the owner of vineyards and wine-cellars. There is even a wine list dating from that time in existence today. The Assyrians carried the craft down along the Lebanese coast and beyond to Palestine; and round the Mediterranean elbow to Egypt. Egyptian wall paintings depict the main stages in the production of wine, with the vines growing on *pergolas* or wooden trellises, much as they do today, and show the grape harvesters using sickle knives identical to those still used along the Mediterranean coast.

---

1 Because all questions appearing as footnotes are answered at the foot of the following page.
2 In the appendixes or glossary, which commence on page 203.

WINE AND RELIGION

The Psalms of King David of Israel speak often of wine and, incidentally, of the contemporary economy of the Eastern Mediterranean. Psalm 104, xv, refers to 'wine that maketh glad the heart of man, oil to make him of cheerful countenance, and bread to strengthen man's heart.' In other words, wine, olives and wheat. And here, already, can be seen a trend which has persisted through all the centuries down to the present day: the strong connection between wine and religion.

Next the Phoenicians, the seafarers from Tyre and Sidon in the Lebanon, took the vine and its secrets along the Mediterranean shores, and even beyond. Soon the Greeks and the Romans had the vine and its precious product, and each in turn dedicated a god to wine. The Greek Dionysus and the Roman Bacchus were both high-ranking deities.

The Greeks brought wine to the people, when originally it had been reserved for the lips of kings and gods, and wherever they set up a colony, from southern France to the Black Sea and from Sicily to North Africa, the vine came too. Not only did they make wine locally, but Herodotus tells of exporting wine to Egypt, while Greek wines from the islands of Chios and Lesbos even challenged the fine wines of Rome in their home city.

THE FIRST ENGLISH VINEYARDS

The Romans set about the task of wine-making with characteristic thoroughness, and were the first to acclimatize the frost-proof vines extolled by Pliny, planting them in the Bordeaux country, in the valleys of the Rhône, Marne and Seine, and along the Mosel and Rhine. They concentrated their vineyards in these and other selected areas, which were expanded and intensively cultivated. New vineyards were established not only in France but also in Hungary, Germany and England. Vines were planted in England as far north as York, and the Domesday Book records some forty vineyards left by the Romans.

Wherever the Eagle flew the Roman legions brought their own wines, made mostly in Italy and Spain, and where vineyards had

---

1 What is the first major characteristic of wine mentioned in the standard definition?
2 Metheglin, an early alcoholic drink, was made from fermented honey. Should we call this wine?

previously been planted, as for example in Carthage, they were uprooted and grain crops sown in their place. The Romans embraced Christianity, and when their empire collapsed, the early Christian missionaries carried the vine further north into Europe. They needed sacramental wines, and wherever they built a church they planted a vineyard. Christianity did not outlaw wine, like the Mohammedan religion which followed it; on the contrary, wine was the very life-blood of the Christian faith. When the Romans left England, abandoning it to the Danes and Saxons, it was the church which kept the craft of wine-making alive. Meagre wine supplies came also from Germany and Holland, through the Dutch ports.

Wine in the Dark Ages

The seventh, eighth and ninth centuries – the Dark Ages – saw little progress in wine production. In England the clergy made their wine as a matter of household catering, and for the Mass, while in Europe the Christian missionaries resisted the Barbarian hordes from eastern Europe who sacked villages, churches and vineyards alike. Substantial wine trade with the Netherlands was eventually brought to a halt

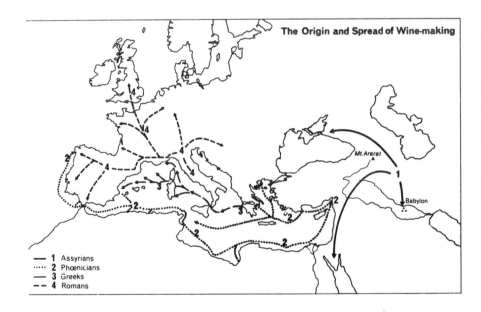

The Origin and Spread of Wine-making

— 1 Assyrians
···· 2 Phœnicians
— 3 Greeks
-- 4 Romans

1 It is alcoholic.
2 No – it was not made from fermented grape juice.

by the attacks of the Norsemen. However, the Moors, who conquered Spain, improved the culture of the vine there.

In the eleventh century the real period of expansion of the wine industry began. The Normans were now to conquer England, and they knew much about wine. But the growth of wine production and consumption did not stem only from France. The wine industry of Italy, for example, had to support a large and growing demand, and it has been estimated that Florence alone accounted for the consumption of some six million gallons a year at this time. The export of wine became an important part of contemporary trading, and sailings from the Mediterranean to Northern Europe increased as the great fairs in the cities of Northern France and the Netherlands were established.

THE ENGLISH WINE TRADE BEGINS

But it was the influence of kings which was destined to shape the wine-drinking habits of the English. In 1153, Henry Duke of Anjou (later King Henry II of England) married Eleanor of Aquitaine, and she brought him as her dowry the provinces of Gascony and Bordeaux – all the land to the south of the Loire. This was the starting-point of the English wine trade, for the people of Bordeaux wanted English wool, and paid for it in wine to a large extent. As the English could not drink it all, a great wine trade grew up with the Hanseatic states of Germany and with the Baltic, and though wine accounted for one-third of England's imports, much was re-exported.

As the French wines came in, viticulture in England fell into decay. Most of the English vineyards were uprooted to make way for more profitable crops, although monastic vineyards survived until Henry VIII seized the monasteries in the sixteenth century.

The entente with France lasted happily for some hundred and fifty years, but then came famines and plagues (including the Black Death which swept Europe) and wars in which France was our enemy or our opponent in foreign policy. During the French Wars, friendship with Spain naturally encouraged increases in Spanish wine imports.

1 In what region did the making of wine originate? Name the city at its centre.
2 The ancient Eastern Mediterranean economy was based on three commodities. What were they?
3 In ancient times, wine-drinking was the right of the privileged few. True or false?

The Treaties with Portugal

In 1353 England signed the Treaty of Windsor, establishing Portugal as England's oldest ally, and granting her great commercial advantages. England now looked also to Portugal to provide her with wine so the English market was no longer a monopoly for France. From Germany and the Low Countries came Rhenish wine, and through Genoa came Commandaria from Cyprus, and other sweet Mediterranean wines. In the sixteenth century, sack, a wine similar to present-day sherry, became the favourite wine in England, coming from Jerez and Tenerife. The discovery of America and the sea route to India, although affecting European trade profoundly, did not alter the pattern of the wine trade in the fifteenth and sixteenth centuries, as the new territories neither produced nor consumed wine.

The pattern of the English wine trade settled down, with imports mainly from Spain, Italy and Portugal, some from France, and a little from Germany and the Low Countries. However, during the seventeenth century, deterioration in the quality of Italian wines and the imposition of heavy duties on French wines decreased their importance.

As a consequence of the falling-off of French and Italian wine imports, there was an increase in the sale of relatively cheap Portuguese wine in England, a development encouraged by the Methuen Treaty of 1703, which revived the spirit of the old Treaty of Windsor, giving Portuguese wines preferential rates of duty. As a result, many English wine-merchants made their headquarters in Oporto and became so important that they set up their own courts of law there. Many descendants remain there to this day. Portuguese wine imports rose steadily during the eighteenth century, until they accounted for two-thirds of all Britain's wine imports.

Early influence of Spirits

The duty on French wine soon became sufficiently prohibitive to induce alternative drinking habits. Taxes were paid on bulk, and therefore spirits, because of their greater strength-to-bulk ratio, attracted less duty. French brandy, under James II, had become a

1 On the slopes of the Caucasus Mountains: Shiraz.
2 Wine, olives and wheat.
3 True.

popular drink by the end of the seventeenth century, but gin received a boost when William of Orange displaced the francophile James in 1688, and introduced Holland's gin which, in its worst form, even the poorest could afford.

Gin could be made cheaply in England – and was. In fact, the poverty-stricken masses took to the poisonous oblivion of gin as their only release from misery and hardship. Hogarth, in a famous cartoon depicting 'Gin Lane', showed the drunken dregs of humanity busy pawning and stealing. The sign over the gin-shop reads 'Drunk for a penny. Dead drunk 2d. Straw free' (see Fig. 1).

THE ERA OF VICTORIAN REFORM

So, as the nineteenth century dawned, the social conditions of England were appalling, as every Dickens-lover will know. But reform was round the corner. As the new century progressed, many hitherto unknown elements affected the national scene, with consequences to the wine and spirit industry. Principally, the growth of British imperial power brought a greater and more diversified trade. Imports of wine from The Cape and Australia appeared for the first time. The policy of Free Trade opened the doors of England to the world's wines and spirits, and this policy was also to be responsible – quite unconsciously – for making Britain the expert in the international wine and spirit industry. Almost every other country supported its domestic wine industry by imposing swingeing duties on imports, and in so doing denied itself this vital knowledge of the wines and spirits of other countries.

After a brief period in the middle of the century, in which Spanish wine formed a major part of Britain's wine imports, French wines again became fashionable, and were imported in quantities comparable with those from Spain and Portugal. Claret was much in demand, and in 1876 seven million gallons of French wines were imported, a record to remain unbroken until 1968.

WINE DUTIES FAIL TO BRING TEMPERANCE

The lower classes had remained faithful to cheap gin however, and strenuous efforts were made, not only to control its production and

1 Why did the Romans destroy some vineyards?
2 With the decline of the Roman empire, did the traffic in wine increase or decrease?
3 Has Britain ever grown her own grapes for wine production?
4 Where did Britain obtain her wine when Roman sources ceased?
5 When was the great period of expansion of the European wine trade?

Fig. 1 'Gin Lane' by Hogarth

Reproduced by permission of the Mary Evans Picture Library

1 To ensure grain production in Gaul and to promote Roman wines.
2 It decreased.
3 Yes, and still does in small quantities.
4 From Northern Europe, particularly through the Netherlands.
5 From the eleventh to the fourteenth century.

sale, but also to wage a war of propaganda against it. In 1860 Gladstone, Chancellor in Lord Palmerston's government, reduced the duties on light wines in an attempt to wean the lower classes off spirits. Eight years later, Gladstone's government was elected on a temperance platform, and introduced much-needed social reforms. But Gladstone failed in his attempt to introduce licensing laws in 1874. Riots ensued in London which were quelled by troops. Instead, the duty on wines was reduced again, and the basis of duty was changed. A hydrometer, devised by a customs officer named Sikes, was introduced to implement a sliding scale of duties on wines and spirits, according to strength.

The wine-merchants of the day were equal to the situation, and it is said that one toured the streets armed with tracts persuading people to 'sign the Pledge'. With the encouraging exhortation 'You can still drink Port, lad – that's not Ardent Spirits' – the wine-merchant would take an order for port on the spot. Port soon became the Englishman's wine.

INFLUENCES FOR MODERATION IN DRINKING

The nineteenth century saw the birth of the Salvation Army, which favoured total abstinence, while the Band of Hope campaigned against intoxicants, largely through the enrolment of children. The cause of temperance was however widely pleaded, for the truth was, and is, that wines and spirits in moderation never did anyone any harm and do many a great deal of good. Pasteur in particular wrote and campaigned about the health-giving qualities of wine.

And so to the twentieth century. Port had remained all the fashion since Gladstone's day and with the Portuguese Trade Treaty Acts of 1914 and 1916, the making of port was as strictly controlled by English law as by Portuguese law. By the late 'twenties, however, port started to lose its general popularity and became more associated with post-prandial drinking. Sherry became the more popular wine for social drinking.

Preferential rates of duty given to Empire wines did much to establish a steady trade with The Cape and Australia during the early years of the century.

1 Why was so much Bordeaux wine exported to England during the thirteenth and fourteenth centuries?
2 Why did the discoveries of the fifteenth and sixteenth centuries not affect the wine trade much at first?
3 What was the importance of the Methuen Treaty to the English wine trade?
4 What countries were the main suppliers of wine to England in the nineteenth century?

Causes of Change in Drinking Habits

Another influence which was quick to affect British drinking habits was the Prohibition legislation of the United States of America, which outlawed all alcoholic beverages. Spirits ousted wines on the undercover market for the very logical reason of their lesser bulk and greater 'kick'; spirits, it will be recalled, were carried in the leg of a boot. Many were of amateur origin, tasted horrid and were distinctly harmful. The taste had to be disguised; and that is how the cocktail was born. The 'cocktail habit remains with us; but today the ingredients are wholesome.

In recent years, drinking habits have been affected more and more by duty changes. Sir Stafford Cripps halved the duty on light wines in 1949, bringing them within reach of the ordinary man, and in 1958 Heathcoat Amory reduced the duty on fortified wines also, which gave a boost to this trade. But successive governments have imposed heavier duties than ever before, and this has held back expansion of sales in the better classes of wine.

In spite of this the habit of wine-drinking is spreading, and inexpensive light wine is being consumed in ever-increasing quantities, thanks partly to the 'package tour' which is taking more and more people abroad, where they drink local wines and return with a taste for them. These light wines carry less duty, many of them are very good, and their price is attractive.

The wine trade, then, has followed the explorer and the flag, and in this way the craft has been disseminated throughout the world and through the ages by the Phoenicians, Romans and Greeks; by the French, Spanish and Portuguese; by the Italians, Germans and Dutch; and in lesser degree by the late-developing countries of the other wine-producing areas of the world.

The European Economic Community

In 1957 the European Economic Community (EEC) was set up between Belgium, France, Holland, Italy, Luxembourg, and West Germany; Denmark, Great Britain, and Ireland were admitted in 1973, followed later by Greece in 1981, and by Spain and Portugal in 1987. One's own country is the *first country*, all other EEC countries

1 Because England ruled western France, including the Bordeaux region.
2 Because the new territories neither produced nor consumed wine at that time.
3 It allowed Portuguese wine to be imported into England at preferential rates of duty.
4 Portugal, Spain and France.

are *second countries*, and all non-EEC countries are *third countries*; in practice, only the last term is current.

The EEC charges a Common Customs Tariff (CCT) on goods from third countries, but no import duties are charged between member States. However, each country levies Excise Duties on goods within its borders, which explains price differences; but in any one country the same duty must apply to Scotch whisky as to French brandy, for instance.

LEVELS OF PRODUCTION

Worldwide, in 1986, over 320 million hectolitres (7,000 million gallons) of wine were produced. As one hectolitre fills 132 standard three-quarter-litre bottles, the world output is equivalent to over 42,000 million bottles a year – about ten bottles for every adult and child on earth. Much of this wine is very unstable and is not exported from its country of origin.

Four-fifths of the world's wine is produced in Europe – well over half in the (enlarged) EEC. The two countries producing most wine annually in the world are France and Italy, with just under 80 million hl each; Italy usually produces more than France, but in some years this is reversed.

Next in order comes Spain, with 37 million hl; then Argentina, USA and USSR with about 17 million; West Germany, Romania, South Africa, and Portugal follow with 8–10 million hl per year. Other significant European wine-producing countries are Hungary, Yugoslavia, and Greece with about 4 million hl each, and Bulgaria, Poland, Austria, Czechoslovakia, and Switzerland with lesser quantities. Significant producers outside Europe are Australia, Chile, Brazil, and Canada. All the other countries of the world together produce less than 13 million hl, and include such countries as Great Britain, New Zealand, Luxembourg, the North African states, China, Japan, India, Peru, and Cuba.

1 Which wines most notably grew in popularity in the period from 1925 to 1950?
2 Which countries offered England wine for the first time in the twentieth century?
3 In the Index, page numbers are printed in **black type,** *italics,* or ordinary type. What does each imply?

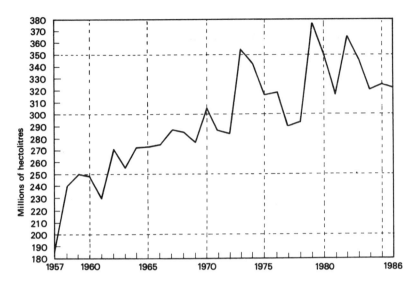

Fig. 2   World Production of Wine, 1957–1986.

FACTORS AFFECTING PRODUCTION

A review of the countries producing wine will reveal that only a relatively small area of the world is 'wine-bearing'. Vines will grow practically anywhere outside the polar regions, but their grapes will only provide juice of the quality necessary for conversion into drinkable wine where two climatic conditions prevail. Firstly, there must be enough sun to ripen the grapes. Secondly, the winter must be moderate, yet sufficiently cool to give the vine a chance to rest and restore its strength for the growing and fruiting season.

In England, for example, there is only sufficient sun to ripen a grape crop in the open in two years out of five; and it is not possible to guarantee a frost-free period when the flowers are forming.

In fact the strength of the summer sun does not become sufficient until the latitude of the Rhineland is reached, and even there the crop may easily be upset. So the northern limit of wine-making in the northern hemisphere is controlled by the first condition, the need for enough sun to ripen the grapes. This condition applies equally to the southern limit of wine-making in the southern hemisphere. This

1 Sherry, 'Commonwealth' wines, and light wines.
2 South Africa (The Cape) and Australia.
3 For your answer, please *now* read the legend, at the beginning of the index on page 227.

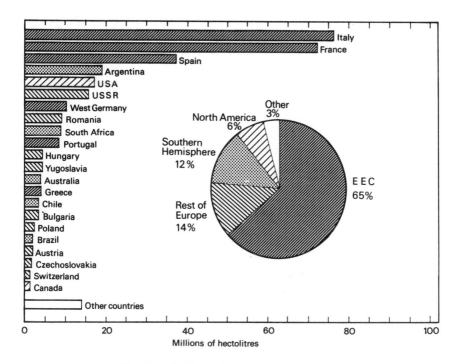

Fig. 3   World Production of Wine in 1986.

'cold' limit lies roughly at latitudes 50° north and south. On the other hand, the tropics and sub-tropics do not get a cool winter, being warm throughout the year, so that vines planted there would not have the chance to rest before the growing season. This, the second condition, therefore controls the southern limit of the 'wine belt' in the northern hemisphere and the northern limit in the southern hemisphere. The 'hot' limit lies roughly at latitudes 30° north and south. The map on page 14 shows the limitations of these northern and southern wine belts.

It may be noticed that some of the regions fall outside the specified boundaries, and also that there are large areas within them where no vineyards are shown. The reasons for this are as follows:

Land-mass: Land heats up and cools down more quickly than water, so the centre parts of the great Continents experience very cold winters and also very hot summers. These are the steppes of the

1 Why did Prohibition in America promote cocktails?
2 The world's annual production of wine in 1986 was enough for (a) 1, (b) 4, (c) 10, or (d) 14 bottles of wine for each person on earth?
3 What share of the world's annual wine production is provided by Europe as a whole?
4. Approximately what proportion of European output does Italy produce?
5. The average annual quantity of wine in millions of hl produced in Germany is about: (a) 20; (b) 10; (c) 2; (d) $\frac{1}{2}$

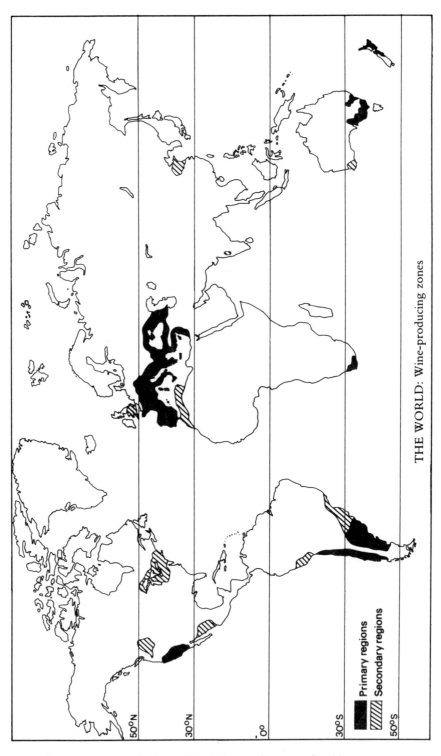

THE WORLD: Wine-producing zones

Primary regions
Secondary regions

50°N
30°N
0°
30°S
50°S

1 The flavouring of cocktails disguised the bad taste of home-made spirits.
2 (c) 10.
3 About 80%.
4 About one-third.
5 (b) 10 million hl (220 million gal).

USSR, the Great Plains of the USA, and the deserts of Gobi (China), Sahara, and Central Australia. Grapes in abundance are grown in Central China, but become raisins before they can be harvested.

Sea-currents: The warm Gulf Stream makes winemaking possible in England and Wales, and contributes to the paramountcy of the European vineyards. The cold polar streams do the opposite for Newfoundland, Korea, Japan, and the southern tip of Argentina and Chile; but on the other hand, their cooling influence enables wines to be made outside the Equatorial boundaries of the South American coast.

Altitude: Temperature decreases with height – mountains are snow-capped. For this reason, winemaking is possible in Peru, Mexico, India, Queensland in Australia, and Zimbabwe.

Religion: Iran, Iraq, and Afghanistan all lie within the boundaries yet produce no wine nowadays because of the Muslim prohibition on alcohol.

Fig. 3. on page 13 gives an approximation of the relative shares of world production provided by countries within the wine belts. The map of Europe on page 17 shows the principal wine regions that provide the world with four fifths of its wine.

WINE-PRODUCING AREAS OF THE WORLD

As well as being one of the world's two largest producers, France excels in producing wines of the very finest quality and diversity, having many distinct wine regions each producing wines unique in character.

Bordeaux, with its output of some 2–4 million hl each year, is subdivided into districts of international reputation – the Médoc, Graves, Sauternes, Entre-deux-Mers, St. Émilion, Côtes de Bourg, and Côtes de Blaye. Burgundy, with a smaller production, has several famous districts, such as Chablis, Côte de Nuits, Côte de Beaune, and Beaujolais.

1 What proportion of world output does the EEC's output represent?
2 Arrange the following countries in increasing order of wine production: France, Germany, Spain.
3 Why do you think Britain is not a commercial wine producer?
4 Is the present world output of wine in millions of hl per year between: (a) 50 and 100; (b) 100 and 150; (c) 150 and 250; or (d) 250 and 350?
5 What are the two climatic conditions which limit the areas within which vines can be grown commercially for wine?

Other great regions in France are Champagne: the valleys of the Rhône and Loire: Provence, Languedoc, and Roussillon in the south-east: and Alsace near the German border.

From Italy comes a full range of sweet and dry red and white wines, in addition to excellent *apéritif* and dessert wines, and sparkling wines.

Unlike the French wines, which are generally known by their area of production, the Italian wines may be labelled according to the grape from which they are made or their place of origin or both.

The best-known wines of Italy include Vermouth, an aromatic herbal wine; Chianti, a light or full-bodied red wine; Orvieto and Frascati, dry and medium-dry straw-coloured wines; Soave, a dry white wine; Barolo, Barbaresco, and Brunello di Montalcino, big red wines improving with age; Valpolicella, a full-bodied red wine; Asti Spumante, the best-known Italian sparkling wine, white and sweet; and Marsala, a rich sweet, fortified wine produced in Sicily.

SHERRY AND PORT

By far the most important wine produced in Spain is Sherry, a fortified wine. The better-known Spanish wines include Valdepeñas, Rioja and Malaga. Despite a varied history, Spanish wines, particularly Sherry, are now enjoying a boom on the British market.

Portugal will forever be associated in the public mind with Port, the superb fortified wine from the Douro. But Portugal exports other wines, notably the *vinhos verdes* or 'green wines', made from immature or green grapes. These wines, usually semi-sparkling or *pétillant* in character, are currently very popular in Britain. A range of red, white and rosé wines is also produced throughout the country, much of it for export.

Germany's production, while greater than Portugal's, is of much lighter character, due mainly to the climate at the north of the wine belt. The light German white wines known as Hocks and Mosels from the Rhine and Mosel valleys are renowned throughout the world.

Good, and an increasing number of great wines, come from The Cape and Australia; Cyprus wines are also reliable and of standard quality. Although their 'sherries' may have been the best known, a full range of wines is exported from these countries.

1 65%
2 Germany, Spain, France.
3 Sufficient sun to ripen the fruit cannot be relied on.
4 (d) Between 250 and 350 million hl (5500 and 7700 million gal).
5 There must be sufficient sun to ripen the grapes every year, and the winter must be cool enough to give the vines a rest.

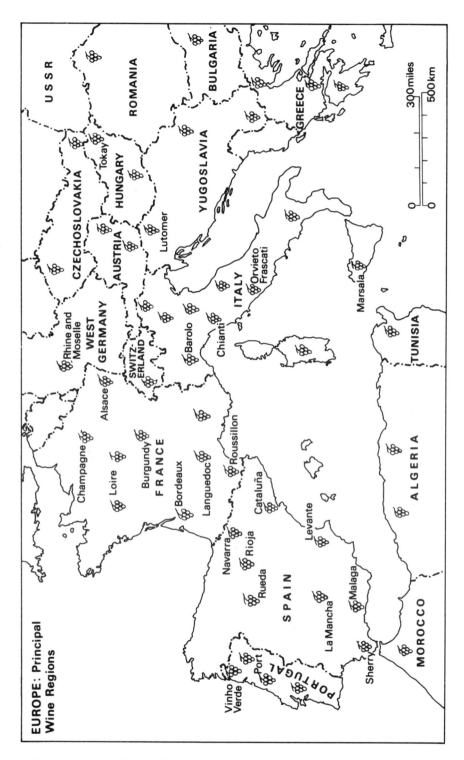

EUROPE: Principal Wine Regions

1 Why are there no wines produced in Central China or the American Mid-West?
2 How is it possible to produce wines in Mexico, Peru, India, and Zimbabwe which are all closer to the Equator than the wine zones?
3 Has Bordeaux a greater or smaller output than Burgundy?
4 Name as many of the main wine districts of Bordeaux as you can.

There are many other countries, not only in Europe but through-out the wine-producing areas of the world, which export little or no wine; examples are Russia, India, China, and South America. It must be remembered that in total only a small fraction of the world's wine output is consumed outside its country of origin, many wines lacking the stability necessary to travel from country to country. However, if such wines are to be found anywhere away from home, it will be in Britain.

1 The central continental climate produces too extreme temperatures.
2 Because the vineyards are at an altitude which reduces temperature.
3 Greater.
4 Médoc, Graves, Sauternes, Entre-deux-Mers, St. Émilion, Côtes de Bourg, and Côtes de Blaye.

2

The Vine and the Grower

So numerous are the varieties of wine that the amateur – the lover of wine – is almost prone to lose heart. However, a logical study of those factors which affect the production of wines and determine their characteristics will rapidly show that a sensible working knowledge of wines is not really so difficult to acquire. But in gaining this knowledge the reader should not expect to become an expert: that may take a lifetime.

1 Suggest three Italian wines for a customer to try.
2 What is the most famous Spanish wine?
3 What is the most famous Portuguese wine?
4 From which countries do the following wines come: (a) Asti Spumante; (b) Loire; (c) Malaga; (d) Orvieto; (e) Sauternes; (f) Tarragona; (g) Valdepeñas; (h) Valpolicella.
5 On which rivers is the German wine industry mainly centred?

IMPORTANCE OF NATURAL CONDITIONS

In each season of the year the vineyard and the vineyard owner or grower (who in France is called the *vigneron*) respond to nature, and in this respect nature works on two levels. Firstly, because of the earth's course in the heavens, the seasons, and hence the hours of daylight and the height and heat of the sun, are predetermined. But nature works also at a secondary level, where such features as the continental land masses and the oceans that separate them set up varying climates, which in turn are affected by other permanent and recurring conditions. Mountains and plains, rivers and valleys, forests and lakes, all contribute to the climate in each country. And although neighbouring regions may share prevalent winds and the same average rainfall, they still have their own very local conditions: spots that will catch the sun or the wind, or where fog or frost will gather. Thus each district has its individual microclimate.

The climate then is a critical factor in wine production. Already, two general bands around the earth's surface have been identified in which the wine-producing vine may grow, one north and one south of the equator. Between them it is too hot, beyond them too cold. The climate varies within these bands, not only from continent to continent and country to country, but also from district to district. Where the microclimate is suitable for wine production, man-made conditions are superimposed on natural conditions in such a way that the wine product of that district is practically unique and can be identified by the expert.

MICROCLIMATES AND TOPOGRAPHY

Traditionally, the growers have made the best use of their microclimate and topography. It will be found that the best vineyards were usually sited away from forest masses, which create excessive humidity, and that the warm aspect was always selected (in Europe this generally means a hill looking to the southeast). The best vineyards have seldom been sited at the top of hills, where exposure to wild weather would damage the crops, or at the bottom of valleys, where cold air and frost may collect. Standing water in a

1 From Asti Spumante, Bardolino, Barolo, Chianti, Frascati, Marsala, Orvieto, Soave, Valpolicella, Vermouth.
2 Sherry.
3 Port.
4 (a) Italy; (b) France; (c) Spain; (d) Italy; (e) France; (f) Spain; (g) Spain; (h) Italy.
5 The Rhine and the Mosel.

valley may rot the vine or lower the temperature unduly in the cold seasons. (Water can also store heat, however, and help to moderate extremes of temperature.) The average yearly temperature should be 14°–15°c (57°–59°F) ideally, and certainly not less than 10°c (50°F), with summer and winter limits of 22°c (72°F) and 3°c (37°F) respectively. To enable the vine to flower, a temperature of 15°c (59°F) or more is necesary.

The grower looks for an average of six to seven hours of sunshine every day from March to September, which may sound reasonable, but he may not always get it. The weather should be cool, even cold for the remainder of the year, so that the sap will withdraw from the canes. In these conditions, the vine will have the rest it needs so that it can flower and bear fruit in the succeeding year. In established vineyard regions, the grower will always have a sufficiently cold winter to rest his vine; the danger is that he will have too much cold.

Fortunately, it is rare for the temperature i to drop to − 15°c (5°F), at which temperature the vine root splits and dies. The effects of such bad luck can be avoided or mitigated by the grower in choosing hardier, if less productive, strains of vine, and by earthing his vines up for the winter. He may be unlucky in a warm winter in not having a frost hard enough to kill the insect and fungus pests, which will then plague him the following year.

CLIMATE AND SOIL

The vine needs plenty of sunshine and warmth in summer to ripen the grapes, but too hot a sun will burn the leaves, and only while the leaves are green do they have power to ripen the fruit. On the equatorial sides of the two wine belts, too much heat can produce dull 'flabby' wines, heavy in alcohol, which are useful only for blending. Hail storms in the vineyard are not uncommon in summer, and there is very little that modern science or the grower can do about it. In early summer, hail may rip the young shoots and reduce the yield. Late in the season, hailstones which strike the grapes break the skins, allowing moulds to form and rot them. Grapes so affected turn a dirty brown colour and give an off-flavour, *goût de grêle*, to the wine. Strong winds also have their dangers,

1 Are Sherry and Port sparkling wines or fortified wines?
2 About how much of the world's wine is consumed outside its country of production? Where is it most likely to be found?

particularly during the flowering season, when the pollen that must be taken from flower to flower by insects or by light winds for fertilization, can be blown away in a gale. Unless the flower is fertilized it will not form a grape.

Quite surprisingly, the growers and all who gain their living from wine shrug their shoulders or smile as they discuss 'the luck of the year' – rain, hail, frost, wind and sun – each of which contributes to their particular microclimates. Usually it is a shrug *and* a smile, for seldom is their luck wholly good or wholly bad. But there are other factors affecting the ultimate wine produced: the soil in which the vine is planted, the vine itself, and the pests and diseases to which it may fall prey.

THE IMPORTANCE OF MINERALS TO THE VINE

It has been said that 'the best wines come from the poorest soils'. While this cannot be taken literally (for some soils are too poor to grow anything), vineyards seem to flourish where other crops will not, and produce less delicate wines from rich soils. In many fields of agriculture the growth potential of soil is judged by its nitrogen content, which stimulates growth of stem and leaf. Important to agriculture, nitrogen is less so to horticulture, and the wine-producing vine marks the boundary between the two. It is an agricultural crop requiring horticultural treatment. What the vine needs far more than nitrogen are the mineral elements in the soil, which are essential to the delicate flavours of different wines. In other words, nitrogen will give quantity but minerals will give quality, and the grower will therefore prune each year to confine growth and concentrate the minerals in his crop of fruit.

It is true that the rich grower today has the resources which enable him to adjust nitrogen and mineral content, acidity and drainage, and so do much to compensate for deficiencies in his soil. Therefore it could be argued that the soil is not the all-important factor in wine production that it once was. However such treatments are expensive, and most growers have to take their soil as they find it.

1 Fortified wines.
2 Only a small fraction. In Britain.

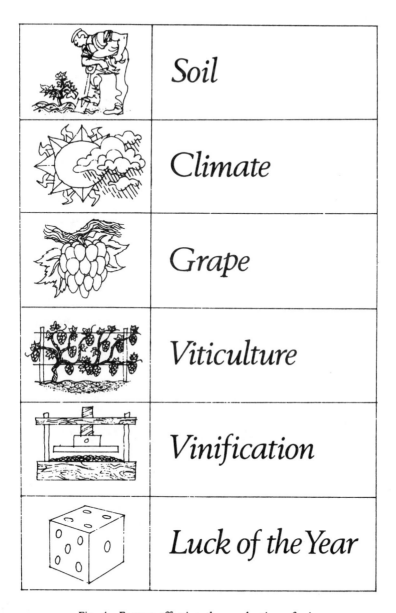

	Soil
	Climate
	Grape
	Viticulture
	Vinification
	Luck of the Year

Fig. 4 Factors affecting the production of wine

1 What topographical features are likely to affect local climatic conditions?
2 Are the best vineyards sited near to forests?
3 What is the ideal average yearly temperature in the vineyard?

Poor Soils produce Fine Wines

Vineyards are grown on a wide variety of soils. The best sherry vineyards of southern Spain have very chalky soil, with some clay. The vineyards perched on the steep hills of the Douro Valley in northern Portugal, where Port is produced, are slaty. In Champagne a poor, thin, loam topsoil covers a chalky base, which drains the vine roots. Bordeaux has poor soils, mostly gravel or pebbles covering a base of limestone, clay and chalk. In Burgundy there is a range from poor granitic soil to alkaline limestone. The weathered granite of Alsace is mixed with sandy gravel and alluvial soils, and in the Rhine and Mosel valleys of Germany the soil is mainly slaty, rich in minerals and limestone. The steep stony hills of Tuscany produce Chianti, Italy's best-known wine, and Piedmont, another region for fine Italian wines, has a limestone soil, with a high proportion of iron.

Vineyards are mainly situated in river valleys, where soils tend to be well-drained gravels, sand, alluvial matter, and weathered igneous rocks. Another reason why the old-established vineyards are found by rivers is the transport facility which the rivers afforded. Before the days of good roads, bulk cargoes of wine could only be moved by water.

TYPES OF VINE AND METHODS OF PROPAGATION

The soils mentioned are all well-drained and have a low organic content but quite a high mineral content. Each differs from its neighbour and, through the grape, produces subtly different wines. There are also hundreds of grape varieties, each with its characteristic flavour. Some vines have definite preferences for certain soils to produce their best wine. As with other plants, some varieties of vine ripen early and others ripen late. The grower's choice of vine must rank as the most important decision in determining the type and quality of his wine, and indeed its colour; and the grower can choose from hundreds, although he may well be limited by local wine laws to no more than a dozen, and for certain wines he is completely ruled both on type and proportion.

1 Mountains, plains, river valleys, forests and lakes.
2 No, forest masses create excessive humidity.
3 14°C to 15°C (57°F to 59°F)

The vine species that grew in the Caucasus in prehistoric times and spread to stock the vineyards of the world was *vitis vinifera*, the 'wine-bearing vine'. This species is one of many hundreds in the botanical family of *Ampelidaceae*, a family which includes Virginia creeper and many other climbing and creeping plants. From *vitis vinifera* all the varieties now planted in Europe have evolved through mutation and cross-breeding, to suit local soils and climates. The same vine variety, grown in different regions and processed in different ways, will produce wines of different characteristics; again, the same vine variety in different regions can be, and often is, given a different name. Of the black varieties, some of the famous ones are the Cabernet-Sauvignon of Bordeaux and the Loire, the Pinot Noir of north Burgundy and Champagne, the Gamay of the Beaujolais, the Sangiovese of Chianti in Italy, and the Grenache of Châteauneuf-du-Pape which, as Garnacha, produces fine Spanish wines.

The white varieties include the Sémillon, which produces the fine sweet Sauternes, the Sauvignon of Bordeaux and Pouilly-sur-Loire, the Chardonnay, producing Champagne and fine white Burgundies, the Riesling and Sylvaner of Germany and Alsace, and the Palomino, used in the production of sherry.

How Grapes become Sweet

Vines are propagated by rooting cuttings and by grafting, rather like roses. New varieties obtained by crossing are raised from seed in the first instance, for example Riesling x Sylvaner. The young plants are transferred from nurseries to the vineyard at various stages of development. Like all vegetable matter, vines need water, carbon dioxide, light and heat, nutrients and minerals. The roots find the water, some roots delving to low levels where it is almost permanently available. Other roots, called day roots, take advantage of water from the least shower. In humid conditions, the vine can also absorb water through its leaves.

The constituent of the grape most important to the making of wine is sugar. How does it get there? Sugar is a carbohydrate, as every slimmer knows, and is a complex molecule; grape sugar comprises a total of 24 carbon, hydrogen, and oxygen atoms – $C_6H_{12}O_6$. The leaves of the vine are the factories. When sunlight falls

1 List the six factors which may influence the production of wine.
2 What property of the soil, other than its fertility, determines the quality of the wine?

on their green matter, chlorophyll, carbon dioxide (CO_2) is drawn from the air to combine with water (H_2O) drawn from the soil via the roots and the vine stem, and they are bound together to make sugar. Some oxygen is left over, and is released to the air. The circulating sap takes the sugar and stores it in the growing grapes. The grower will take care to cut back long-growing shoots in summer, as they would consume some of the sugar for their own growth.

All growing and decomposing organic matter produces carbon dioxide, and its concentration in the air is greatest at the end of the night. The process of assimilation – of turning this into sugar – is therefore most effective on southeasterly slopes, which receive the energy of the early morning sun. Also at this time haze and dust are least, so that the sun's rays are not obscured. Moreover, in the high latitudes nearer to the poles, it is not only the winter cold that limits grape production, but also the greater absorption of the sun's energy in having to penetrate the atmosphere at a more oblique angle.

PRUNING AND TRAINING

Pruning of the vine takes place during winter. This time of year is chosen because the sap has withdrawn from the canes, and the vine will not therefore 'bleed' when cut. As with roses, nearly all the previous year's growth is cut away, leaving a selected few buds to provide the new year's growth. It is important to prune the vine hard, for each cane may grow as much as fifteen feet every year. The time of pruning also is important: the later it is pruned, the later it will flower. However, while there is more danger of bleeding with late pruning, which will weaken the vine, there is less danger of a late frost killing the shoots.

But the question arises: when is the grower pruning, and when is he training the vine, as both involve cutting part of the vine's growth? For the answer it is necessary to look at the objectives. Fundamentally, pruning is the cutting out of unwanted growth with the object of conserving quality in a reduced quantity of produce; pruning ensures that the vine will use the sun's energy to store sugar in a controlled crop of grapes which have taken the optimal goodness from the soil, rather than squandering that energy in luxuriant foliage and long shoots. Training, on the other hand, is the cultiva-

1 Climate, soil, grape, viticulture, vinification and 'luck of the year'.
2 The particular mineral content of the soil.

tion of an eventual plant shape which is conducive to production of the best fruit. Therefore, when the grower prunes he will be selective, taking away only those parts of the vine which are not essential to the eventual vine shape, which will be determined by tying the remaining shoots to a stake or to wires. It must be remembered that the essential shape of the vine is dictated not by the grower, but by the natural condition of the vineyard – latitude, height, part of slope and microclimate.

Training Systems for varying Natural Conditions

So as the vines grow, the grower sets about training them from year to year. If there is danger of too much frost, the vines will be trained higher from the ground. Or, if it is desired to get maximum heat from the soil, the vines will be trained near to the ground. Incidentally, too much heat can also be a disadvantage, and in very hot regions it may be necessary to grow the vines on trellises high above the ground. Fig. 5 shows the methods of training the vine adopted in a number of regions.

In the Guyot Double system, much used in northern Europe, two shoots are first trained, from which the fruit-bearing shoots develop over a period of four years. Generally, the planting distances are 1.2 m between vines in one row and 1.5 m between rows. However, the Lenz Moser system, introduced as an economy, provides 2.7–3 m between rows to admit tractors for cultivation, spraying, and harvesting purposes. Typical of the bush system is the Gobelet, used in the Beaujolais, where the shoots are tied together at the top, simulating the shape of a goblet. The Alsace and Mosel methods show the tall vines best shaped to cope with ground frosts or steep slopes. In parts of southern Europe, where the sun is very hot, the trellis method is ideal; here the grapes are suspended high over the surface, where they suffer less from overheating by reflection of the sun's rays from the ground.

PESTS AND DISEASES

Like all agricultural crops, the vine is subject to pests and diseases, in the form of birds, insects, fungi, viruses and weeds. The vigneron

1 *Vitis vinifera* is the name given to: (a) a species of vine; (b) a particular variety of vine; (c) a type of wine.
2 Of which species are practically all the varieties of European wine-producing vines members?
3 What natural resources do vines need?

Guyot Simple   Guyot Double   Gobelet   Bush

Low Styles

Alsace   Mosel   Trellis

High Styles

Fig. 5   Styles of vine training

1 (a) A species of vine.
2 *Vitis vinifera.*
3 Water, carbon dioxide, light, warmth, nutrients and minerals.

has steadily mastered the catastrophes of the last century, but the battle with nature is a constant one.

Birds can cause severe damage, and there is no real answer to the problem. Children beating saucepans with spoons help to scatter them, but deterrents such as scarecrows are soon treated with the familiarity they deserve. Sprays are unsatisfactory because they affect the grape and the vine. It can only be said that birds present a problem which the grower is happy to share with neighbouring fruit farmers. One can understand why roasted ortolans and thrush pâté are available in vineyard areas.

Because the English were keen botanists and inveterate travellers plants from all over the world came to Kew Gardens. Unfortunately, some brought pests and diseases with them. One of the earlier fungi to reach Europe was *Oïdium tuckerii*, a 'powdery mildew' which covered the grapes, splitting and rotting them. Hardly had this been conquered, when the dreaded *Phylloxera vastatrix* arrived accidentally on the American species *vitis riparia*, imported to various European countries from the eastern states of North America between 1858 and 1862. By the end of the century most European vineyards had had to be uprooted because of this louse-like, almost invisible aphid, producing an acute shortage of wine. In this situation, blended and poor quality wines were marketed.

THE KILLER PHYLLOXERA AND THE REMEDY

Since *vitis riparia* and the other American varieties *v. rupestris* and *v. berlandieri* did not seem to suffer from the pest, and bore grapes, some growers planted them and made wine from them. The wines had an unmistakable, pungent flavour, repugnant to those who liked the fine wines of earlier years; nevertheless people drank them, and hoarded their remaining stocks of pre-*Phylloxera* wine for great occasions. Some, however, acquired a taste for the 'fox wine' as it was called, and grew even to prefer it. A few peasant farmers still make wine from these vines for their own use, and the trouble is that such grapes can unknowingly be bought in by the wine cooperatives. A small quantity of fox grapes will give a distinct off-flavour to a whole vat of wine, much as wild garlic, eaten by one cow, can taint a whole county's milk. So these varieties, and hybrids bred from

1 How does the process of assimilation produce sugar in the grape?
2 On which slopes is assimilation most effective in the northern hemisphere?
3 What is the process of cutting out unwanted shoots of the vine called?
4 Why is it necessary?
5 When does pruning normally take place?

them, are banned in nearly every region, and severe penalties are imposed on those who grow them.

The cure, if cure be the eradication of the pest in one vineyard, was to uproot and burn the vines, and to sterilize the soil. But that hardly touched the cause, and certainly did nothing to meet the effect – no vineyard, no wine. Scientists provided the answer. The American vine species, which had brought the pest to Europe, were found to be resistant to it whereas the European *vinifera* species was not. As *Phylloxera* caused its worst damage to the roots, grafting was found to be the answer. European 'scions' could be grafted on to resistant American root-stocks, and this practice has become standard throughout the world where *vitis vinifera* is grown. The *Phylloxera* is so hardy that there is no absolute remedy, and the dangers that it represents will always be with the grower. Before replanting a vineyard, therefore, the soil is always dressed with strong insecticides.

METHODS OF GRAFTING

The partial defence against *Phylloxera*, the grafting of European *vinifera* scions on to American stocks, presented little problem to the French. Their nurserymen were already experts in the art of grafting, and soon perfected techniques to meet an enormous demand for grafts to restock the lost vineyards of Europe.

A straightforward graft may be made by taking a scion of the desired, non-resistant variety and a root-stock of the resistant American variety, each of the same diameter, cutting each through on the diagonal, and binding the upper section of the scion to the lower section of the stock. More safely, a slit is cut in the stock, and the scion cut into a pointed section to fit into it.

The French use a 'whip and tongue' graft, which combines these two principles, giving a maximum surface area of 'cambium' in contact. Fig. 6 shows the principle of these grafts. The French call the whip and tongue graft *la greffe anglaise*, which suggests that it may have been of English origin. The *maître greffeur*, whose uncanny skill enables him to cut and fit a graft by eye with the precision of a

1 Carbon dioxide from the atmosphere is combined with water from the soil, by the action of chlorophyll in the green leaves.
2 The southeasterly slopes.
3 Pruning.
4 Without it, the vines would grow rapidly and expend their energy on growing wood instead of fruit.
5 In the winter.

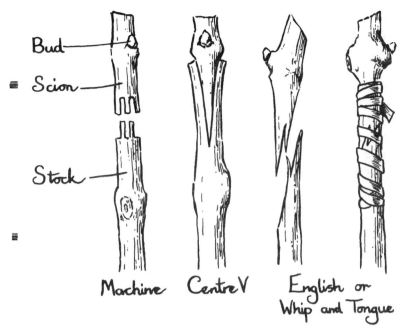

Fig. 6   Grafting – the principal styles

cabinet-maker, complements the grafting machines which promptly appeared on the market after the great *Phylloxera* plague.

In bench grafting, the method used in colder climates, the grafts are packed in boxes, covered with charcoal and soil, and left to grow together in greenhouses. After about three months, those which have taken are planted out in nurseries to grow and harden off during the summer and following winter. Thence they go for final planting in the vineyards in the following spring. In warmer climates, where bedding-out is an unnecessary expense, the root-stocks are planted straight into their final position in the vineyards. When spring comes, their shoots and leaves are removed, and scions from *vitis vinifera* are grafted straight on to the bare stocks (field grafting).

THE ANNUAL VINEYARD CYCLE

The successful vineyard proprietor with a technical training and long experience of the climate, the soil, the vine, the methods of pruning

1 To what sort of climate would the trellis method of training be most suited?
2 In general, what are the enemies of the vine?
3 What insect pest devastated vineyards in the nineteenth century?

and training, the pests and diseases, and the hazards of nature, is equipped to take them all in his stride, and his yearly cycle of vineyard management will start after the vintage has been finished, in October or early November each year. First he will tidy up, and providing the soil is dry, the winter ploughing will begin and continue into December. He will plough the soil up to the roots of the vines for winter protection and the roots may also be mulched with compost for the same purpose. From December to February the vine needs light frost to kill disease and also to help it to rest. From January onwards the vineyard will be pruned, and the aim is always quality, not quantity. Pruning is not only a very skilled task but it is also compelled by law in France and many other countries. In the spring, as soon as the vine shoots start to grow, they will be attached to stakes and wires in many districts. If manure is spread, it will be ploughed under, and, at the same time, the soil that has been ploughed up to the roots in November will now be ploughed away from them. Young grafts brought from the nursery in their second year will be planted out. Rain is now wanted to make a good spring growth. Late frosts are a real danger, and to combat these, fires are lit in the vineyards to create air circulation, for frosts at this time of year only form when the air is still.

In late May or early June the vine will flower, and the grower's annual battle with pest and disease will begin. Indeed if meteorological conditions have been bad he may already have started spraying against mildew during April. When the flowers are on the vine, mild weather is wanted, for too much wind will scatter the flowers and the pollen will be lost. To encourage pollination, the grower may have planted roses at the end of the rows in the vineyard; the vine flower is insignificant to look at, and the roses will attract the bees and set them about their task.

RIPENING AND HARVEST

Not only does the grower need clement weather during flowering, but the weather in the hundred days which follow before the grapes are ripe is critical. Some rain at first, to swell the grapes, is needed, followed by hot sunshine to ripen them. But if all goes well, at the end of September or early October, the grapes will be fully ripe and

1 A hot climate.
2 Birds, insects, fungi, viruses, and weeds.
3 *Phylloxera.*

they can be picked. This is hard work demanding a great deal of labour for about three to four weeks. People come from all over the country, and even from abroad, to help with the vintage.

Usually the pickers in the vineyard use wooden baskets, cutting the grape bunches carefully from the vine with knives or secateurs. Their baskets are emptied into bigger baskets or hods, carried on the backs of stronger members of the team. The loaded weight at this stage is about 50 kg (1 cwt) and the hod is then carried to the road for transfer to large tractor-drawn tubs or modern tipper lorries. And so the grapes make their way to the winery, handled tenderly and carefully at every stage in order to be perfect for vinification.

1 What is the only known effective precaution which can be taken against *Phylloxera*?
2 Name three methods of grafting.
3 Are pruning and training the vine important activities of a viticulturalist?

3

The Making of Wine

As the hot hundred days draw to their end, the ripened grapes are harvested and brought to the winery in baskets or other containers in much the same way as they have been for a thousand years or more. In a matter of minutes, their transformation into wine will begin. But the process will bear very careful study, for the chemical action of fermentation – the conversion of sugar into alcohol – is fundamental to all alcoholic drinks; not only to still, sparkling and fortified wines, but also to spirits, liqueurs and beers, even though some variations and further processes will be applied for individual beverages.

1 Replanting with scions grafted on to American roots, which are resistant to *Phylloxera*.
2 From: machine, centre V, English or whip–and–tongue, and bud.
3 Yes, very.

THE GRAPE

First, a study of the grape itself will explain much that is to follow. If a grape, say a black grape, is put into the mouth and the teeth burst the skin, instantly a fruity sweetness is noticeable, quite different from the flat sweetness of cane sugar. From this, and from the moisture, the presence of sugar and water in the grape is instantly established. But also a taste quite different from the taste of wine is apparent; this comes from the fruit acids and their compounds within the grape. If the grape skin is next crushed between the teeth, a sensation of bitterness follows, coming from the tannin in the skin; and if a small part of the grape stalk were also bitten, the same bitter taste of tannin would be apparent. However, if one of the pips is crushed by the teeth a different and altogether unpleasant bitterness would be tasted, a bitterness quite unacceptable in wine.

Next, observation of the grape yields more essential information. If a black and a white grape are sliced through the centre, and the cross-sections of each are compared, it will be seen that the jelly-like substance in the middle, composed of juice and pectins, is a pale green or yellow in colour. So the colour of red wines cannot come

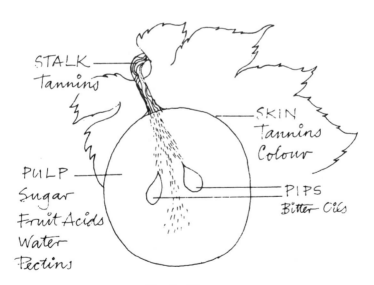

Fig. 7   The grape

1 (a) When is the grape harvest in the northern hemisphere? (b) How long after flowering is this?
2 What weather is necessary during ripening and harvest and for what purposes?

from the centre, it must come from the skin of the black grape. Red wine can only be made from black grapes, but white wines can in fact be made from white or black grapes, provided that, in the latter case, the grape skins are removed before fermentation begins.

WINE YEASTS AND WILD YEASTS

On the outside of grapes is a whitish bloom, more easily seen on a black grape, although still quite apparent on a white grape. This waxy substance has trapped a mass of organisms, of which three main kinds are important to the wine-maker. Firstly, there are wild yeasts, of which there are some ten million per grape. Secondly, there are about 100,000 wine yeasts, or one for every 100 wild yeasts. The wine yeast *saccharomyces ellipsoideus* ('the potato-shaped fungus that lives on sugar'), is in fact first cousin to the truffle and second cousin to the mushroom. And thirdly, there are bacteria, principally acetobacter, of which there are also about 100,000. The yeasts and bacteria are carried on to the grape by insects, mostly fruit flies, and also float in the air and stick on the grapes. These are all microscopic single-celled living organisms, containing enzymes which will work on the constituents of the grape. Of great importance to the wine-maker is the fact that the wild yeasts and the acetobacter are 'aerobic', that is to say, they can only work in the presence of oxygen. Only the wine yeasts are anaerobic (able to work in the absence of oxygen), so the unwanted wild yeasts and acetobacter can be put out of action by excluding air from the process.

Yeasts feed on sugar, changing it to alcohol by means of their enzymes, on contact. As the enzymes do their work, performing much the same role as machine tools in a factory, gas is given off, so that the whole mixture bubbles and ferments. The wild yeasts, sometimes called 'apiculate' because of their lemon shape, start to work immediately and ferment violently until 4% vol. alcohol has been produced, at which concentration they will die. The wine yeasts, although slow starters, will then go on producing alcohol up to 16% to 18% vol. Acetobacter is a real danger, for all that it does is to work on the alcohol and produce vinegar, so it must be prevented as effectively as possible at the earliest opportunity

1 (a) At the end of September or beginning of October. (b) 100 days.
2 Clement weather during flowering, wet weather to swell the grapes, and hot sunshine to ripen them.

VINIFICATION

The atmosphere of a European winery, whether it be a château on
the Gironde, a Schloss on the Rhine, or a monastery on the Danube,
is essentially ageless; stone predominates, and its worn surfaces bear
evidence of the workings of machines, some of them primitive,
which have served the wine-maker through the ages. It is here that
the vintage is received into the first year *chai*. This low building
houses the crusher–destalker, which separates the stalks and breaks
the skins of the grapes, putting the yeast into contact with the sugar.
This equipment has almost entirely displaced the old *lagar*, the
shallow trough in which men trod the grapes, either with bare feet or
with special boots, enabling the grape skins to be broken without the
pips being crushed. Under lagar conditions, the wild yeasts started
the natural fermentation process and died at 4% vol. alcohol
concentration. The wine yeasts took over the fermentation and
continued until either an alcohol concentration of 16% to 18% killed
them or no sugar was left to convert. Meanwhile, the lagar being
open to the air, the acetobacter would convert the alcohol to vinegar,
and, if the lagar were abandoned, other bacteria would eventually
turn the vinegar to water, completing the natural cycle.

Replacing the original lagar, a crushing machine and a destalking
apparatus were devised. Then came a crusher–destalker, combining
both operations, from which the grape pulp was pumped into open
wooden vats holding hundreds of gallons. Modern vats, which can
be sealed, are made of stainless steel, or of cement lined with tiles or
glass. The grape stalks together with the spent grape skins recovered
later (known in English as pomace and French as *marc*) are boiled
down to produce a spirit of varying quality called *eau-de-vie-de-marc*,
or colloquially *marc*.

FERMENTATION

The crushed grapes are now known as 'must', and in the vats the
yeast will work on the sugar in the process of controlled fermentation. The first step, even before fermentation can begin, may be to
add sulphur dioxide. This is called 'sulphuring' and it has two effects.

1 What two colours are used to describe the grapes?
2 Why is the taste of a grape different from that of wine?
3 The jelly-like substance in a white grape is pale green or yellow in colour. What colour is
it in a black grape?

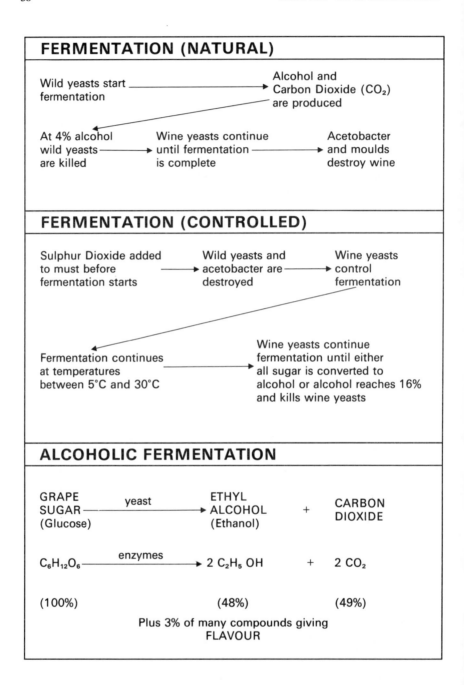

FERMENTATION (NATURAL)

Wild yeasts start ⟶ Alcohol and Carbon Dioxide (CO_2) are produced
fermentation

At 4% alcohol wild yeasts ⟶ Wine yeasts continue until fermentation is complete ⟶ Acetobacter and moulds destroy wine
are killed

FERMENTATION (CONTROLLED)

Sulphur Dioxide added to must before fermentation starts ⟶ Wild yeasts and acetobacter are destroyed ⟶ Wine yeasts control fermentation

Fermentation continues at temperatures between 5°C and 30°C ⟶ Wine yeasts continue fermentation until either all sugar is converted to alcohol or alcohol reaches 16% and kills wine yeasts

ALCOHOLIC FERMENTATION

GRAPE SUGAR (Glucose) ⟶[yeast] ETHYL ALCOHOL (Ethanol) + CARBON DIOXIDE

$C_6H_{12}O_6$ ⟶[enzymes] $2\ C_2H_5\ OH$ + $2\ CO_2$

(100%)   (48%)   (49%)

Plus 3% of many compounds giving
FLAVOUR

Fig. 8   Principles of Fermentation

1 Black and white.
2 Because of the fruit acids and their compounds in the grape.
3 The same.

Firstly, the sulphur dioxide, being hungry for oxygen, will take up oxygen from the must, and secondly it will form a coating over the top, preventing the air from getting to the must. This coating stops the wild yeasts and the acetobacter from working, because they are aerobic. The anaerobic wine yeasts are left to carry on the fermentation alone. The principles of natural and controlled fermentation are demonstrated in Fig. 8.

The sugar, produced in the fruit by assimilation, is ready for its transformation by yeast into alcohol, ethyl alcohol (not to be confused with the poisonous methyl alcohol contained in methylated spirits) and carbon dioxide. Mostly the sugar found in grapes is glucose, but there are many other types of sugar. As individual enzymes will only work on particular sugars, it is perhaps fortunate that the yeasts peculiar to one vineyard usually contain the best enzymes for its wine.

The glucose molecule, being sugar, is composed of six atoms of carbon, twelve of hydrogen and six of oxygen, as shown in Fig. 8. It is, in fact, a carbohydrate. All that the yeast with its enzymes is doing is to rearrange this molecule in a different way, to produce two other molecules. This classic equation sets out correctly the molecular change from glucose to alcohol and carbon dioxide, but it conceals behind its simplicity a complex chain of processes by which the conversion actually comes about.

While it is sufficient here to remember that grape sugar influenced by yeast enzymes is turned into ethyl alcohol and carbon dioxide, one fact of the greatest importance must not be overlooked. In the complex reaction that produces this result, fractional quantities of sugar and intermediate compounds get lost on the way and react with other substances like the fruit acids and tannins in the must. These compounds fail to become alcohol and are turned instead into other organic compounds, aldehydes, ketones and esters, which give flavour to the wine. For this the world should be truly grateful, for a plain, simple mixture of ethyl alcohol and water would have no taste at all.

CONTROL OF ALCOHOL POTENTIAL

In order to control the production of his wine, the wine-maker needs to know certain facts about the must. It is vital that he knows the

1 Why must care be taken when crushing or pressing the grapes, not to crush the pips?
2 Does 'bloom' on the grape refer to: (a) the flowers on the vine which are the basis of the fruit; (b) the coating of yeasts and other moulds on the outside of the grape.
3 What are the three groups of organisms in the bloom on the grape?
4 What are the two conditions, apart from temperature, under which natural fermentation will cease?
5 What is must?

sugar content, for this will tell him how much alcohol the must is capable of making. There are laws in most countries which specify the minimum alcoholic strength of wines; alcohol is a powerful preservative and will ensure that the wine will remain at its best. A hydrometer is used to measure the specific gravity of the must, which indicates the sugar content accurately, and hence the alcohol potential. The law may allow the wine-maker to add limited quantities of sugar, should the must show insufficient alcohol potential. This process of enrichment, or improvement, is generally called *chaptalisation*, after the French scientist Chaptal who first devised the method. It is important to remember that additional sugar may only be used to increase the alcohol potential of the wine, and not to increase its sweetness. The must is sucked up from the vat below and put through a mixing machine where ordinary cane sugar is added. If too much is added the flavour of the wine will be spoiled, hence the strict legal control.

The wine-maker needs also to know the acidity of his must, because the fruit acids in the grape affect the working of the yeast. The wine-maker may, as allowed by local laws, control the acidity by adding water or acidifying agents such as gypsum.

As the fermentation gets under way there is need for strict control, and a vat control chart logs the progress of the fermentation. Each day the specific gravity is plotted, showing the wine-maker the progress made by the yeast in converting the sugar to alcohol. As the alcohol increases, the sugar decreases and the specific gravity will drop.

TEMPERATURE CONTROL

Another line is plotted on the chart, and this relates to the temperature. Temperature control is very important indeed, because fermentation generates heat, and the *saccharomyces* yeasts are very sensitive to heat and cold. They cannot operate below 5°C (40°F), nor above 30°C (90°F). Nor is this the only difficulty, for if the must temperature goes outside this range, fermentation will stop. This is known as 'sticking'. It may not be possible to restart fermentation, particularly if it has been too hot, as changes may have taken place in the sugars to spoil the wine. To avoid this danger the must has to be cooled in

1 Because the pips contain substances which would spoil the flavour of the wine.
2 (b) The coating of yeasts and other moulds on the outside of the grape.
3 Wild yeasts, wine yeasts and other moulds including acetobacter.
4 Either all the sugar has been converted into alcohol and carbon dioxide, or the alcohol level has reached about 16% vol.
5 The juice which has been squeezed out of the grape (sometimes including the grape skins as well).

hot countries and may have to be gently warmed in cold countries.

Within the safe temperature range, heat will accelerate fermentation, and the quicker the must ferments within this range, the less risk there is of acetobacter breaking down the alcohol. There are various ways in which the wine-maker may keep the temperature within safe limits. Sometimes the wine must be pumped through heated radiators to keep it at a sufficiently high temperature, but more usually it must be cooled. The simplest way is to pump must drawn from the bottom of the vat up to the top, cooling it as it passes through the pipe outside the vat. If a drastic reduction in temperature is necessary, the wine may be pumped through cooling radiators before being pumped to the top of the vat. This process has another advantage. In making red wine, grape skins are included in the must, and form a floating 'cap' in the vat; and in red wine production the colour must be drawn out of the skins. This can only be done by constant contact with the alcohol in the must, and the pumping of the must over the skins ensures this continual dissolving of colour by the alcohol.

There are other methods of cooling the must. Where modern vats of stainless steel are used, a constant film of cold water may be run over the sides, and in other cases water is sprayed on to hessian wrapped round vats in the open, cooling them as the water evaporates in the sun and breeze.

'Bubble caps', valves which enable the carbon dioxide to escape without admitting any air or bacteria, may be fitted on the tops of vats. The caps can be adjusted to give fermentation under regulated pressure. This method is often referred to as *maceration carbonique*.

WINE-MAKING – RED WINES

After a day or so, the first violent fermentation dies down. The wine will go on fermenting for a further period of up to four weeks, depending on the kind of wine being made. For red wine the must contains the skins, which will continue to be fermented in the vat until the required amount of colour and tannin has been drawn from them. At this point, the vat will contain a mixture of liquid (for most of the juice will have been drawn out of the grapes) and skins. The

1 What, in general terms, is the chemical reaction of fermentation?
2 What type of sugar is found in grapes?
3 What compounds give flavour to wine?
4 What is added to must to neutralize wild yeasts and acetobacter?

liquid, 'running wine' or *vin de goutte* as it is called in France, will be run off from the bottom of the vat, into casks or another vat, leaving the vat partly filled with marc.

There will, however, be a large quantity of liquid left in this mass, which will not be wasted. In old types of vat, the mass had to be shovelled out of the top of the vat for further pressing, but modern designs include hatches at the bottom, which facilitate removal of the marc.

Today, the marc is moved into a press, where the remaining juice is recovered. Naturally, this juice – the *vin de presse* – is much stronger in tannin than the vin de goutte. The wine-maker must decide whether he will add all, some, or none of this press wine to his vin de goutte.

TYPES OF WINE PRESS

The first presses were of vertical design, worked by a screw or hydraulic pressure. Slightly more gentle than the hydraulic press is the horizontal press shown in Fig. 9. The mechanism of this horizontal press rotates, drawing two end-plates together so that the marc between them is crushed. As the mechanism is reversed, chains break up the squashed mass of grape skins, so that they are ready to be pressed several more times.

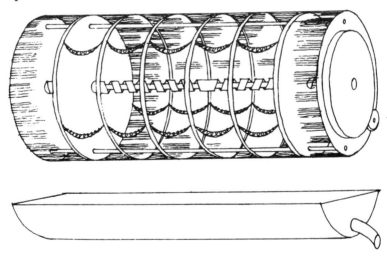

Fig. 9   Horizontal press

1 Sugar, under the action of yeast, is converted into ethyl alcohol and carbon dioxide.
2 Glucose.
3 Aldehydes, ketones, and esters.
4 Sulphur dioxide.

Delicate wines require an even gentler pressing process, which can be provided by another type of cylindrical press which contains an inflatable rubber bag. The press is filled with marc and rotated, and the large rubber bag is then inflated, gently and firmly pressing the grape skins against the side. The pressure is then released, rotation being continued to allow the grape skins to break up again. Then the process is repeated, as often as required.

In the large cooperatives the volume of production does not allow such individual treatment, and batteries of continuous presses are used, working on the principle of a mincing machine, with the mass being pressed forward against the resistance of its own weight, or of a restricted orifice.

The skins and pips coming from all these presses will eventually be quite dry, but still contain a little sugar. After wetting, they will be fermented again, and then distilled to produce eau–de–vie–de–marc in France, (called *grappa* in Italy, *tresterbranntwein* in Germany, *aguardiente de orujos* in Spain, and *bagaçeira* in Portugal) so nothing at all is wasted.

MATURATION

Although the initial fermentation is over, the process will continue for up to a month, or even longer, depending upon the temperature, and so the still-fermenting wine is put to mature in large casks. The casks are mostly made of wood, and vary somewhat in size; in the Gironde small casks of 225 litres, called *barriques*, are used. The casks have to be carefully purged of lurking acetobacter, even though the casks may be new. So first they are scalded with steam, and then either sulphur dioxide is pumped into them, or sulphur candles – pieces of paper or cloth impregnated with flowers of sulphur – are burned inside them.

The casks of red wine are put in the cellars of the winery, where they will mature, according to the wine variety, from two to ten years. This is known as 'cellaring'. Small glass conical weights seal the bungholes of the casks in some cellars, allowing any carbon dioxide to escape from inside, but preventing any air from getting in. The casks must be kept topped up, in order to exclude air and the

1 Would you expect the sugar content of must to increase or decrease as fermentation proceeds?
2 Why should the wine-maker know the sugar content of his must?
3 (a) Will fermentation proceed faster at 13°C (55°F) or 24°C (75°F)? (b) What happens to fermentation at 2°C (35°F) or at 35°C (95°F)?
4 What are 'bubble-caps'?

possibility of bacterial spoilage. The wine shrinks as it cools, and a certain amount soaks into the wood, so it is necessary to fill the casks brim full at least once a week.

RACKING AND FINING

During the first three months of maturation the wine will throw a sediment called lees, consisting of dead yeasts which have either starved having consumed all the sugar or expired from a surfeit of alcohol. The wine must be removed from the dead yeasts because these will decompose quite quickly, and give an off-flavour to the wine. The wine is therefore carefully pumped from one cask to another, leaving the lees at the bottom of the first. Air is pumped into the first cask, forcing the wine into the new one, by 'pushing'. To suck it up might disturb the lees at the bottom, frustrating the whole operation. This process is called 'racking'.

As the last of the wine is transferred to the new cask, it is examined with great care for the first signs of any sediment; and at that moment the racking stops. The lees are not wasted; they go for distillation into eau-de-vie.

The operation of racking is done for red wine once every three months because the alcohols and tannins combine to form a much heavier deposit than in white wines. Tannin is very important, however, in clearing wine, as it gathers a lot of the jelly-like protein substances which would otherwise make a wine cloudy. But tannin will not clear all such substances, and more help is necessary, so wines are 'fined' before they are bottled. Fining may be done with a gelatinous substance such as isinglass or white of egg. In Bordeaux, egg whites – usually about six per barrique – are mixed with a little wine in a bowl, using a small heather whisk. This mixture is then thoroughly stirred into the wine in the cask. The tannin and egg whites combine to form a gummy substance which drags all the protein matter down to the bottom of the cask, leaving the wine above clear and crystal bright. After settling for three weeks the wine is again racked.

Another method is to mix the wine thoroughly with an absorbent earth, such as kieselguhr or Bentonite, which will absorb the protein haze, and then to filter this through very fine filters.

1 Decrease, as the sugar is converted.
2 So that he knows how much alcohol it is capable of making and how much sugar he may add to make more.
3 (a) 24°C (75°F). (b) It will 'stick'.
4 Valves which enable carbon dioxide to escape from the top of vats without admitting any air or bacteria.

The period of cellaring serves two purposes. It allows the wine to clear, or 'fall bright' in wine-makers' language, and to mature.

WINE-MAKING – WHITE AND ROSÉ WINES

The making of white wine differs from the making of red wine, in that the skins are not required. For this reason grapes for white wine, which may be either black or white because the juice of both is white, are not generally crushed and vatted with their skins, as in the production of red wine. Instead, usually after destalking, they go straight to the press before they have a chance to start fermenting; the the juice pressed out of them is immediately pumped to the fermentation vats. Enough of the yeasts will have been washed off the skins to make fermentation possible, and the dry skins are put to distillation. Because they lack the tannin from the skins, white wines do not take quite so long to mature as red wines – usually six months to a year.

Rosé wines can be made in several ways. The classic method is to start the process as for red wine, but to remove the juice from the skins after only a short while. This period could vary from twenty-four to forty-eight hours, depending on the amount of colour required in the wine, and the temperature. A second and very simple method of producing rosé wine is by mixing a very little red wine with a large quantity of white wine, but this is generally forbidden in the EEC. Or again, a small quantity of black grapes may be fermented on the skins with a large quantity of white grapes. It should however be noted that white wine made by fermenting white grapes on their skins may tend to be harsh from the resulting high tannin content. The maturation time for rosé wines may be a little longer than for white wines.

Maturation periods will vary quite considerably for different wines of the same colour; furthermore, light wines will continue to mature in storage, whether in a tank, vat or bottle. Wine is a mixture of many things which continue to act on each other until the wine is finally consumed. There is the alcohol, there are the fruit acids, and

1 Will the wine-maker always add the 'press wine' to the 'running wine'?
2 Were the earlier wine presses of horizontal or vertical design?
3 What two conditions should a storage container for wine fulfil?

there are other substances, such as pectins and tannin, which existed in the original grape. The long interaction during maturation produces a gradual and constant change, so that a young wine does not taste or look the same as an old wine.

1 No; only if he requires additional colour and tannin.
2 Vertical.
3 It must be airtight, and it must not contaminate the wine.

4

Light Wines

FRENCH WINES

Reviewed in the light of certain facts, it is not surprising that the wines of France are held up to the whole world as examples of character and quality. The latitude of France is ideal for wine production, and most of her 200,000 square miles is fertile agricultural land. For these reasons the grape crops are heavy. Wine production in France has become a major industry to an extent which no other country of Europe can match.

The continuous production of wine in volume and variety from the medieval period or earlier has given France a knowledge which is

1 Give two reasons why the level of wine in a cellar cask may fall during maturation.
2 What would happen to this wine if the casks were not topped up regularly?
3 Why are wines racked and fined during storage?
4 (a) Is it possible to make white wines from black grapes? (b) Is it possible to make red wines from white grapes?
5 Which will benefit from a longer maturation – a red wine or a white wine?

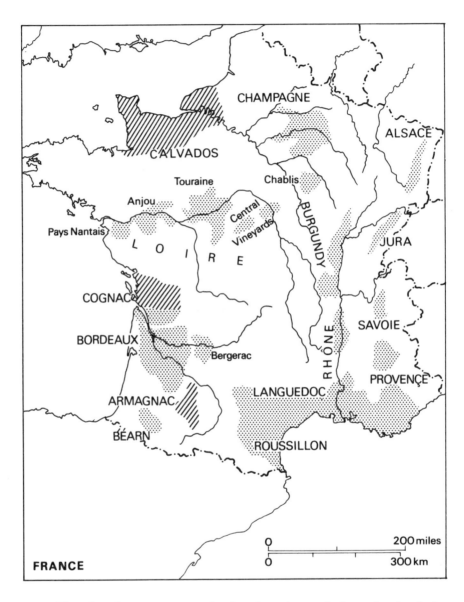

Note: The dotted areas are predominantly wine-producing; the hatched, spirit-producing.

1 Cooling after fermentation; evaporation of wine which has soaked through the cask.
2 It would deteriorate.
3 To clear them of any cloudiness due to particles suspended in the wine.
4 (a) Yes. (b) No.
5 A red wine.

yet unequalled. The vines have been selected and bred to complement the soils; the craft of the vineyard has been perfected; the taste for wine of differing characteristics has been assessed; the methods of making wine have been adapted to present-day requirements and have made full use of modern scientific developments; and the benefits of research are in the bottle.

Appellation Contrôlée

The *Appellation Contrôlée* system (AC for short) set up under French law classifies all major vineyards, and such vineyards have been given a right to use certain place-names as an indication of origin. They must be within the official area of *Appellation* and obey many constraints concerning the density of vines, the types of vines planted, the production per ha, and alcoholic strength. This ensures that a Beaujolais AC is a genuine wine from the legally limited Beaujolais area. French law is sufficiently hard on the transgressor for the purchaser to believe in the label.

These controls have grown from the roots planted by the medieval guilds, who traditionally used to try the contents of each cask and burn bad casks (having first emptied the bad wine down the public drain). Much as with the craft Guilds of the City of London, their power declined in intervening centuries, only to be revived in the present one. Following two disastrous vintages in the early 1930s the vignerons and négoçiants of Burgundy revived the *Confrérie des Chevaliers du Tastevin*, inducting some prominent persons to give publicity to the wines of Burgundy and enhance their prestige. Similar wine brotherhoods now exist in all the main French regions, and in some Italian ones also; they will be mentioned in their appropriate places.

THE WINES OF BORDEAUX

The areas of France where some of the finest still wines are produced centre on the regions of Bordeaux and Burgundy. The red wines, or clarets, of Bordeaux have been described as the best-known and most popular light wines in the world. There are both red and white Bordeaux wines, but the production of claret is somewhat in excess

1 Why does a young wine neither taste nor look like an old wine?
2 Why are the grape crops of France heavy?

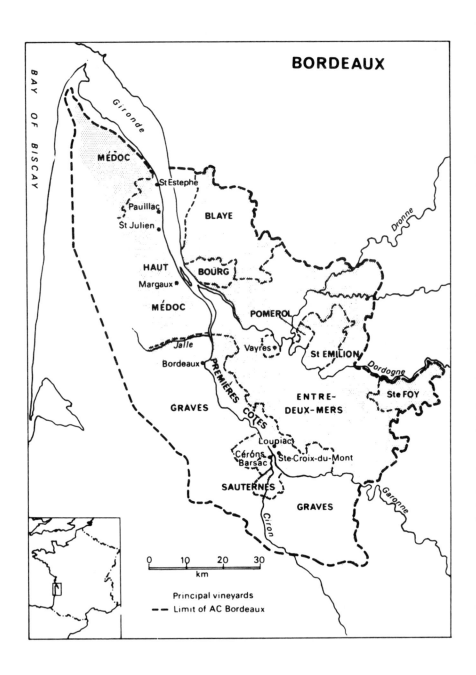

1 The long interaction during maturation produces a gradual and constant change.
2 Because her latitude is ideal for wine production and her 200,000 square miles is mostly fertile agricultural land.

of that of white wine. The Bordeaux region has two rivers, the Garonne and the Dordogne, which meet about 15 km north of the city of Bordeaux; their estuary then takes the name Gironde, as the river broadens out and flows on some 65 km to the sea. This river, the Gironde, gives its name to the *Département* in which all Bordeaux wines are produced.

The valleys of these rivers and the land lying between them are covered with vineyards. The region is divided into six principal districts; in each district there are many small villages known as *communes*, and within these lie individual *châteaux*, or vineyards. By these distinctions, the qualities of all Bordeaux wines are indicated on their labels. The mere description 'Red Bordeaux' or 'White Bordeaux' denotes the cheapest of them, but those bearing the name of a district will be of better quality, and individual characteristics will start to be noticeable. If the label also states the village of origin, the wine should again be of better quality, while those bearing the names of the great châteaux vineyards will be the best.

There are great châteaux, and humble: a classification founded on quality, not quantity, for some of the finest châteaux produce little wine. Classifications based on popularity, as measured by price, have been made for a long time; the most famous was the classification of the 1855 Paris *Exposition* which classified the wines of the Gironde into five categories of Great Growths (*Grands Crus Classés*), followed now only by the Bourgeois Growths, classified by the Courtiers in 1932. This ordering of estates is today questioned, but is still generally acceptable as a guide. The 1855 classification is a valuable aid to the understanding of Bordeaux labels, and is reproduced in Appendix 2.

The Médoc, Graves and Sauternes

The area to the northwest of the city of Bordeaux is the Médoc, where the finest claret is produced. South of Bordeaux, to the west of the Garonne, lies the Graves district, taking its name from the gravelly soil; this district is famous for both red and white wines, which are of excellent quality, but which lack the repute of the equivalent wines of the Médoc. Though the wines of Graves are often looked upon as being white and dry, Graves also produces

1 What is the Appellation Contrôlée system?
2 Which was the first of the medieval French wine brotherhoods to be revived, and when?

good quality red wines and some sweet and semi-sweet white wines. Château Haut-Brion is the most famous red Graves, an 1855 'first-class growth'.

Enclosed by the Graves district, 50 km south of Bordeaux, the Sauternes district lies on the left bank of the Garonne. Here the world-renowned sweet white wines of Sauternes and Barsac are produced, from grapes which have been affected by *botrytis cinerea* in ideal weather. This produces the condition known as *pourriture noble* ('noble rot'), in which the grapes shrivel to a raisin-like state and their sugar becomes very concentrated.

Entre-deux-Mers, St. Émilion and Pomerol

Across the Garonne from Graves is the district known as Entre-deux-Mers, 'between two rivers', the triangular area formed by the confluence of the Garonne and the Dordogne and the Département boundary. Here less distinguished wines, predominantly white, are made, which nevertheless are entitled to their own particular quality wine designation. Two famous districts lie to the north of the River Dordogne: the area surrounding St.Émilion, and Pomerol, where exquisite clarets challenging those from the Médoc are made.

Only the principal districts of Bordeaux have so far been mentioned. But there are minor districts of the region whose finest wines are just as good as the lesser wines of the better known districts: these include Côtes de Blaye, Côtes de Bourg, Côtes de Fronsac, Premières Côtes de Bordeaux and Cérons.

Most clarets are dry or medium-dry and of lighter texture and body than the red Burgundies and Rhône wines. This is due largely to the proximity of the Bay of Biscay, which tends to temper the climate. Even the clarets of St. Emilion, produced some 80 km inland, are slightly heavier.

Local Foods of Bordeaux

The local foods of Bordeaux are no less distinguished than its wines. Oysters from Arcachon, lobsters, and sea bass are admirably accompanied by dry white Graves. On the other hand lampreys, eel-like sucker-fish, are cooked in red wine, and red Graves should accompany them; they must be delicious, for it is recorded that King John

1 A system controlling the production of and naming of the better-quality French wines.
2 The Confrérie des Chevaliers du Tastevin, in the mid–1930s.

died from eating too many of them! 'Entrecôte Bordelaise' is a dish met in many restaurants, being a sirloin steak, or thick slice of topside (*contrefilet*) with a sauce made from chopped shallots, seasoned butter, and claret. The lees left after decanting wine for the table may be used for the sauce.

The white wines of Bordeaux have been mentioned in conjunction with fish – but only the dry wines. The sweet wines are more generous, and it is pleasant to sample the wines of Loupiac or Ste. Croix-du-Mont as an apéritif or mid-morning snack with fresh walnuts or almond biscuits. This immediately invokes the counter proposal of *pâté-de-foie* or of cheese. Sauternes is not just a dessert wine, magnificent though it is with peaches or strawberries. It can be appreciated with spicy foods too.

Bordeaux Wine Brotherhoods

The wine brotherhoods of Bordeaux are many, but the most famous include the *Jurade de St. Émilion*, whose livery is of scarlet trimmed with gold, and who announce permission for the harvest to start (*le ban de vendange*) with fanfares from the dizzy heights of the Tower of St. Emilion; the *Commanderie du Bontemps du Médoc et des Graves*, whose hat is modelled on the bowl in which egg-whites are whisked with wine for fining; and the *Commanderie de Sauternes-Barsac*, whose golden robes are evocative of the wine.

Bordeaux wines when young can be hard and astringent, although they will age into wines far more delicate than the full-bodied Burgundies. The analogy has been drawn with man and woman – Burgundy the heavier and stronger, soft in youth and duller in old age; Bordeaux the more delicate, yet harder in youth and mellowing into a far more attractive old age. Moodiness, seen in Bordeaux wines which can occasionally fall out of condition, is perhaps also in the feminine character.

The range and quality of Bordeaux wines should not be underestimated. They range from light golden to deep purple in colour, and between them suit almost every taste and every pocket. Amongst them are some of the finest of the world's wines, yet, by a process of classification, the quality varies down to the *vin rouge* enjoyed by the French labourer.

1 Would an AC wine of Bordeaux, marked with a commune name, probably be superior to one marked 'Bordeaux'?

2 Is the 1855 official classification a list: (a) ranking the best of the Bordeaux wines in order of quality; (b) indicating the vineyards with the largest output?

3 Which is of higher classification – Château Latour or Château Talbot?

4 If you buy a 1961 Château Margaux, will it be the product of the best wines from the Château of that year, or the product of the best wines of several years?

THE WINES OF BURGUNDY

The very word Burgundy conjures up thoughts of Chablis, Beaune, Nuits St. Georges and Montrachet or Romanée. In the heart of the Burgundy region, running south from Dijon to the Beaujolais district north of Lyon, a wide range of red and white wines, both still and sparkling, is produced. These are almost entirely dry in character. The volume of red wine production is three times that of white.

The Burgundy range and variety is second only to that of Bordeaux, but, because of the inland climate, the Burgundies are generally bigger and fuller than the clarets, although not so long-lasting. In fact, the Mâconnais and Beaujolais wines are better drunk young, when they are fresh and fruity.

Chablis and the Côte d'Or

The Burgundy region is long and narrow. Going southeast from Paris, the first of the Burgundy districts is Chablis, where white wines of a remarkable freshness and flavour are made. Their rather dry and flinty character causes many to aver that they are the only wines to drink with shellfish. About 100 km to the southeast of Chablis, the compact wine district known as the Côte d'Or begins, comprising the Côte de Nuits and the Côte de Beaune. In the middle of the Côte d'Or is the town of Beaune, famed not only as a wine centre, but also for the Hospices de Beaune, which must rank among the most interesting buildings on the Continent. The Hospices, a charitable institution, was bequeathed a number of vineyards for its upkeep. Yearly sales of the Hospices wine, held in November each year, go back for many centuries. These wines are generally rather expensive, having regard to their charitable purpose, and are easily identified by their special label. However, the relationship between the prices fetched by the various Hospices wines gives a guide to Burgundy prices in the following year.

The Côte d'Or stretches from Dijon to Santenay, just north of Chalon-sur-Saône, and here the fine red and white Burgundies are made. The villages of Gevrey-Chambertin, Chambolle-Musigny, Vougeot, Vosne-Romanée and Nuits St. Georges produce some of

1 Yes.
2 (a) A list ranking the best of the Bordeaux wines in order of quality.
3 Château Latour is a first growth; Château Talbot is a fourth growth.
4 It will be the product of the best wines of Château Margaux of 1961.

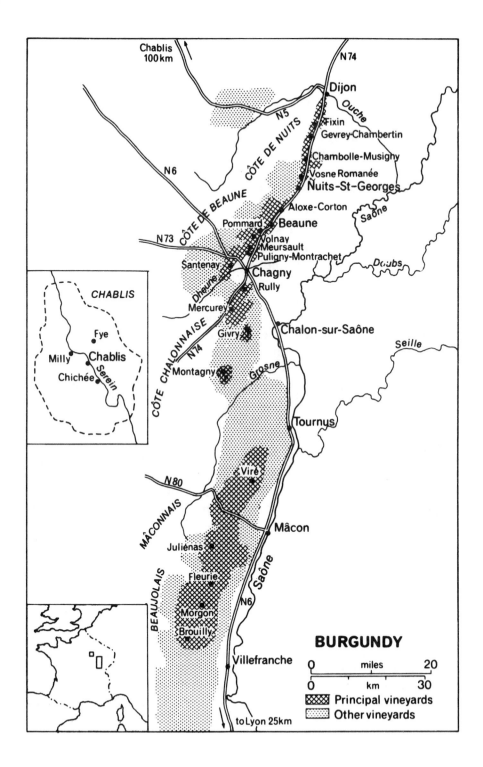

1 In which district are Barsac wines produced?
2 How does *pourriture noble* affect grapes?
3 Which area generally produces the better-quality wines: Graves or Entre-deux-Mers?
4 Which of the following districts are more important for red wine than for white:
   (a) Médoc; (b) St. Émilion/Pomerol; (c) Entre-deux-Mers; (d) Bourg and Blaye?
5 What are the names of the wine brotherhoods of (a) Médoc; (b) St. Émilion?

the finest red wines of the Côte de Nuits. Equally famous, from the Côte de Beaune, are Aloxe-Corton, Beaune, Pommard and Volnay. At the southern end of the Côte de Beaune, fine white wines are made in Puligny-Montrachet and Meursault, names familiar throughout the world.

The Côte Chalonnaise, Mâconnais, and Beaujolais

In the Côte Chalonnaise are Mercurey and the Rully area, which produce fine red wines and wines suitable for conversion into sparkling Burgundy. Some 65 km further south is Mâcon at the head of the Mâconnais and Beaujolais vineyards. Here the wines, though still classified as Burgundy, are somewhat lighter in texture and lack the body or fullness of a Vougeot or Meursault. Consequently, they tend to develop more quickly, and should be drunk young, for some of them are at their best when only a few months old, and make a fresh and fruity drink. In summer, the light red wines of the Beaujolais may, with advantage, be served cool, contrary to the usual practice. Generally, the red and white Mâcons are good value for money. Pouilly-Fuissé, a white wine without the delicacy of Chablis or the body of the Côte de Beaune white wines, is one of the best-known.

The light red wines of Beaujolais may be sold under the district Appellation of Beaujolais or Beaujolais Supérieur; certain villages, however, are allowed to sell their wines under the name of their village as an Appellation, or where these village wines are blended together, under the name Beaujolais-Villages (the same principle applies to the white wines of the Mâconnais). Beaujolais wines can nevertheless be made to keep and improve in bottle, when some of them will develop a character more like the wines of Mercurey.

Labelling of Burgundy Wines

The system of labelling the wines of Burgundy is logical and relatively simple to follow. Firstly, a wide variety of wines may bear the name of the same village, even though produced in different qualities by different growers and at varying prices. Secondly, the villages or communes attach to their own name that of the most famous vineyard in their district. Thus Puligny (the village) attaches

---

1 Sauternes.
2 It shrivels the grapes to a raisin-like state, and concentrates their sugar.
3 Graves.
4 (a), (b), and (d).
5 (a) The Commanderie du Bontemps du Médoc et des Graves; (b) The Jurade de St. Émilion.

the name of Montrachet (the famous vineyard) and calls itself Puligny-Montrachet, as does the next village, Chassagne-Montrachet. There are many wines entitled to be called by their village names, but there is only one vineyard area which can produce wine to be labelled 'Le Montrachet', and of course this vineyard stretches over both villages.

Certain vineyards, whose superior products have been recognized since the Middle Ages, have been entitled '*Grands Crus*'; these are listed under the name of the commune in which they lie, in Appendix 1. Other vineyards, whose products are not quite so superior but are better than normal, are designated '*Premiers Crus*'; these are too numerous to list in this book.

Local Foods of Burgundy

Unlike compact Bordeaux, Burgundy is spread over such a wide area that it is difficult to select one dish that is characteristic. Many will say 'Boeuf Bourguignonne' which is certainly a world-renowned dish; but what of ham cooked in, and eaten with, Chablis? Or eggs poached in red Mâcon, covered with a sauce made with the wine they were poached in? Or steaks 'au poivre' marinated in Beaujolais, with green peppercorns beaten into them, grilled to taste and covered with a sauce of butter, shallots, and Beaujolais? For the best results the steaks should be 'flamed' with marc-de-Bourgogne before adding the sauce.

There is an apocryphal story about 'escargots de Bourgogne'. The snail is a pest of the vineyards, as it feeds on the leaves and, from time immemorial, sweeping the snails from the vine has been one of the labours of the vineyards. At one time in the Middle Ages, the lord of the manor was so mean, and the snails so large, that the peasants had to resort to eating them: they didn't like them, but their clever wives concocted a sauce of butter, salt, garlic and shallots which concealed the flavour and even equated it to the best mutton. The peasants flourished under this protein-rich diet until the lord said, 'What are my peasants stealing – they grow fat.' On being told that they were not stealing, but had been reduced to eating even the pestilent snails, he said, 'Eugh' and then, 'Give me one'. Unfortunately, they gave him one with its delectable sauce, whereafter he claimed all snails for his own table. Incidentally, it is a disgusting misrepresentation to

1 How do the wines of Burgundy differ from those of Bordeaux?
2 Is Chablis renowned for its fine red wine or white wine?
3 Which two areas does the Côte d'Or comprise?

suggest that modern tinned snails, with their accompanying housing of plastic shells, are English slugs rather than Burgundian snails – even if slugs are also gasteropods, and larger!

Burgundy Wine Brotherhoods

It is mentioned earlier that the modern wine brotherhoods stem from the Chevaliers du Tastevin, who have their headquarters in the ancient monastery of the Clos de Vougeot, and celebrate annually with a grand banquet preceding the auctions of the Hospices de Beaune. Chablis has its own brotherhood, the *Piliers Chablisiens*, with gold and black livery; as has Mâcon, with the *Confrérie des Vignerons de St. Vincent-de-Mâcon* (St. Vincent is one of the patron saints of the vine). Beaujolais has its *Ordre des Compagnons du Beaujolais*; unlike most of the others, who are attired in grand style of scarlet and gold, their livery is the traditional green apron of service with black coat and hat. Their accoutrements are the tastevin and the pruning-knife.

OTHER FRENCH LIGHT WINES

Until recently, few people who had not visited France were aware of regions other than Bordeaux or Burgundy. Fortunately for all wine-lovers, wines from these 'other regions' are being shipped to, and sold in, the United Kingdom, and their qualities appreciated throughout the world.

RHÔNE

The Rhône valley wine region lies south of Burgundy from Lyon to Avignon along the banks of the river, and divides into clearly defined northern and southern subregions. From the granite and sandstone cliffs of the north come red Côte Rôtie, Hermitage and Cornas among others, and white Condrieu. In the south, after traversing the thirsty plain of Montelimar for 40 km, the traveller will find the heady red wines of Châteauneuf-du-Pape – the 'new castle of the Pope' – recalling the time when the Cardinal Bishop of Bordeaux was elected Pope and, fearing to leave his beloved France, invested

1 They tend to be fuller and stronger.
2 White wine.
3 Côte de Nuits and Côte de Beaune.

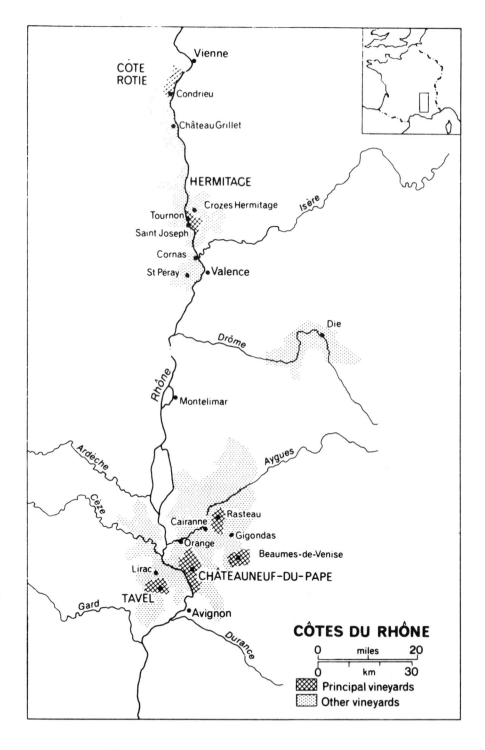

COTE
ROTIE

Vienne

Condrieu

Château Grillet

HERMITAGE

Isère

Crozes Hermitage

Tournon

Saint Joseph

Cornas

St Péray

Valence

Drôme

Die

Rhône

Montelimar

Ardèche

Aygues

Cèze

Rasteau

Cairanne

Gigondas

Orange

Beaumes-de-Venise

Lirac

CHÂTEAUNEUF-DU-PAPE

TAVEL

Gard

Avignon

Durance

CÔTES DU RHÔNE

```
0        miles       20
0         km         30
```

▨ Principal vineyards

░ Other vineyards

1 Name the six districts of the Burgundy region, and the colours of the wines each produces.
2 Identify the meaning of the two hyphenated names Puligny-Montrachet.
3 Name the famous dish associated with Burgundy.

Avignon with the Papacy as Clément V. His vineyard in Bordeaux is
still famed as Ch. Pape Clément.

The chief wine brotherhood of this region is *L'Échansonnerie des
Papes*, who are richly attired in purple and white and bear a symbolic
golden key; at their banquets they will often eat chicken in a rich
sauce of chicken and veal stock with onion, carrots, herbs, and wine,
served with fried button mushrooms. The Échansonnier differs from
the Sommelier in that he is a trusted nobleman, and does not merely
pour the wine, but also has the duty of tasting it, to ensure that his
chief is not poisoned.

Châteauneuf-du-Pape, raised from its excessively stony soil, is an
expensive wine. Yet the southern Côtes du Rhône have many others
to refresh the traveller or local at moderate prices. Côtes-du-Rhône
itself, and the more select Côtes-du-Rhône-Villages, are satisfying
red wines: some may even aspire to carry the name of their village
alone, like Gigondas, or Lirac.

Seventeen villages, including Cairanne and Vacqueras, are entitled
to add their name to 'Côtes-du-Rhône' or to describe their product as
Côtes-du-Rhône-Villages.

PROVENCE AND LANGUEDOC

The tumultuous Rhône, born in the glaciers of Switzerland and long
confined in narrow rocky valleys, breaks out into the broad plains of
Provence and Languedoc, and here all is vines and wine. This is the
land of van Gogh and of Bizet, of bulls in the arenas of Nîmes and
Arles, of olives, garlic, and hard little *saucissons* which complement
the wines so well.

This 'sea of vines' continues south to the Pyrenees and west, past
Toulouse, almost to Bordeaux. Some of the wines are rough, but
they are fine companions for the local specialities of food, and will
satisfy. 'Pork and beans' conjures up the thought of plebeian
indigestion, but Cassoulet, although its prime constituents *are* pork
and beans, is a different matter. Garlic, goose, spices, truffle, bread,
wine, all contribute to one of the great dishes of all time. The pot is
seldom emptied, but frequently refreshed; the constituents vary from
village to village, from house to house, but all, with wine, satisfy.

1 Chablis (white); Côte de Nuits (red); Côte de Beaune (red and white); Côte Chalonnaise
  (red and white); Mâconnais (red and white); Beaujolais (red).
2 The first half is a village; the second half a famous vineyard.
3 Boeuf Bourguignonne.

ROUSSILLON

There are many other parts of France, south of Paris, producing wine: Languedoc has been mentioned stretching from the Rhône to Bordeaux. Provence lies east of this, from the Rhône to the Italian border; generally light red, white, and rosé wines are produced which accord well with Provençal cookery – the cookery, however, is more famous than the wines! South of Languedoc, Roussillon produces sound red and white wines, but is renowned in France for its fortified wines called *vins doux naturels*; these are seldom seen in England, which is a pity, for they have a pleasant flavour of Muscat grapes or sultana raisins and, chilled, make a refreshing apéritif.

VAL DE LOIRE

The river Loire is the longest in France: it rises in the Auvergne, south-west of Lyon, flows north for 500 km to Orléans, then west for another 500 km to join the sea at Nantes. For almost the whole of its length it is bordered by vineyards. In the upper reaches this is evidenced by the little-known wines of the Côte Roannaise and St. Pourçain (VDQS); and, lower down, by the steely white AC wines of Sancerre and Pouilly-sur-Loire (Blanc Fumé de Pouilly) of the Central Vineyard region, and by others further downstream. But before going further, linger in the chalky hillocks between Nevers and Orléans to enjoy trout and pike from the river and steaks from the beef of the Charollais mountains which alone separate the Loire from Burgundy.

From Orléans downstream lies the Loire valley as most people know it. Touraine produces fine white Vouvray, still or sparkling and, south of Tours itself, red wines of great fruity elegance and vinosity. A bowl of fresh strawberries, liberally sprinkled with red Bourgueil, is a dish for kings; for this and neighbouring Anjou were the home of the Plantagenet kings of England – they were buried at Fontevrault Abbey at the junction of the two districts.

The Rosé wines of Anjou

Anjou recalls sweetish pink wine, taken with a picnic on the river on a fine summer's day. Yet not all Anjou rosés are sweet, nor are all

1 Where is the headquarters of the Confrérie des Chevaliers du Tastevin?
2 What are the names of the wine brotherhoods of (a) Chablis; (b) Mâcon?
3 Name wines coming from the north of the Côtes-du-Rhône.
4 From what region do Châteauneuf-du-Pape and Condrieu come?

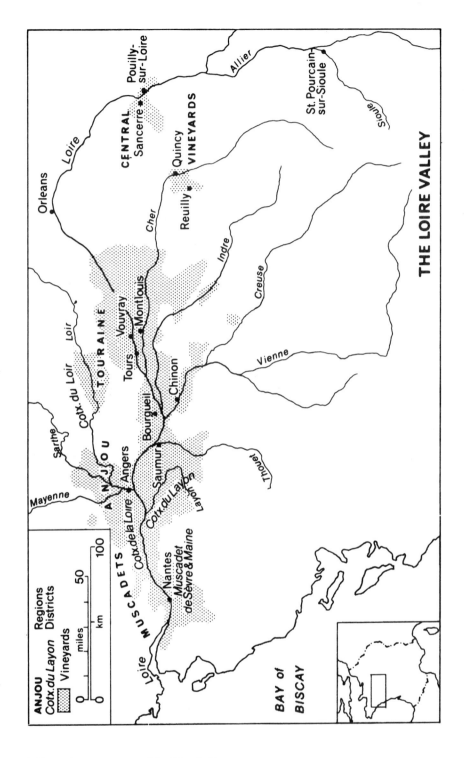

THE LOIRE VALLEY

1 The ancient monastery of the Clos de Vougeot.
2 (a) The Piliers Chablisiens. (b) The Confrérie des Vignerons de St. Vincent-de Mâcon.
3 Côte Rôtie, Hermitage, Condrieu, and Cornas – among others.
4 The Rhône region.

Anjou wines rosé. This is the land of Rabelais, of gargantuan meals, of laughter, and of song. The *Chevaliers du Sacavin* are perhaps the jolliest of all the brotherhoods, and enjoy such dishes as eels stewed in wine with mushrooms, carrots and onions; fine lamb and veal; and fruits accompanied by the sweet white wines of the Coteaux du Layon which rival Sauternes in all but price.

The 'land of Nantes' is more austere, reflecting the nearness of the unrelenting sea. Almost all the wines are white – typified by Muscadet – to be drunk young and fresh with the abundant seafood. True, there are better wines: Chablis springs to mind when oysters are mentioned, and Meursault with sole. But Muscadet with lobster, sole, oysters or mussels is an admirable choice.

ALSACE

Bordering Germany – just across the Rhine – Alsace has suffered a chequered history, being the battleground of many wars. It is strangely unchanged: its people speak French and German with equal facility: its towns have German-sounding names, but are most definitely French. It is almost separated from France by the Vosges mountains; some of its grapes are French in origin, others German. Its wines are unique – they are Alsace. Alsace is famed for wines akin to the German Hocks and Mosels; practically all are white wines, the majority being dry or medium-dry, although a good year may produce a sweet Alsatian wine. The Alsace wine label differs from other French wine labels inasmuch as the wines are named for the grape, the Riesling or Sylvaner for example, and not for the place name, such as Beaune. The place name can be added, however, as for example Riesling de Barr. The general Appellation is 'Vin d'Alsace'. Bottles labelled either Sylvaner or Pinot are usually very good; a cheaper, blended wine is Edelzwicker. Generally, Alsatian wines need to be served cool and crisp, but not chilled excessively. In the summer they make a splendid thirst-quencher.

Chief among the wines is the noble Riesling, golden and full-bodied. Such a statement provokes disagreement from those who would place the Gewürztraminer first, with its delicate, pungent,

1 Name some of the Côtes-du-Rhône Villages.
2 What is the local dish of Languedoc?
3 How does the River Loire run from its source to Orléans? Name wines found near its banks in this reach.
4 How does the River Loire run from Orléans to the sea? What are the names of the districts on this reach?
5 Name three wine regions of southeast France, other than Rhône.

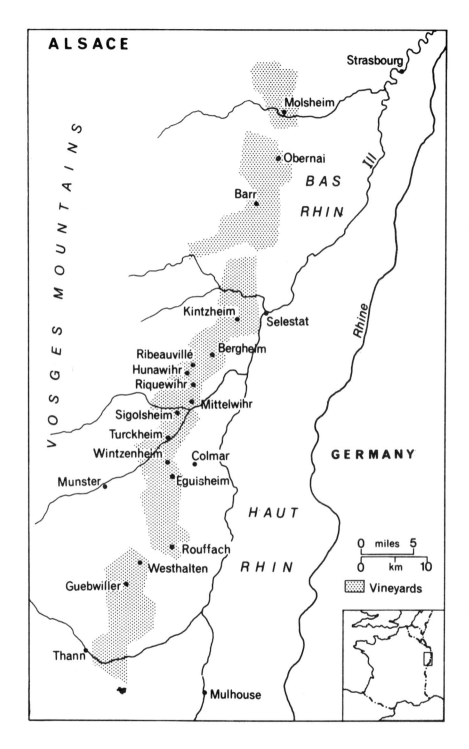

ALSACE

Strasbourg

Molsheim

Obernai

BAS

Barr

RHIN

Ill

VOSGES MOUNTAINS

Kintzheim

Selestat

Rhine

Bergheim

Ribeauvillé

Hunawihr

Riquewihr

Mittelwihr

Sigolsheim

Turckheim

Wintzenheim

Colmar

GERMANY

Munster

Eguisheim

HAUT

RHIN

Rouffach

Westhalten

Guebwiller

0   miles   5

0   km   10

Vineyards

Thann

Mulhouse

1 Cairanne and Vacqueras, with fifteen others, are AC Côtes-du-Rhône-Villages; other villages such as Gigondas and Lirac, have their own AC.
2 Cassoulet, a superb stew of garlic, sausage, goose, pork, and beans.
3 North, for 500 km. Côte Roannaise VDQS; Sancerre AC; Blanc-Fumé de Pouilly AC; and Pouilly-sur-Loire AC; are the most important.
4 West, for 500 km. The districts, from Orléans, are Touraine, Anjou, and the Nantais.
5 Provence, Languedoc, and Roussillon.

spiciness. Well, one can disagree about feminine beauty too – perhaps it depends on the vintage! There are other wines: the rare Muscat, absolutely dry, one of the only wines with enough character to balance smoked fish: or Pinot Gris which balances well the local dish of sauerkraut with sausages. But the classic dish of Alsace is Coq au Vin, not cooked in red wine as it is in Burgundy, but in Riesling, with peeled grapes. Alsace has a mighty cheese, the square Munster – much milder than the nose suggests – which Riesling accompanies well. To finish the meal, what better than a Tarte St. Étienne, for St. Étienne is the patron saint of Alsace. Its very active wine brotherhood, in scarlet livery, is the *Confrérie-de-St. Étienne d'Alsace.*

JURA

One last important district should be mentioned before leaving France: the Jura, lying between Burgundy and the Swiss border on the slopes of the mountains of that name. The soil is of the same hard limestone that is found in Yorkshire, appropriately called jurassic as is the geological era when the soils were laid down. Pasteur lived here, and praised the wines as health-giving; the district not only has red and white wines, but also rejoices in wines called 'mad', 'grey', and 'yellow'! The 'mad' wines are sparkling; the 'grey' are rosé; and the 'yellow' are attacked by the Sherry yeast, which turns them that colour. The district is famed for its gastronomy, particularly for the AC Poulets de Bresse (from the nearby plains) cooked in *vin jaune*.

GERMAN WINES

Germany is the producer of light wines ranking only second to France. In fact Germany is unsurpassed in her own white varieties, coming from the Rhine and Mosel valleys. Because the area of cultivation is almost at the northern limit of the wine belt, the growers are very much at the mercy of the weather. They have many difficulties with which to contend, so that production is comparatively small and the price reflects these difficulties. Practically all Rhine and Mosel wines have a magnificent bouquet and fine

1 What is the name of the wine brotherhood of Anjou?
2 Where, in the lower reaches of the Loire, would you find: (a) a sweet; (b) a dry, white wine?
3 In what region would you find Muscadet, and what sort of wine is it?
4 What French light-wine-producing regions are there other than Bordeaux and Burgundy?

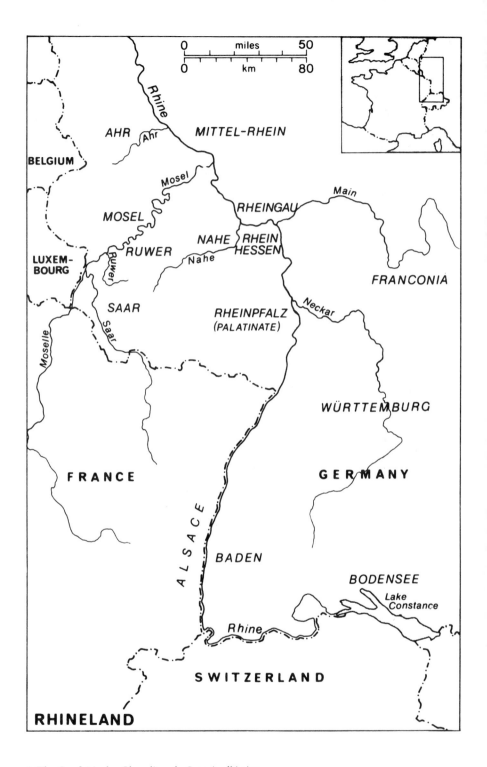

RHINELAND

1 The Confrérie des Chevaliers du Sacavin d'Anjou.
2 (a) Coteaux du Layon, in Anjou. (b) Muscadet, in the Nantais.
3 Loire. Dry white wine.
4 Alsace, Loire, Rhône, Jura, Provence, Languedoc, and Roussillon.

colouring. The rich Hocks, produced in limited quantity and only in good years, are among the world's most expensive wines.

Queen Victoria's favourite wine came from Hochheim in the Rheingau. The Queen used to visit the area frequently and she would say, 'Bring me a glass of *mein hock*', so that the name Hock came into the English language as describing Rhine wines in general. But incidentally, the good Queen (and her son Edward VII) used to dilute it with soda water – for moderation's sake!

GERMANY'S MAIN WINE REGIONS

The most important districts of the Rhine, extending from Coblenz to Mannheim are: the Rheingau, Rheinhessen, Nahe and the Palatinate. Each district has its famous villages, giving their names to wine. From Rheingau come the wines of Rüdesheim, Johannisberg, Oestrich, Hattenheim, Erbach, Winkel, Kiedrich, and Hochheim. From Rheinhessen come the wines of Worms (whose church, the Liebfrauenkirche, gave its name to 'Liebfraumilch'), Oppenheim, Nierstein, and Nackenheim. The Nahe is the home of Schlossböckelheim, Niederhausen, and Kreuznach wines, and from the Palatinate come the wines of Ruppertsberg, Deidesheim, Forst, Wachenheim, Dürkheim, and Kallstadt, among others.

These Rhine wines tend to be bigger, fuller and longer-lasting than the Mosel wines, which come from vineyards on the precipitous slate hills rising from the River Mosel and its tributaries, the Saar and Ruwer. The Mosels have a touch of acidity, derived from the soil as well as from their northern habitat, which makes them taste delightfully crisp and fresh when correctly chilled. They should be drunk when young.

The best-known wines from the Mosel valley are those of Trittenheim, Piesport, Brauneberg, Bernkastel, Graach, Wehlen, Zeltingen, Urzig and Traben-Trarbach. From the Saar, Ockfen, Wiltingen, Oberemmel and Ayl are among the finest names, and from the Ruwer, Casel.

Some red wines are made in Germany, but as red grapes need more warmth than white grapes to ripen satisfactorily, these red wines tend to be harsh, and are little-known outside Germany. Sparkling wines called Sekt or Schaumwein are also produced, and find a limited market in Great Britain.

1 Name three grapes in Alsace which give their names to wines.
2 What is the name of the wine region lying between Burgundy and the Swiss border? What is its soil?

WINE LAW AND QUALITY CONTROL

Germany has a new wine law and quality control, intended both to guarantee the value of German wines and establish their identity. Government officials supervise both viticulture and vinification, and analysis of the wines in approved laboratories ensures that they conform with legal requirements. After examination in a laboratory, wines are divided into three categories: *Deutscher Tafelwein* (table wine, which is no longer allowed to bear the name of a vineyard), *Qualitätswein* (quality wine of a designated region), or *Qualitätswein mit Prädikat* (quality wine with special attributes). Six special attributes (*Prädikaten*) can be awarded: *Kabinett*, elegant mature wines of superior quality; *Spätlese*, full-bodied wines made from late-gathered grapes left to ripen further after the main harvest; *Auslese* and *Beerenauslese*, noble aromatic wines from bunches of individual grapes which have been affected by 'noble rot'; *Trockenbeerenauslese*, the crowning achievement of German viticulture, made from raisin-like grapes shrivelled by noble rot, and comparable with the fine Sauternes; and *Eiswein*, a description which must be attached to one of the other five attributes, denoting a rare wine made from grapes harvested in the depths of winter and crushed while still frozen. The two quality wine categories must bear an official certificate number (Prüfungsnummer) on the label.

In addition, the label may indicate the vintage, the vineyard, the grape variety and the name of the 'wine-grower'. With a patient understanding of all these disciplines, the wine-lover can learn much from German wine labels.

Drinks for German meals

The foods enjoyed in Germany tend to be heavier than their French equivalents, possibly because the winters tend to be much colder, and many people prefer to drink beer with their Kalbshaxe (knuckle of veal), Wildschweinschnitzel (wild boar steak), or Fasan mit Rotkohl (Pheasant with red cabbage). Wines are often drunk after the meal with delicious sweets such as Apfelstrudel, and the wines of Germany (and of Austria) complement these perfectly.

---

1 Riesling, Gewürztraminer, and Muscat – there are others, not mentioned in the text.
2 Jura. A region of jurassic limestone, like that found in Yorkshire.

ITALIAN WINES

The wine regions of Italy generally take their names from the provinces, and the individual wines are either named after grapes or districts. The Barbera and Nebbiolo red wines and the white Moscato, all from Piedmont, have grape names, while Bardolino and Valpolicella, red wines from Lake Garda, and the famous white Soave are all place-names from Veneto province. Piedmont also has wines named for places – Asti, Barbaresco and Barolo are three.

The red wines of Chianti and the white wines of Tuscany have been put up in the same-shaped straw-covered flasks down through the centuries, but in the modern economy this bottle has become too expensive to survive generally. This applies also to the dry (*secco*) and sweet (*abboccato*) white wines of Orvieto. None of these wines will suffer from a conventional shape of bottle. Furthermore, legislation in Italy during the last two decades gives the consumer a far greater guarantee of quality than he has ever enjoyed in Italy's 2,700 years of wine-making.

Italy – land of pastas

Italy has a variety of foods to offer the visitor as wide as those of France. *Spaghetti* is not all the land has to offer and, although this form of *pasta* is ubiquitous, there are many other forms: *tagliatelli* in thin strips, *lasagne* in wide sheets to interleave between layers of meat and vegetables, *cannelloni*, of larger bore than *macaroni*, which can be stuffed with minced meat, *ravioli*, best described as 'stuffed postage stamps', and *vermicelli*, thin threads to thicken a fine broth, are only a few of these. Pasta goes equally well with meat or fish, and the regional variations consist of the sauces, always incorporating the wine of the region.

Wines worthy of greater popularity

The wines of Italy are not as popular in the UK trade as they deserve to be, and there seems to be no reason for this except perhaps that the British are unable to spell or to pronounce the names. For the wines themselves are delectable, and give just as good value for money as do their French counterparts; their names may even be easier to

---

1 In which Rhineland quality regions are the following towns? (a) Nierstein; (b) Kallstadt, (c) Johannisberg; (d) Kreuznach.
2 Name the four most important Rhine districts extending from Coblenz to Mannheim.
3 Are Hocks usually red or white wines?
4 In which quality region are the villages of Piesport, Wehlen and Zeltingen?

1 (a) Rheinhessen, (b) Palatinate, (c) Rheingau, (d) Nahe.
2 Rheinhessen, Rheingau, Nahe, and the Palatinate.
3 White.
4 Mosel-Saar-Ruwer.

pronounce, for in Italian every letter is pronounced, and none of them in the back of the nose as is necessary in French.

Italian Wine Brotherhoods: It is hoped that the wine brotherhoods of Italy will do as much to promote the wines of their country as the French brotherhoods do for theirs. Two of the leaders are the *Lega del Chianti* presiding over the region between Florence and Siena; and the *Company of Paladini* of Sicily, which is influential in that important wine-growing province.

WINES OF SPAIN AND PORTUGAL

Spain and Portugal call to mind Sherry and Port, but these are fortified wines, and will be dealt with in a later chapter. These two countries also produce fine light wines, which are coming on to the British market.

SPANISH WINE REGIONS

When the Protestants were persecuted in France, many fled from Bordeaux over the Pyrenees into Spain, and planted vineyards in Rueda, and in the valleys of the Duero and the Ebro, with its tributary the Oja; these regions of Rueda and Rioja provide the best light wines of Spain, both red and white. The Ebro flows into the Mediterranean near Tarragona, and in the coastal hills between the Ebro and the French frontier the region of Cataluña yields a variety of wines – heavy reds, strong rosés, and white wines that range from light delicacy to sweet fullness.

Further south on the Mediterranean coast comes the region of Levante, between Valencia and Alicante; the wines of this region are heavy and strong, as visitors to the resorts of Benidorm or Calpe will know, and are an indispensible accompaniment to the rich *paella* of rice, chicken, and prawns; such is their strength that it is wise to order a bottle of *acqua minerale*, and to drink it glass for glass with the wine. These wines have long been known by the English, who found them during the course of wars in the Low Countries before Shakespeare's time, for his characters speak of 'Tent' as being a Spanish wine: this was the English soldier's attempt to pronounce

1 What does the new German wine law and quality control guarantee?
2 What does Prädikat Trockenbeernauslese mean?
3 Where can the wine-lover find much useful information about German wines?
4 (a) How are Italian wine regions named? (b) How are Italian wines named?

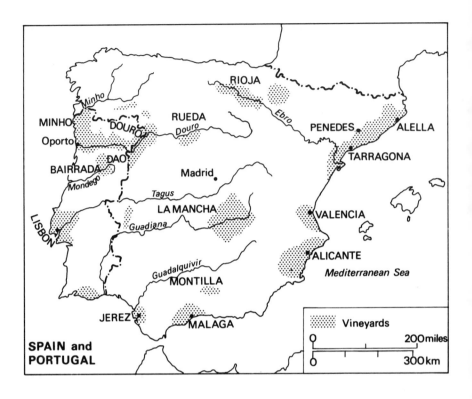

SPAIN and
PORTUGAL

'Tinto' (red), just as 'Plonk' was his 1914 descendant's attempt to pronounce 'Blanc' (white)! The largest wine-producing region of Spain, however, lies inland, occupying the whole of the high central plateau of the Peninsula; La Mancha is a vast, windy plain, dotted with isolated hills crowned with windmills, and the scattered vineyards produce over 10 million hl a year – half Spain's total production. The wines are hardly noteworthy, except for Valdepeñas, and much of them is made into brandy.

WINE REGIONS OF PORTUGAL

The wine from Portugal most likely to be encountered in the UK or America is pink, sweetish, and semi-sparkling; or white, also

---

1 The value and identity of German wines.
2 That the wine is made from grapes which have been allowed to remain on the vine until shrivelled. They are picked singly.
3 On the bottle labels.
4 (a) From Italian Provinces. (b) From grapes or districts.

semi-sparkling, known as *vinhos verdes*, and meaning 'green wines'. These wines are 'green' in the way that little unripe apples are 'green', and it is the excess of malic acid that, with a malolactic fermentation, causes the wine to become semi-sparkling. The excess of malic acid comes from the grapes having been grown on high trellises and thus getting no reflected heat from the soil; they are grown thus because this takes up less room and provides shelter for crops of maize, beans, and cabbage below. Vinhos verdes provide a balancing acidity to cut through the greasiness of grilled *sardhinas* – more like herrings in size than sardines – and the meal is most satisfyingly rounded off with a maize and cabbage soup. Peasant fare, yes: but peasants know how to make the best of Nature's gifts and take pride in doing so.

Other regions of Portugal are Dão and Bairrada in the central highlands, producing red and white wines of distinction which are matured, in the fashion of the Peninsula, in wood for three or four years: and north of Lisbon, the red and white wines of Estramadura – Bucelas and Torres Vedras, and Palmela to the south; their most celebrated wine was Colares, planted in clay thirty feet down through sand, so that *Phylloxera* could not attack the vines. But the vineyards are now planted with holiday cottages, which bring in a better income with less risk of being buried in sand.

OTHER LIGHT WINES OF EUROPE

Greece: Until recently, the name 'Greece' in connection with wine conjured up the thought of *retsina*, tasting heavily of pine resin, or of white wines so oxidized that they were dark brown and bitter. But times have changed, and fine red and white wines are produced in northern Thessaly, notably in the district of Naoussa, and in southern Attica and the Peloponnese. The islands, Crete in particular, produce wines, though most of them are resinated; a rosé wine, Kokkineli, comes to mind as a suitable accompaniment to Greek dishes such as dolmas (vine leaves stuffed with aromatic mince).

Yugoslavia: The wines of the Lutomer district near the Italian and Austrian borders have long been popular in the UK, being excellent value for money; but it must be noted that the Yugoslav 'Riesling' is

1 Whereabouts in Italy is Chianti produced?
2 Name two important wine brotherhoods of Italy.
3 Which regions of Spain produce the finest light wines, and where are they situated?
4 Where is the Spanish region of Levante, and what are its wines like?

not the grape of the Rhineland, nor even a direct relative, but one common to many Eastern European countries and called variously Laski, Olasz- and Wälsch-Rizling.

Austria: This important wine-producing country has an output exceeding two million hl each year; production is mainly of white wine from the Grüner Veltliner grape, and is centred on the Danube valley and its tributaries to the north of Vienna. Fine wines from the Wälsh-Rizling and other grapes are made in the region on the shores of the Neusiedlersee in the east; some red wine is made in the south of the country. Quality wines are known as *Spitzenweine*, and their names are recognized by the EEC; table wines are called *Tischweine*.

Switzerland: White wines from the Chasselas, and red from Pinot Noir and Gamay grapes, are found on the shores of Lake Geneva in the canton of Vaud under the names of Salvagnin and Dorin respectively; from the Rhône valley in the canton of Valais they are known as Fendant and Dôle. They are good value for skiers.

Hungary: Famed for white Tokay, Hungary is probably best known for 'Bull's Blood of Eger'; both come from the mountains in the north-east of the country. However, very fine white wines from Olasz-Rizling and Furmint grapes are made on the northern shores of Lake Balaton (the largest lake in Europe), and some very drinkable reds come from the eastern shore of the Neusiedlersee, opposite Austria.

Romania and Bulgaria: The quality of wines exported from these two countries has improved enormously in recent years with the widespread introduction of the Cabernet Sauvignon grape. Bulgarian Cabernet in particular is good value for money.

LIGHT WINES OF THE MIDDLE EAST AND ASIA

USSR: The Soviet Union is the sixth largest producer of wines in the world; its vineyard regions lie in Moldavia on the border with Romania, in the Crimea, and on the northern slopes of the Caucasus mountains in Georgia. It is unlikely that her wines will be encountered in the west, however, because home consumption accounts for 98% of them.

---

1 Between Florence and Siena in Tuscany.
2 The Lega del Chianti and the Company of Paladini of Sicily.
3 Rioja and Rueda. In the valleys of the Ebro and Duero in the north of Spain.
4 On the Mediterranean coast between Valencia and Alicante; the wines are heavy and strong.

Cyprus: The wine industry of Cyprus is well-established, largely under British influence; but the island is better known for 'Cyprus Sherry' than for its light wines which resemble those of Greece.

Turkey: This country has a large vineyard area, but most of the grapes are harvested for the table, as in all Muslim countries. Much excellent wine is produced, however, coming notably from Anatolia in the south, and from the Black Sea shores of both European and Asian Turkey.

Lebanon and Israel: Both countries produce wines in quantity, but the only one likely to be found readily in the UK is that from Château Musar in the Beka'a valley of Lebanon.

India: Wine production on a commercial scale has recently been instituted in the Deccan Hills north of Poona, about 300 km from Bombay. At this latitude (18°N) the vine flowers twice a year, in May and November; all the flowers are removed in May so that the vine can conserve its strength, but the November flowering is allowed to ripen during the mild winter months, to be harvested in March. The wine, made sparkling by a second fermentation in bottle, is surprisingly good.

China: There is an expanding wine industry centred on the peninsula south of Shanghai, and a growing interest in wine among the Chinese people.

Japan: As far as viticulture is concerned, the Japanese suffer from an even worse climate than England, but nevertheless persevere and produce enough to be quoted in the production 'league tables'. It has been described as thin and watery, but no doubt the selection of suitable vine varieties will change that.

LIGHT WINES OF THE SOUTHERN HEMISPHERE

Australia: The wine industry of Australia is only 200 years old, and has progressed through many vicissitudes to become one of the healthiest in the world. Once known (and often reviled) for 'Burgundy' and 'Port', its light wines rank among the foremost in the world. They are more often known by the names of their producers and the grapes from which they are made than by the districts from which they come, but the districts of Barossa and Coonawarra in Southern

1 Describe the wines of Portugal now most exported to the UK and America.
2 *Vinhos verdes* translates as 'green wines'. Why is this so, seeing that the wines are not green in colour?
3 From what parts of Greece do the finest wines come?
4 Name the Yugoslavia district supplying wines popular in the UK.

Australia, Milawa in Victoria, and the Hunter River Valley in New South Wales are becoming better-known. The main grapes for white wines are Sémillon (known as 'Hunter River Riesling') and Chardonnay. For red wines they are Cabernet Sauvignon and Shiraz (the Syrah of the Rhône Valley, sometimes known as Hermitage in Australia); the two are sometimes blended together with great success. Besides these states, wine is produced in the southern part of Queensland, and near Perth in Western Australia.

South Africa: The Cape received the grape rather earlier than Australia, through the original Dutch settlers, and therefore its wines, mostly fortified, became popular earlier. The vineyards are mainly concentrated in Cape Province to the north of Capetown on the slopes of the Drakensberg Mountains, where the soil and climate are ideal for viticulture. For red wines, Cabernet Sauvignon and Shiraz are grown; Hermitage (the French Cinsaut, *not* the Syrah), and a cross called Pinotage between the Pinot Noir and (Cape) Hermitage are also cultivated. For light white wines, the French Chenin Blanc is paramount and may be called Steen. Cape wines are fine and are subjected to rigorous examination and classification.

Argentina: Although Argentina is the world's fourth largest producer of wines, she is also the world's fourth largest consumer, which means that less than one per cent of her production is available for export. The producing regions are located to the east in the foothill plains of the Andes in the provinces of Mendoza and San Juan; the wines are generally unremarkable, with the exception of some made from the Malbec and Cabernet Sauvignon grapes.

Chile: On the west side of the Andes, Chile has a very different story to tell. The country has for a long time been reputed for fine wines, particularly red from the Cabernet Sauvignon grape. The cold polar current restricts the climate suitable for vineyards to the north, where cool fogs covering the land produce ideal conditions. With a prevailing easterly wind, the dreaded *Phylloxera* never crossed the Andes, so that *Vitis vinifera* can be grown here on its own roots. As the vineyard regions stretch for 2000 km along the narrow coastal strip the climate varies from very wet to very dry; in the central section the finest light wines are produced. Just as in the first place the vines were brought to South America by the Spanish Conquistadores, so now it is Spanish winemakers who are modernizing the industry.

1 Pink (sweetish and semi-sparkling) and *vinhos verdes* (semi-sparkling).
2 The grapes are picked when they are still unripe, or 'green'.
3 Northern Thessaly and southern Attica.
4 Lutomer.

Brazil: This country also has a significant wine industry, with production about equivalent to that of Austria: there, the similarity ceases. The principal grapes grown are not *Vitis vinifera*, but hybrids such as Isabella and Jacquet; however, the Brazilians must like it because they drink it all and import quite a lot from Portugal too!

Uruguay: Situated between Brazil and Argentina, Uruguay has a smaller population and smaller production than either. The wines are not of great quality, but the population drink all of them.

LIGHT WINES OF NORTH AMERICA

Was it because they found vines there that the Norsemen who first discovered North America called it Vinland? The vine is certainly native to the country, but not *Vitis vinifera* (see Chapter 2).

USA

Grapes are grown for wine in the State of Texas, and in the eastern States of New England, particularly New York and Ohio; they are also grown in the north-west States of Washington, Oregon, and Idaho; but it is in the State of California that the winemakers' fortunes are made, aided by the quirks of nature.

Traditionally, wines in the north-east were made from the indigenous wild vines, *V.riparia* and *V.rupestris*, and have a flavour described as 'foxy' which persists even when these vines are crossed with *V.vinifera*. Such crosses are known as hybrids, and are resistant to cold as well as to *Phylloxera* – hence their popularity. Modern hybrids like Seyval Blanc, Vidal Blanc, and Maréchal Foch (locally pronounced MAIRSHAL FOSHE) lack the 'foxiness', but also lack any other notable flavour. Some success is now being obtained with true *V.vinifera* grapes.

California lies between the latitudes of Rome and Cairo, so that heavy wines of no better than average quality would normally result; but the Arctic current flows along its shoreline (as the Antarctic current does in Chile), allowing fine grapes to be grown for the making of fine wines, under the moderating influence of coastal fogs. The further inland, the hotter it gets, so eastern California is

1 Is 'Yugoslav Riesling' the same as the Riesling of the Rheingau in Germany?
2 What are the principal grape varieties for white wines of (a) Austria; (b) Switzerland?
3 Name two wines of north-eastern Hungary and give their colours.
4 Name the grape of western Europe that has done much to improve Romanian and Bulgarian wines in recent years.
5 What countries in Asia produce wine?

more suited to the production of wines for quaffing and fortified wines.

The Napa and Sonoma valleys and neighbouring Carneros, all to the north of San Francisco, and Santa Ana, Santa Clara, and Monterey to its south, produce wines equal to those of Europe, the Cape, and Australia. The grapes generally used for white wines are Chardonnay, Chenin Blanc, and Colombard; for red, Cabernet Sauvignon and the difficult Pinot Noir are favourites, and Italian Barbera and Grignolino are highly thought of. But it is the Zinfandel – the American descendant of another Italian grape – that may prove to be the true glory of California.

Mexico: Although nearer the Equator than the wine-growing belt, the compensation of altitude allows wine to be made from *Vitis vinifera* grapes along the Central Plateau which stretches from the US border almost to Mexico City.

Canada: The 49th parallel of latitude which marks the border with the USA is just 96 km south of the limit for commercial winemaking to be successful. Nevertheless, an industry is thriving in British Columbia near Kelowna in the Mackenzie valley, and in Ontario near the Great Lakes. In both regions *V.vinifera* stocks are gradually replacing hybrids, with consequent improvement in wine quality. The winters are so cold, particularly in the Okinagan district of British Columbia, that the whole vine has often to be buried during the winter if it is to survive.

---

1 No. It is the Italian or Laski Rizling, a completely different grape variety.
2 (a) Grüner Veltliner; (b) Chasselas.
3 White Tokay and red 'Bull's Blood of Eger'.
4 Cabernet Sauvignon.
5 Russia, Turkey, India, China, and Japan.

5

Sparkling Wines

Very occasionally a discovery of great importance can make a significant contribution to civilization. For the wine trade, the discovery of the principle of secondary fermentation during the early eighteenth century was such an event. For many centuries an inferior cloudy wine that bubbled had been known, but soon wine was to sparkle with crystal clarity. By definition, a sparkling wine is one where natural gas from fermentation is retained in the bottle, or one where the wine has been artificially impregnated with gas. A Customs definition of sparkling wine is 'a wine with a wired cork'.

1 Name three well-known wine districts in eastern Australia.
2 Which produced wine first – the Cape or Australia?
3 What is the difference between the variety called 'Hermitage' in the Cape and Australia?
4 Which South American country produces (a) the most wine; (b) the finest wines; (c) principally hybrid wines; and (d) insufficient for itself?
5 Which is the principal wine-producing state of the USA?

HISTORY OF SPARKLING WINE

The discovery of sparkling wines coincided with the first use of corks, and it was noticed, particularly in the northern parts of Europe, that in the springtime certain of the wines were given to popping their corks. These were called 'devil wines'. It is now obvious that some sort of fermentation must have been taking place in the bottle, although this fermentation did not necessarily leave any sediment. As it did not leave a sediment, and these were dry wines, it could not have been the normal fermentation of sugar to form alcohol and carbon dioxide. It is now known that the fermentation was due to a changing in the acids of the wine. One of the most important fruit acids is malic acid, found in apples, and as drinkers of rough cider will know, it is very acid indeed. This malic acid is attacked by minute organisms, particularly at the time of the year when the sap is rising, and turned into lactic acid, which takes its name from milk and is a much softer acid. In this process carbon dioxide is created, so that after this malolactic fermentation the wine becomes less acid and slightly sparkling, or pétillant as they say in France. This can be enough to make the usual wine cork pop out of the bottle, letting the wine escape.

This phenomenon was particularly evident in the cold northern land of Champagne, where the monks of the Abbey of Hautvillers studied it carefully. They concluded that if they had stronger bottles and tighter corks the bubbles could be contained. They put their theory into practice and the wine became popular. It also occurred to the monks that if a little extra sugar and yeast were added to the still wine before bottling, a stronger fermentation would give the wine even more sparkle.

THE 'FATHER OF CHAMPAGNE'

The must for sparkling wine, wherever and however made, is fermented naturally and completely to produce a still white wine. It is quite probable that the making of Champagne originated in the fact that in northern climates it is very cold just after the harvest, and therefore difficult to keep fermentation of the must going. This 'stuck' fermentation will normally restart in the spring if the winter

1 Barossa, Murray River, Coonawarra, Miláwa, Hunter River, and many more.
2 The Cape.
3 The Cape 'Hermitage' is a clone of French Cinsaut; the Australian is a clone of French Syrah.
4 (a) Argentina; (b) Chile; (c) Brazil; and (d) Uruguay.
5 California.

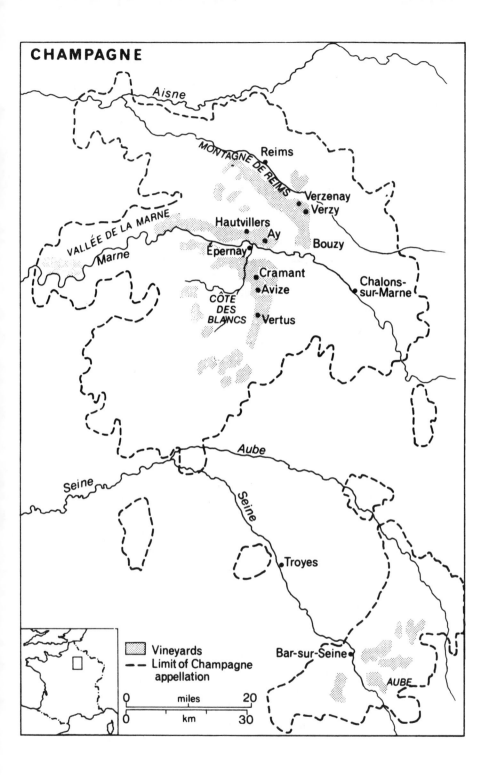

CHAMPAGNE

Aisne

MONTAGNE DE REIMS

Reims

Verzenay
Verzy

VALLÉE DE LA MARNE

Hautvillers
Ay

Marne

Épernay

Bouzy

Cramant

Avize

CÔTE
DES
BLANCS

Vertus

Chalons-
sur-Marne

Aube

Seine

Seine

Troyes

Vineyards

Limit of Champagne
appellation

0   miles   20

0   km   30

Bar-sur-Seine

AUBE

1 What geographical condition makes it possible to make delicate light wines in western
   USA at the latitude of Malta?
2 Name two wine districts (a) north of San Francisco; and (b) to its South.
3 Name three grapes most used in California for (a) white wines; and (b) red wines.
4 In which Provinces of Canada are wines chiefly made?

has not been too cold, and will continue until all the sugar has been converted, although some yeast will have been lost.

The cellar master of Hautvillers at this time (the year 1700) was Dom Pérignon, and in Reims may be seen a statue erected to his memory, for he is regarded as the 'Father of Champagne'. Although he may not have invented the process which led to the second fermentation, he undoubtedly perfected the system of blending together the wines from various grapes and districts.

However, the addition of sugar and yeast to the wine before bottling has one unfortunate consequence. Besides producing extra carbon dioxide and a little extra alcohol, it also produces a mass of dead yeast cells. In the first fermentation, dead yeast cells are normally left in the cask or vat when the wine is racked from them, but when they are in bottle under a pressure that must not be lost, it is more difficult to get rid of them. For many years people grew accustomed to drinking the wine of Champagne in a cloudy, yeasty condition – not at all like the Champagne of today.

METHODS OF PRODUCTION

Since Dom Pérignon's discovery, four methods of making a clear sparkling wine have been developed – the Champagne method, the tank method, the transfer method, and the carbonation method (see Fig. 10). All four systems may be used in the making of other sparkling wines, but only the Champagne method is allowed by French law in the production of Champagne: this is known as the Cava method in Spain. By French and EEC law 'Champagne' means wine produced by the Champagne method in the Champagne region, and no other.

The four methods of making sparkling wines fall into two categories. The first three are natural, with a second fermentation, maturation, and removal of the sediment; the fourth is artificial, carbon dioxide gas being injected into a vat of still wine, and the gasified wine then bottled under pressure.

1 Cooling fogs produced by the cold Arctic current running south along the shores.
2 From (a) The Napa and Sonoma Valleys, and Carneros; and (b) Santa Ana, Santa Clara, and Monterey.
3 (a) Chardonnay, Chenin Blanc and Colombard; and (b) Cabernet Sauvignon, Pinot Noir, and Zinfandel.
4 British Columbia and Ontario.

(A)	2nd Fermentation and Maturation	Clearance of Sediment
Champagne or Cava Method	In Bottle	Remuage and Dégorgement
Tank method (Cuve Close)	In Tank	Filtration
Transfer method	In Bottle	Vatting under pressure, then Filtration
(B) **Carbonation** (Gazefié)	Carbon Dioxide (CO_2) injected into chilled vat of still wine, which is then bottled under pressure. Much cheaper.	

Fig. 10   Modern production of sparkling wine.

THE MÉTHODE CHAMPENOISE

The Champagne or Cava method comes first, and undoubtedly this method produces the finest sparkling wine. The grapes, black or white, are placed with their stalks in a press and pressed several times. The wide Champagne vertical press is more usual, but horizontal presses are coming into use; in either case, the amount of must that may be extracted from a given weight of grapes is strictly limited.

After fermentation the wine is racked in the usual way and after about four to five months, depending upon the area, it is ready to be made sparkling. At this stage in the Champagne method, liquid sugar and yeast are added to the wine in carefully measured quantities, and the wine is then bottled in special strong bottles, and corked firmly with the cork clamped down. The cork bulges out like a mushroom above the head of the bottle, because it is much bigger than the neck of the bottle and has had to be forced in. There is a 'V' cut in the top of the cork to locate the clip or *agrafe* which fits over it

1 What happens in malolactic fermentation?
2 Why do you think a sparkling wine has a wired cork, and a bottle heavier than the bottles used for still wines?
3 Where is the Champagne district in relation to the wine belt in the northern hemisphere?
4 What happens to the natural gas produced by the second fermentation in the making of sparkling wine by the Champagne method?

and is secured under the ridge in the neck of the bottle. The modern method of crown corking is now being used in Champagne as elsewhere, and is perfectly satisfactory and acceptable. After the mixture of wine, sugar and yeast has been bottled and tightly corked, the bottles are taken down to a cool cellar – about 10°C (50°F) – and are laid on their sides.

The fermentation proceeds just as the first one did. The yeast turns the sugar into carbon dioxide and ethyl alcohol but, unlike the first fermentation, the carbon dioxide cannot escape and becomes dissolved in the wine. This creates a considerable pressure of about 6 atmospheres (95 pounds per square inch, similar to the pressure in the tyres of a double-decker bus). So the bottles have to be extremely strong and the corks clamped very firmly. In the old days, when there was uncertainty about the quantities of sugar and yeast to add, there were many breakages during fermentation, and the men who attended the bottles in the cellars were paid danger money. Now, with the benefit of the scientist François's device to measure the exact amount of sugar, and the use of uniformly and strongly made bottles, breakages are rare.

Remuage

The bottles stay binned on their sides until the second fermentation is complete, which may take up to six months. Every few weeks they are taken up, shaken, and put down in a slightly different position, so that the sediment does not stick to any particular part of the inside of the bottle. When this ripening period is completed, the process of removing the sediment begins. In the Champagne method this is done by a process called *remuage*, which means shaking, developed by the Widow Clicquot in about 1800.

The object of remuage is to remove the sediment in the bottle on to the cork. It might be asked why the bottles were not stacked upside down in the first place, so that the sediment would naturally fall on to the cork. The answer is that the sediment is of two types: first, a heavy granular sediment is formed; then, as the fermentation proceeds, the sediment becomes finer and is more easily disturbed.

1 Harsh malic acid is turned into softer lactic acid, releasing small amounts of carbon dioxide.
2 To prevent the pressure from the gas inside the bottle blowing out the cork or bursting the bottle.
3 It is at the northern limit of the wine belt.
4 It is retained in the bottle.

The art is to get this fine sediment to go down on to the cork first, so that the heavier granular sediment can sit on top of it and thus prevent it from clouding the wine, which it would otherwise do every time the bottle was moved in the slightest degree. Fig. 11 shows the oval holes in the *pupitre* or rack, which is so constructed that a bottle may be held quite firmly in the nearly-horizontal or the nearly-vertical position, as the smaller diagram shows. Each day the *remueur*, who is a very skilled man, gives each bottle a little shake and a slight twist. It is a most dexterous operation, difficult to perform. Nevertheless, after a long and arduous apprenticeship, a skilled remueur can treat 30,000 bottles every day.

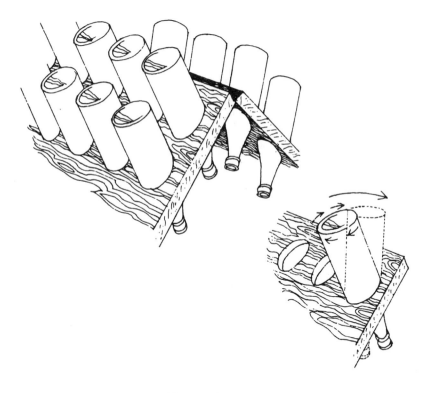

Fig. 11   Remuage

1 Who was Dom Pérignon?
2 What are the four methods of producing sparkling wine?
3 What is the accepted definition of Champagne?
4 Could the tank method be used in the production of Champagne?
5 What is 'CAVA'?

Ageing of Champagne

As the remueur shakes each bottle each day, he tilts it gradually, degree by degree, from the horizontal up to the vertical. After two or three months the sediment will have moved down to lie on the cork. The first stage of removing the sediment has now been finished, and the wine is put aside for ageing. The bottles are stacked very carefully, so that the cork of each rests in the hollow of the bottom of the one below, thus ensuring that the sediment remains on the cork. For non-vintage Champagne, the legal minimum period of ageing is one year, but most are aged for at least three years. Vintage Champagne *must* be aged for three years.

The process outlined above needs much skilled manpower and is therefore very expensive; however, recent developments have produced a machine which will do the job automatically, called the *giropalette*, into which boxes containing hundreds of bottles laid horizontally are loaded. The boxes are shaken, turned, and tilted under computer control until the bottles in them are vertical, when they are removed from the machine to age.

The bottles resting *en masse*, as they say in Champagne, may however stay there for a very long time; the wine will go to sleep and mature until it is wanted. No matter for how long it ages, the second stage of eliminating sediment must ensue. This process, known as *dégorgement* in France, consists of getting all the sediment out of the bottle, without losing the wine.

Dégorgement

By the old-fashioned, manual process, the bottles were taken upside down to the *dégorgeur*, who skilfully removed the agrafe while holding the cork in position, and then eased the cork out of the bottle, at the same time bringing the bottle upright. The pressure in the bottle forced the sediment with the cork out of the bottle. After a quick sniff to ensure all the sediment was gone and the wine clean, the bottle was replenished and recorked with a new cork held down by a wire muzzle. A little sugar was usually added to the replenishing wine, to sweeten the product to the extent required by the market. This was the traditional method of dégorgement and was occasionally a little wasteful of wine.

1 Cellar master of the Abbey of Hautvillers in the year 1700.
2 The Champagne method, the tank method, the transfer method, the impregnation method.
3 Sparkling wine produced only in the Champagne district by the Champagne method.
4 No.
5 The Spanish term for (a) a cellar; (b) the method of making wine sparkling in bottle and removing sediment by shaking onto the cork before disgorgement.

Nowadays an automatic procedure is available, in which the bottles are brought from the cellar upside down and immersed in a bath of chilled brine, so that the quarter inch of wine above the cork freezes. In this pellet of ice all the sediment is imprisoned. The cork can then be take off (a crown cork can be removed automatically), and pressure in the bottle expels the pellet of ice; the bottle is stopped up, recorked, and shipped out, in the knowledge that it is sound. A special machine adds the little sugared *dosage* to the bottle, to bring it up to the market sweetness required.

STYLES OF SPARKLING WINE

There are several styles of sparkling wine, the driest of which is Brut and the sweetest Rich or Doux; the percentage of sugar syrup in the dosage which is added varies from nil – filling up with just plain wine – to filling up with wine that has been mixed with 10% of sugar syrup (see Fig. 12). This mixture of wine and sugar is shaken up with the rest of the wine under pressure in the bottle, either by hand or by a machine which gently turns the bottles over and over. The bottles are then put down into the cellars again so that the dosage can 'marry' with the wine. Finally the bottles are brought up for labelling and capsuling with gold foil, after which they are ready for marketing.

Sparkling wine comes in many different sizes of bottle, ranging from the quarter bottle up to the Nebuchadnezzar, holding the equivalent of twenty bottles. These two ends of the scale would be quite impossible to clarify by remuage; the quarter bottle would be too trifling to handle, while the loss from a burst twenty-bottle Nebuchadnezzar would be too great. So, it is normal to bottle in the ordinary-size bottle of 80 centilitres (28 fluid oz) and to a certain extent in half bottles or in magnums, equivalent to two bottles. For larger and smaller bottles, the wine is withdrawn from the original bottle after dégorgement and is then filled into the appropriate bottle under pressure, so that none of the sparkle is lost. Obviously for this purpose the magnum would be a more efficient size, as the remuage and dégorgement could be done at twice the speed of the single bottle.

1 What happens to carbon dioxide gas that cannot escape?
2 What is the purpose of the process of remuage?
3 How many bottles per day can a skilled remueur treat?

Style	Equivalent
BRUT, NATUREL	Very Dry
EXTRA DRY, EXTRA SEC, TRÈS SEC	Dry
SEC	Medium Dry
DEMI-SEC	Medium Sweet

Fig. 12   Styles of sparkling wine

OTHER METHODS – THE SEALED TANK

Curiously, the wine coming from the magnum seems to be better than that which is made in the ordinary bottle, so much so that a scientist named Charmat conceived the sealed tank method to get rid of the sediment more easily and cheaply. After carrying out the second fermentation in a closed tank it was possible to filter the wine under pressure, so that the sediment was left behind, and then to bottle the wine, still under pressure. The French term *cuve close*, often appearing on wine labels, simply means 'closed tank'. It was found that this method did not make such a fine sparkling wine, and the French Government ruled that it could not be used for Champagne or for any sparkling wine bearing Appellation Contrôlée. However, this method is widely used in other countries.

The Champagne method is expensive because it involves so much work by skilled craftsmen. The tank method, being less labour-intensive, allows sparkling wine to be made more cheaply. The sparkle lacks the permanence of the Champagne method, however, the bubbles usually being larger and not remaining in the wine so long. So a compromise was sought to maintain the excellence of the Champagne method and the cheapness of the tank method. This resulted in the transfer method.

1 It is dissolved in the wine.
2 To encourage the sediment to fall through the wine and collect on the inside of the cork.
3 30,000.

The Transfer Method

Here the second fermentation takes place in bottles and the wine is matured or ripened lying down in cellars just as in the Champagne method, but at this point the method changes. Instead of undergoing the expensive remuage and dégorgement processes, the bottles are taken, very cold, straight to the point of disgorgement. As soon as the corks are removed the sediment rises up in the wine and clouds it. All this clouded wine is then sucked out of the bottle through a filter; and after the addition of a dosage, the filtered wine is pumped, still under pressure, into clean bottles of the size required, which are then firmly corked and muzzled. The apparatus for this looks remarkably like an automatic dégorgement and dosage machine in Champagne, or the machine that withdraws wine from the Champagne magnums to fill them into smaller- or larger-sized bottles. The difference is that the wine taken out of bottles in the transfer method contains sediment which has to be filtered out. It is possible to confuse the transfer of cleared wine in the Champagne method, with the transfer, filtering and rebottling of clouded wine in the transfer method. Certainly, the transfer method may not be used for any AC wine in France, though it may be used for quality wines elsewhere.

The 'Sparkled' or Carbonation Method

Finally, in the carbonation method, the wine is cooled to a very low temperature in a closed vat, so that frost forms on the outside. A special apparatus injects carbon dioxide gas into the still, chilled wine, and the wine is then bottled under pressure. Wine made by this method is not so much sparkling as 'sparkled'. When the cork is removed, the bubbles will very soon disappear, just as they do from an open bottle of artificial soda-water or fizzy orangeade.

Sparkling wines are nearly always white, although there are a few pink ones. Sparkling red wine *can* be found, but it should be remembered that red wines tend to throw a deposit in bottle, and

1 What is the purpose of dégorgement?
2 The topping-up process after dégorgement is known as dosage. What is used to fill up the bottles?
3 What is the capacity of a magnum of Champagne?

that sparkling wines cannot be decanted as still wines can. Just as white wines generally have a shorter life than red, so do sparkling wines; as a rule, they will have a maximum life of ten years after dégorgement and recorking, but there have been notable exceptions due to superlative vinification, corking and storage.

CHAMPAGNE

Not all wines made by the Champagne method are Champagne, yet Champagne is acknowledged as being the finest of them all. Why should this be? Consider the main factors which determine the quality of production in Champagne. The grapes used are the Pinot Noir and the Pinot Meunier; yet these grapes, with the Chardonnay, are also used in other areas to make sparkling wines. So the answer must lie in two other factors, the climate and the soil.

The Champagne region is generally divided into three areas, the Montagne de Reims, which lends backbone or a framework to the wine, the Vallée de la Marne, which gives it bouquet, and the Côte des Blancs, where the wine is made entirely from the white Chardonnay grape, adding finesse. Sometimes the wine from the Côte des Blancs is marketed on its own as 'Blanc de Blancs' – a white wine from white grapes – but this wine is too light and delicate for popularity.

The Champagne region lies northeast of Paris, and being some 300 km inland, has a more continental climate than the maritime provinces, having colder winters and hotter summers. The soil of Champagne, below a thin topsoil, is pure chalk, similar to that found in the North and South Downs of England. Calcareous soils, chalk and limestone, always accentuate the flavour of the grape in the wine. Moreover, in this most northerly French vineyard region, every calorie of heat in summer is important: this is stored up in the chalk soil during the day, as in a night-storage heater. The heat is then transmitted anew to the vines and grapes at night, enabling them to continue ripening.

1 To remove the cork and sediment with minimum loss of wine and pressure.
2 The same Champagne, with or without sweetening.
3 Two bottles or 160 cl.

QUALITY BEFORE QUANTITY

Although the viticultural methods used are similar to those used in other areas, in Champagne greater care is necessary and indeed is exercised. When it comes to the time of the vintage, all unripe and rotten grapes, and those which have been damaged by hail, are cut out. So also with the vinification of each charge of four tonnes (4000 kg) of grapes in the press, only ten barrels of juice, amounting to 2000 litres are taken for the finest wines. After the first pressing, which yields this amount, the press is raised, the grapes are broken up, and then again pressed to give a further one and a half barrels of must. This process is repeated once more, but the must produced by these two *tailles* is not used for the finest Champagnes. Finally, the mass of grapes, which still contains much juice, is pressed harshly to produce the *rebêche*, which is usually used for local drinking and for the making of the very fine *marc de Champagne*.

One factor which has not yet been mentioned is luck. Luck is particularly important in northern climes; for until the harvest is gathered, the wine fermented, and the blending done, it is not known whether the wine will make a vintage Champagne. And even in years which produce wines fine enough to stand on their own with their year's name, it is not certain whether there will be sufficient yield to allow it to be marketed as such. Fine wine is too valuable to the wine-maker for improving the quality of his normal blended wines in poorer years, for him easily to allow himself the luxury of declaring a vintage.

OTHER SPARKLING WINES

There are several other sparkling wines of France entitled to Appellation Contrôlée, but none with such fame, nor is the magic word 'Champagne' allowed to be associated with them: even the words, 'Méthode Champenoise', are frowned on, although they must be made by that method in order to qualify for AC.

From the Loire Valley come Saumur Mousseux AC, Vouvray Mousseux AC, and Sauvignon de Touraine (or de La Loire) Mousseux AC; Bourgogne Mousseux from Burgundy, Clairette de Die and

1 What do the following mean on a sparkling wine label: (a) sec; (b) demi-sec; (c) brut; (d) rich?
2 How does the producer of sparkling wine by the tank method remove the sediment?
3 (a) How is the sparkle put into the wine by the impregnation or carbonization method? (b) Does this sparkle last long in the glass?

St.Péray from the Rhône Valley, and Blanquette de Limoux from the Pyrenees are all entitled to AC. Much sparkling wine is made in Bordeaux and elsewhere in France which is not entitled to AC because it is made by other methods and is therefore sold under trade names; but it is mostly worthy of appreciative drinking and, being much less expensive, excellent value for money.

The Cava method used in Spain is almost identical to that used in Champagne, but the yeasts used 'clump' better and make remuage easier so that the giropalettes do not need to be driven by motors but merely turned on to their next hexagonal side with a thump to disturb the lees.

Excellent sparkling wines are made by the same method in Trentino in Northern Italy, in California, and in Australia; the USSR has it 'Champanski', no doubt made by the same method. Other sparkling wines worth mentioning are Sekt from Germany, and Asti Spumante which is made by its own special method to leave the product sweet and low in alcohol. Deutscher Sekt can be QbA.

Sparkling wines do indeed 'make glad the heart of man' – why else should they be the perfect wine for weddings – and there are enough sound sparkling wines at reasonable prices to make any couple happy. But however good other sparkling wines may be, when all is said and done there is no wine to equal 'The wine of Kings and the king of wines' – Champagne.

1 (a) Medium dry; (b) medium sweet; (c) very dry; (d) sweet.
2 By filtration under pressure.
3 (a) By forcing carbon dioxide from a cylinder into chilled still wine. (b) No.

6
Fortified Wines

Fortified wines have a greater proportion of alcohol than light wines, because they have been strengthened or fortified with spirit during manufacture. While light wines have a strength of 9%–18% alcohol, fortified wines have a strength of 17%–24% vol. The added spirit is usually, but not always, local brandy made from wine. The brandy has an affinity with the wine, and is also cheap because surplus wine is always available in the vineyards for distillation into spirit. Substandard wine can also be used, as for instance the lees of the wine, and wine from the last pressing of the grapes.

Fortified wines may be of many types: they may be sweet or dry; they may be red, white, rosé or brown; they may be given a special

1 What are the three districts of the Champagne region, and what does each give to the blended wine?
2 What is a 'Blanc de Blancs' Champagne?
3 What is the soil like in the Champagne region?
4 Which pressing yields the best Champagne?

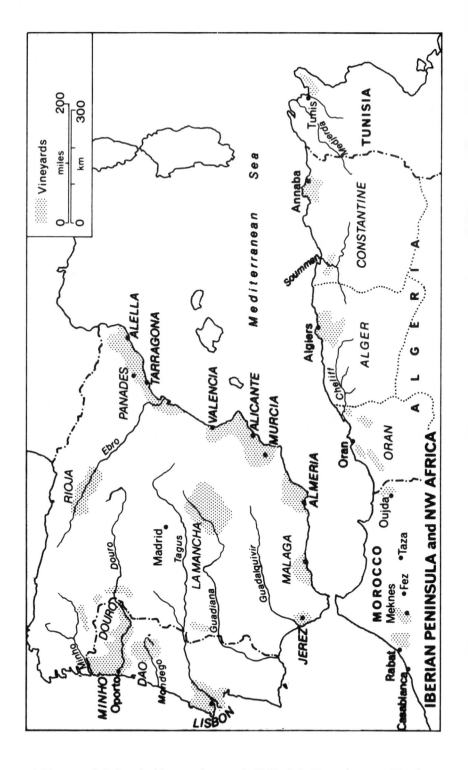

IBERIAN PENINSULA and NW AFRICA

1 Montagne de Reims, backbone or framework; Vallée de la Marne, bouquet; Côte des Blancs, finesse.
2 Champagne made entirely from white grapes. /
3 Thin topsoil over solid chalk.
4 The first pressing. This is called *vin de cuvée*.

flavour. They are produced in many parts of the world, in any area where wine and brandy can be made.

SHERRY AND PORT: THE DIFFERENCE

The two most important fortified wines come from the Iberian Peninsula. These are sherry and Port, each made in a distinctive way; their methods of fortification are classic, and the 'sherry method' and 'port method' are used in a variety of other fortified wines.

In the sherry method the spirit is added *after the wine has fermented to dryness and consumed all the sugar of the grape*. The group of fortified wines made by this method includes the original Spanish sherry, the 'sherries' made in Australia, South Africa, Cyprus and Britain, Vermouths and some Madeiras.

In the port method the spirit is added *during fermentation in sufficient quantity to arrest fermentation*. When the alcoholic strength is raised above the level at which the yeast can continue to work, the natural sugars cease to be converted into alcohol, and the wine is left sweet. Some madeiras, and the sweet wines of southern France called vins doux naturels (natural sweet wines), are made in this way. These are mostly made from the Muscatel grape. What are called *mistelles* in France, such as Pineau des Charentes, or *mistellas* in Italy, are not strictly wines at all, being merely grape juice which has been fortified with brandy before it has a chance to start fermentation at all. They can be distinguished from wine because they taste of grape juice and not of wine.

LEGAL PROTECTION OF SHERRY AND PORT

The names of Sherry and Port are protected by law in the United Kingdom, Sherry because of civil cases and Port because of treaties, ratified by Act of Parliament.

Although the name 'sherry', on its own, describes a wine which must come from Spain, a label showing, for instance, 'Australian Sherry', is legal in the United Kingdom provided that the words 'Australian' and 'Sherry' are of the same size, and immediately next to each other.

1 Name three AC sparkling wine districts in France other than Champagne.
2 (a) Name a DOC Italian sparkling wine. (b) Name a QbA German sparkling wine.
3 By what name other than the 'King of Wines' is Champagne known?
4 What are fortified wines?
5 Is it possible to produce naturally fermented wine containing 20% vol. alcohol?

The word 'Port' is more strongly protected, in that it may not be used by itself to describe *any* other wine. The Australians and Californians make wines similar to Port which they may call 'Port style' or 'Port type', but they may not call them Port and the label may not show, for instance, 'Australian Port'.

SHERRY

The sherry country is the Jerez region of Spain, and is shown on the map on page 97. The name 'Jerez' in modern Spanish derives from the Moorish 'Sheris', recognizable from the works of Shakespeare. Although Jerez de la Frontera is the centre of the region, there are some other important towns which are noteworthy for sherry. Sherry is shipped around the world from the port of Cadiz and from Puerto de Santa Maria, the little port from which Columbus sailed to discover the Americas. Another important village to the north of the region is Sanlúcar de Barrameda, noted for one particular wine, Manzanilla, which gains its peculiar salty quality from maturation by the sea.

Different shadings on the map denote Albariza, Barros and Arenas soils, which have an important effect in the region. Albariza is a very chalky soil, rather crumbly but gummy in the wet season, due to the presence of clay. The Barros soils are darker in colour and have more clay, while Arenas are more sandy; neither produce quite such fine wines, as the Albariza soil contains a greater proportion of chalk, which always accentuates the flavour of the grape. This very white soil also reflects the sunlight brilliantly, helping to ripen the grapes.

Grapes for Sherry and their Treatment

The grapes used for sherry are the Palomino, the Pedro Ximenes and the Moscatel. The Palomino is the most important, Pedro Ximenes and Moscatel being used for sweetening only.

In the modern scene, baskets for collecting the grapes are giving way to plastic containers which are lighter and easier to keep clean, besides being less expensive.

1 From: Vouvray, Saumur, St. Péray, Gaillac, Die, and Limoux.
2 (a) Asti Spumante. (b) Deutscher Sekt.
3 'The Wine of Kings'.
4 Wines which have been strengthened or fortified with spirit during manufacture.
5 No. Fermentation ceases when the alcohol level exceeds about 18% vol.

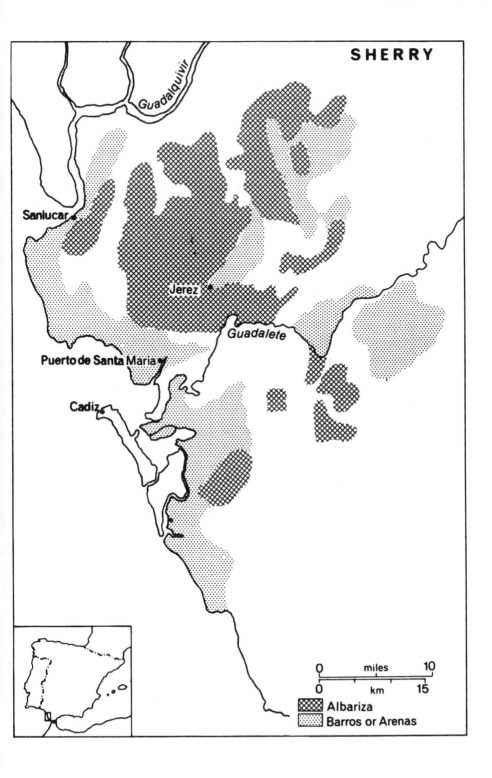

1 Is Sherry fortified before or after natural fermentation is complete?
2 Is Port fortified before or after natural fermentation is complete?
3 Will the stage at which fortification takes place affect the sweetness of the wine?
4 How does a mistelle differ from a fortified wine?

As the Jerez region is so hot, the grapes develop a great deal of sugar, which for sweetening wine is concentrated by laying the grapes on mats in the hot sun, but covering them very carefully at night against the dew. This is done in order to evaporate some of the water, and thus increase the concentration of sugar in the grape. Nevertheless, a hot climate means that there will be less acid in the grapes, and wine must have sufficient acid if it is to have a balanced flavour. Therefore, before the grapes are trodden or pressed, they are often 'plastered' – that is to say gypsum, the raw material of plaster of Paris, is scattered over the grapes. This will react to produce tartaric acid to balance the wine.

TRADITIONAL AND MODERN SHERRY PRODUCTION

When ready, the Palomino grapes are taken to large warehouses called *bodegas* for pressing. Traditionally the grapes were trodden in open shallow troughs called *lagares*, which were usually about twelve feet square, with sides some two feet high. The men wore traditional Jerez boots with nails driven into the soles at angles so as to avoid crushing the pips, which contain bitter oils. When they had crushed the grapes, the juice ran off and was collected.

In this method, the soft pulp residue was gathered up into a pyramid around a screw in the middle of the lagar and long, plaited grass lanyards were wound round, covering it completely. A plate was put on top and screwed down so that more juice could be pressed out of the grapes. This pressing operation was repeated two or three times, but the juice from the later pressings was only used for making brandy.

The lagar has now largely been superseded by modern rotary presses, which extract the juice without danger of the grape pips being crushed (see p. 42).

The juice or *mosto* runs from the lagares or presses into vats or barrels, where it ferments furiously for three or four days. The fermentation continues more quietly for about another three weeks, until the yeast has consumed all the sugar, leaving a still white wine. This wine is run off its lees into casks, called butts; confusingly, this new wine also is known as mosto. The wine is left to mature in the casks without the bungs on and without topping up. At this stage the

1 After natural fermentation is complete.
2 Before natural fermentation is complete.
3 Yes.
4 Mistelles consist of grape juice prevented from fermenting by the addition of spirit. They are not wines.

first fortification is made, bringing the alcoholic strength up to about 15% vol. During this first stage of maturation, an important development in the making of sherry takes place.

Random Formation of Flor

On some casks, quite at random, a substance known as *flor* forms. Flor is a yeast, rather like cream cheese in appearance, which floats on the surface of the wine. The casks being open, the aerobic flor can take oxygen from the air and feed on the wine itself. In the process, it changes the flavour of the wine, while also increasing the alcoholic strength slightly. It may be that, of two casks filled with must at the same time from the same press, one will grow flor and the other will not.

At this stage the *catador* or taster comes on the scene. With the help of the *venenciador*, who inserts a *venencia* (a small cup on the end of a long whalebone stick) through the bunghole to gather a sample of mosto, the catador tastes, or rather noses, the sample from each barrel and classifies it. Those which have flor are classified as *Finos* and their casks are cut with a Y-shaped mark called a *palma*. Those which do not are classified as *rayas* and are marked with a stroke or raya.

Classification of Sherries

Fig. 13 shows the family tree of sherry, with mosto at the top, and the first important classification into Finos and Rayas. On the Fino side, from the casks which have developed flor, will be seen Fino itself, a well-known style of sherry, and in addition Manzanilla and Amontillado. If Fino is matured at Sanlúcar de Barrameda, near the sea, it will acquire a salty tang which is readily distinguishable as a separate style, known as Manzanilla. Finos kept for a long time will become what the trade calls 'fat' – slightly darker in colour and fuller in flavour, with a pleasant nutty tang. These are called Amontillados. Their name derives from the wines of similar character produced at Montilla near Cordoba, which were greatly sought after before Jerez

1 What are the three main types of soil in the Jerez region?
2 What is the most important grape used for Sherry?
3 Name the two grapes used for sweetening wines in Jerez.

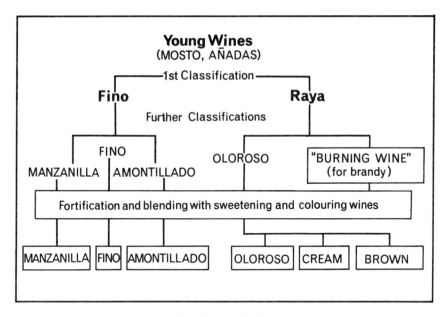

Fig. 13   Sherry development

became famous. The Montilla wines were so popular that the people of Jerez called their wines 'Amontillado' – 'like the wines of Montilla'.

On the Raya side of the figure, the wines develop into Olorosos, or alternatively are relegated into 'wines for burning'. Wines left open to the air do not generally do well, and can easily turn sour. Flor protects the Finos from this fate because it covers the surface of the wines, but Rayas do not have this advantage. Some are strong enough to stand it and develop into Olorosos, but some go bad. These are immediately detected by classification and testing, and are put aside to be made into brandy, hence the name 'wines for burning'.

The chart shows expansion of the Olorosos into different styles of sherry, entirely due to blending with other wines. Another sherry type called Palo Cortado is occasionally found. This is a very rare wine, an Oloroso which develops Fino characteristics, and is usually very expensive.

1 Albarizas, Barros and Arenas.
2 Palomino.
3 Pedro Ximenes (PX) and Moscatel.

BLENDING AND THE SOLERA SYSTEM

There are no vintages in sherry. All sherries are blends of many years and the blending is done by a special method known as the *solera* system. The wines start by being all of one year, and remain so in their individual butts for several years, until it is decided whether they are going to become Finos or Olorosos. Very few Rayas manage to become Finos. It is usual after the first classification for a further fortification to be given to the Rayas. They cannot then become Finos, because flor will not stand a percentage of alcohol above 18%. Even within the broad classifications of Fino and Raya, there will be very different characteristics: individual butts will assume different qualities, just as members of a family may resemble each other very closely or may be quite different. The catador's task is to categorize each butt frequently, so that he can see which of his standard soleras it resembles most. He keeps all the different styles in different casks.

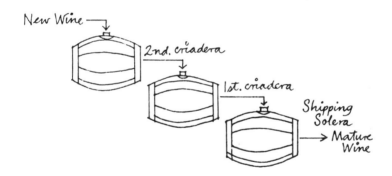

Fig. 14   The solera system

PREPARING SHERRY FOR THE SHIPPING SOLERA

It is a characteristic of sherry that if a small amount of similar, although younger, wine is added to a large amount of older wine, the younger wine will gradually take on the characteristics of the older, rather as children learn from their elders at school. In fact the Spaniards think of it this way – they put each wine from its *añada*

1 Why are sherry grapes 'plastered' before pressing?
2 What are lagares?
3 What is flor? Describe the classification of sherries associated with it.
4 What is a 'raya'?
5 Where is Manzanilla matured?

stage (wine of a single year) to its appropriate nursery school, called a
criadera (reminiscent of a nursery) after which it progresses through
successive stages. Just as children move up their school as they
develop, so the wines from the criaderas progress through the scales
of the solera. A solera consists of a variable number of casks arranged
in scales. To give an idea of how the system works, imagine six
scales, the first consisting of 40 or 50 butts. The wine from the first
scale is the one ready to be sold. This scale is often known as the
'shipping solera'. The scale backing it up has an equal number of
butts of wine about a year younger, and so on until the sixth and last
scale, where the wine will be about five years younger than that of
the first. When wine is drawn from a butt in the first scale, this butt
will be replenished with equal quantities from each of the butts in the
second scale. These butts in turn will be similarly replenished from
the butts in the third scale, replenished in their turn from the fourth,
and so on until the sixth, which is replenished from the añada.

Because wine changes as it matures, it varies in quality from year
to year, usually acquiring more strength, body and colour. The
solera system tends to compensate for this change. But the system
will only work if the transfers of wine are made gradually, one jar at
a time. A jarful is 'called' through a siphon from the younger scale
and poured through a funnel into the next older scale. The funnel
used for 'running the scales' has a very long spout so that the wine
may be introduced at all levels throughout the butt.

Sweetening and Colouring Additions

The Palomino grape is the source of Fino and Raya sherries, but two
other varieties, the Pedro Ximenes and the Moscatel, have very
definite usefulness. The grapes of these varieties are usually left to
dry in the sun for two or three weeks so that they become quite
shrivelled and very sweet; they are then fermented normally to
produce a very sweet wine of low alcoholic content, for excessive
sugar inhibits fermentation. Wines for sale in cold northern climates
need sweetening to be acceptable, and we know that the solera wines
are all bone dry. So the sweet wine obtained from grapes sun-
shrivelled on mats, is added to the dry wine before shipment. Again,
wines from different butts may vary greatly in colour, but the final

1 To increase the acidity of the must.
2 Shallow troughs in which grapes were trodden by men (and women!), now largely
  superseded by modern rotary presses.
3 It is a wine yeast appearing as a whitish film on the surface of the wine. Finos.
4 The stroke marked on the butt of Sherry that does not develop flor.
5 At Sanlúcar de Barrameda.

blends must be identical in colour to previous shipments. To achieve this, 'colouring wine' or *vino de color*, is added. This is made from the fermentation of one part unfermented must with two parts grape syrup obtained by boiling down grape juice until it caramelizes. The blend ferments slowly and, when it has been aged in cask, a highly aromatic and very dark vino de color is obtained. This looks rather like gravy browning, and is in fact the best possible basis for a brown sauce.

When the sherry shipper receives an order for a particular brand for one customer or another, he will look up his blending book, take the wines he needs from his shipping soleras, and blend them, together with sweetening wine and vino de color.

The sherry soleras are housed in bodegas, which are above ground. With high roofs and thick walls, they have been designed to maintain a temperature exactly suited to the maturation of sherry. Stainless steel vats are also used in the soleras, not for maturing sherry, but for conditioning the final blend prior to shipment. The final blend, which has also to be fortified up to shipping strength with more brandy, is placed in these vats and refrigerated. This is done to precipitate tartrates and other soluble salts, so that the wine may thereafter keep clear and bright in all conditions.

PORT

The other great fortified wine is Port, which comes from the Douro valley in the north of Portugal. The town of Porto, often called Oporto (the 'O' meaning 'the'), is on the north bank of the mouth of the Douro river; across the river is its suburb Vila Nova de Gaia. The port wine brought down from the vineyards must by Portuguese law be stored here for its maturation. Some 65 km up the Douro from Porto is the town of Regua, in the middle of the most productive district of the Douro valley. The port-producing region of the Upper Douro extends up the river to the Spanish border. But although the Douro rises well within Spain, near to Madrid, nothing like Port is produced from its vineyards outside Portugal.

1 Name, from the driest to the sweetest, the three sherries derived from Finos.
2 Name the three sherries derived from Rayas.
3 What is 'burning wine'?
4 Is there such a wine as a vintage Sherry?

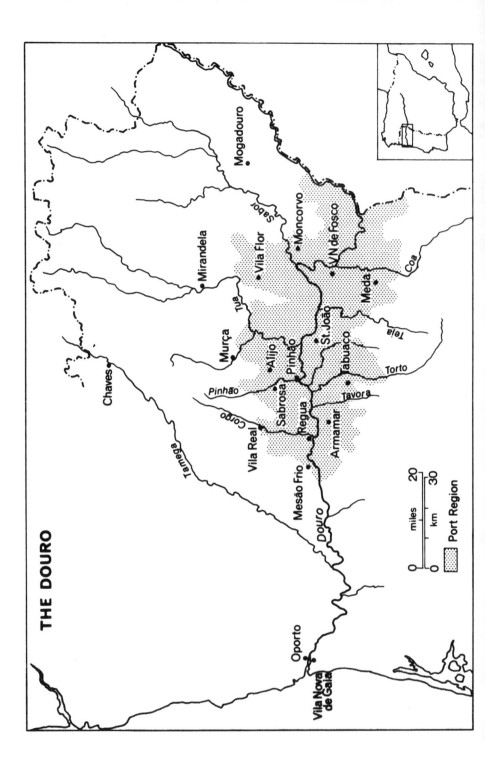

THE DOURO

Port Region

1 Manzanilla, Fino, Amontillado.
2 Oloroso, cream, and brown.
3 Raya that has gone bad, and is distilled for brandy.
4 No. All sherries are blends of wines of a number of different years.

The Difficult Douro Region

The country is very mountainous and rises steeply from the twisting river. This region has very cold, wet winters with some 130 cm (50 inches) of rain, considerably more than in the United Kingdom. But in the summer it is hot and dry. The steep mountainsides guarding the river have to be terraced, to make reasonably flat areas for growing the vine. This creates continual work, especially as the torrential winter rains wash much soil to the bottom of the valley, whence it must be carried up again. Olives are planted among the vines to help hold the slaty soil together. The vines grow below the critical 400-metre line, above which grapes may not be used for Port. Even below the 400-metre line only a proportion of the grapes is allowed to be used; they must be very carefully chosen, the remainder being used for light beverage wines.

Several grapes are used for making Port, contrasting with Sherry which is almost entirely made from one grape, the Palomino. The vines grow in schistous soil, which is sometimes so hard that pickaxes cannot break it, and explosives have to be used to make holes for new vines. When the grapes are picked they are taken to the nearby wineries of the *quintas*, where they enter the press house.

Traditional and modern Port Production

By traditional method, the grapes are put into a lagar as for sherry; but in this case, the lagar is stopped, that is to say the juice is not allowed to run off as the pressing continues, but is left in the lagar. The grapes for Port are fermented on their skins, and therefore most of them are of the black varieties, producing a red wine. White ports are also fermented on their skins, unlike sherries.

The treading used to be a test of manhood, the lagar of the Douro being rather deeper than that of the Jerez, and indeed treading grapes was a very hard job. The heat of the body helped to accelerate the fermentation. When enough colour had been produced in the wine after treading, the fermenting must was run off into barrels called *toneles*, in which a quantity of spirit had been placed. This arrested the fermentation and the wine was then left to mature. This traditional method, although still used in some places, is becoming

1 What are (a) añadas; (b) criaderas?
2 What two conditions must be fulfilled if a solera is to be satisfactory?
3 What are the five main stages of treatment of Sherry after it has passed through the solera?
4 Name three of the principal features of sherry production.

less common in the Douro, because workers tend to leave the countryside and migrate to the towns where they can get better wages. So modern methods have been introduced.

AUTOVINIFICATION

In these methods, a crusher-destalker is used, as in the making of light wines. Thence the crushed grapes are pumped into large vats or *cubas*. As it is important to extract the maximum colour from the fermenting must as quickly as possible, a technique of autovinification is used: Fig. 15 shows how this process works. The crushed grapes are pumped into the siphon vat up to a predetermined level. Once the fermentation starts, gas pressure forces the fermenting liquid in the sealed vat downwards, and up the side funnel and fills the trough, showing how much colour has been extracted. This siphon autovinificator works rather like a cross between a coffee percolator and an automatic flush. There is a hydraulic valve, quite separate from the wine, which opens when the pressure reaches a certain level, and allows the wine to drain from the upper outside trough, back into the vat through the central tube. By its concentric arrangement, this tube forces the returning must to bounce off the inside roof of the vat and to spray down on to the cap of skins with considerable force, beating the colour out of the skins as it does so.

The siphon vat is an improvement on the lagar, which left the whole fermenting mass open all the time, not only to the air but also to bacteria. However, it still leaves part of the must in the open for some time, and it still brings the skins into full contact with the fermenting must only at fairly long intervals. The ideal situation is to keep the skins in constant circulation throughout the fermenting must. This can be done by another method of autovinification, in which sealed vats of stainless steel are used. In these an electrically driven shaft with vanes drives the cap of skins into the centre; attached to this central shaft is an Archimedean screw which forces the cap of skins down a central tube to the bottom, whence they emerge and again float to the top, thus ensuring that the skins are continually in contact with the fermenting must. By this method, the required colour is produced more quickly and without risk of contamination. The vats are thermostatically controlled to ferment at

---

1 (a) Wines of a single year. (b) Cradle butts in the solera system, which act as 'nursery schools.'
2 The wines must be of similar quality, and must not be added in large quantities.
3 Blending shipping solera wines. Addition of colouring wine. Addition of sweet wine. Fortification up to shipping strength. Refrigeration to precipitate tartrates.
4 Fermentation to dryness; the appearance of flor; and maturation by the solera system.

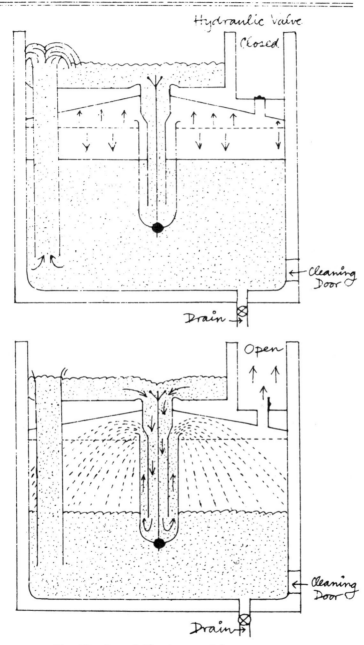

Fig. 15 Autovinification – a siphon vat

1 Does the Douro valley have a greater or a lesser rainfall than the United Kingdom?
2 Sherry is made almost entirely from one grape. Is this true of Port?
3 Is the soil of the Upper Douro like that of Jerez?

the best temperature. Although temperature control is also possible in the siphon vat, the wine, being open at the top to the air, is subject to oxidation and contamination by bacteria.

MATURATION: FROM QUINTAS TO SHIPPERS' LODGES

Whatever method is used, frequent tests are taken in a small white porcelain bowl, looking rather like an American sailor's hat, so that when the right amount of colour is achieved, which should be with the maximum sugar, the wine can be run off into the maturing vats or toneles, into which spirit has been placed to stop further fermentation.

The wine, muted by the spirit, is allowed to remain in the quintas in the Upper Douro region until the spring. In the old days, the wine had to wait until the Spanish snows melted and the River Douro started to flood, as only then was it possible to move the wine in boats, the ancient Barcos Rabelos, which travelled down-river to Porto. It was a very treacherous journey, as there were many rapids. This journey is nowadays impossible, because dams have been constructed across the river for power; but for some time the wine has been moved in casks or tanker, by rail or road, down to the shippers' lodges at Vila Nova de Gaia, where it is checked by the inspectors of the Instituto do Vinho do Porto.

CLASSIFICATION OF PORTS

There are as many different styles of Port as there are of Sherry. Fig. 16, page 110 summarizes their maturation. Some styles of port are 'vintage', that is to say they are all wines of one year. Others, shown by shaded casks, are blends of several years. Yet there is only one Vintage Port and the rules controlling its production are very strict. It must be bottled between the second and third year after harvest. Ports, being red wines, throw a considerable sediment and young port bottled for vintage will throw this in the bottle. Such ports must therefore mature on their lees. The lees are heavy and the wine thus needs to be very carefully decanted from the bottle before serving.

The second column of Fig. 16, 'Late-Bottled Vintage' deals with wine that has been kept a little longer in cask, with production

---

1 Greater. About 130 cm (50 in) per year.
2 No. Port is made from several grapes.
3 No. It is a very hard schistous slate.

strictly controlled. It must be bottled between the fourth and the sixth year after the harvest. Some of the sediment will have been thrown in the cask before the fourth year. Much more is thrown in the fifth year, so that a port bottled as a Late-Bottled Vintage in its fourth year will be suitable for laying down and will mature slowly. Although throwing much less in bottle than vintage, it will require decanting in the same way as a Vintage Port. This system is particularly suitable for ports which, though not from the finest years, can be softened a little by accelerated ageing in cask.

However, a Late-Bottled Vintage Port which has been bottled during the fifth or sixth year will have thrown most of its deposit in the cask and is bottled ready for immediate drinking, as is indicated in Fig. 16 by the bottle standing beside a glass.

'DATED' PORTS

'Port with Date of Harvest' is another category allowed by the Portuguese authorities. This may not be bottled before the eighth year. The date of vintage may be stated on the label but it is not vintage port even though it is from a single year.

These three wines are all ports of a single year; nevertheless there is a fourth 'dated port' known as 'Port of Indicated Age'. This is a blend of wine of different ages, adjudged by experts to be similar in character to wines of a single vintage matured in cask. The only ages which may be indicated on the label are ten, twenty, thirty or over forty years old. They are in fact fine old 'Tawny' ports, tawny in colour through ageing in the wood. Oxidation dulls the bright red or purple of the original wine, which pales as the years go on. Oxidation also changes the fruitiness of the original wine to a more nutty flavour. Thus two port wines, both twenty-five years old, one a vintage and one a tawny, could readily be distinguished by eye and 'on the nose'. To the eye the vintage would look a garnet colour and the tawny would look a lovely light tawny brown. The vintage would smell fruity and the tawny would smell nutty. Each is beautiful Port, each for its own occasion.

1 Are all ports still made by treading in a lagar?
2 What are the two types of autovinification used in the Douro?

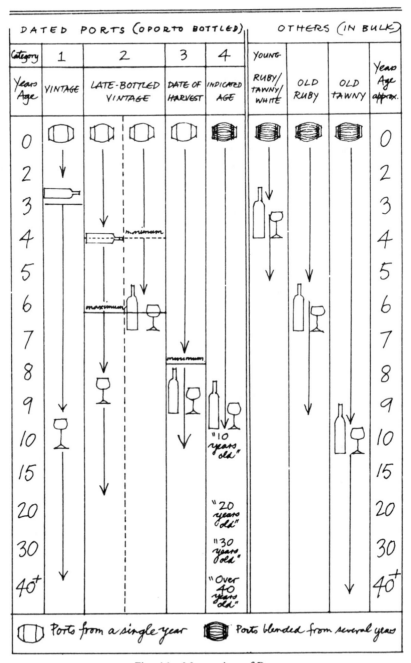

Fig. 16   Maturation of Ports

1 No, modern appliances save labour.
2 The siphon and the sealed Archimedean screw type vats.

COMMERCIAL PORTS

All four wines so far described must be bottled in Oporto, or more correctly in Vila Nova de Gaia. They must, in short, be Portuguese-bottled. On the right-hand side of Fig. 16 are the commercial ports, all blended, which may be bottled in the United Kingdom. 'Ruby' is a port which has been aged in wood for about three to five years and is blended from wines of two or three years. White Port has been made from white grapes in exactly the same manner as that made from red grapes – fermented on the skins, but golden in colour. Young tawny is probably a commercial blend of ruby and white ports. It will not have the quality of the older tawnies, but will find a ready market because of its reasonable price.

Shippers in this country might, for economic or other reasons, get a good young ruby blended from three fairly good years, bottle it and lay it down. After a few years, when it has thrown a crust, they could sell it as a 'Crusted' port at a better price than they would otherwise obtain. If late-bottled vintage port should become very expensive and the taste for 'Crusted' port persists, this could be a very reasonable commercial alternative.

Next comes 'Old Ruby'. These ports have been blended and matured for a minimum of seven years, going up to about ten years, after which they will become fine old tawny ports, as shown in the last column: again these are blended ports, bottled in the United Kingdom. They cannot be called 'Ports of Indicated Age' like '20-year-old Tawny', because they have been bottled in the United Kingdom and not in Portugal.

OTHER FORTIFIED WINES

There are other fortified wines besides Sherry and Port, and they too have their individual methods of production. The most important of them is Madeira, taking its name from the Portuguese island where it is made, some seven hundred miles out in the Atlantic from Lisbon.

1 How does the Douro cellarmaster decide when to halt fermentation?
2 What does he do then?
3 Why will a Vintage Port not be produced every year?
4 Name the ages permitted on the labels of 'Ports of Indicated Age'.

MADEIRA

Though Madeira is a very small island, some of its mountains are about 2,000 m (6,000 feet), considerably higher than any in the British Isles. Only the coastal belt is cultivated and that is very steep indeed. The vineyards are perched on terraces, ranged up the cliffs from the sea. The island was discovered in 1410 when a Portuguese captain named Gonçalvez, known as Zarco (cross-eyed), landed in the bay of Funchal and decided to settle his people there. As the island was heavily wooded, he started a fire to make a small clearing. The fire raged for seven years and all the trees on the island were burned. Now the island rises gaunt out of the sea. Its volcanic rock is of great value in that water accumulates in its crevices, but nevertheless drains well; and of course the trees burning for seven years made a great deal of potash, a very good fertilizer, thus creating ideal conditions for the vine.

The vine is not the only crop grown on this island. Next in size to the vine crop comes sugar-cane and then bananas. Cultivation of the vine in Madeira is hard work. Everything has to be carried up or down the precipitous paths by hand. This applies to fertilizers as well as to the grapes themselves, or their juice at harvest time. The vines are trained mostly in two ways: either on high wires as in Alsace, or on the traditional trellises where the grapes hang down from the top. This island is at the equatorial side of the northern vineyard band, and therefore the sun is hot. Keeping the grapes away from the soil ensures that they do not get too much heat, which would burn the leaves and prevent the grapes from ripening properly.

The Vines of Madeira

Of the noble vine varieties grown on the island in the last century, four, the Sercial, the Verdelho, the Bual, and the Malmsey, gave their names to styles of Madeira: as listed, they are in increasing order of sweetness. They are now largely supplanted by the Tinta Negra Mole, also a noble variety, which has the amazing ability to reproduce the qualities of each of the 'standard' varieties according to the height at which it is grown.

1 By the colour of the must.
2 He runs the must into toneles containing spirit which will stop the fermentation.
3 This depends on the 'luck of the year', especially volume yield from harvest.
4 Ten, twenty, thirty, or over forty years old.

Estufado

The unique factor which singles out Madeira from all other wines, fortified or otherwise, is the process of *estufado*. This is literally cooking the wine. In the eighteenth and nineteenth centuries, there was an active shipping trade between Europe (and England in particular) and South America, Australia and South Africa. The ships sailed out with the merchandise needed in those distant markets and returned with skins, wool and grain. Before the ships sailed through the tropics, however, their captains were careful to top up their water tanks, and Madeira was well known for its water supply. Having, on the outward journey, a certain amount of space, and being businessmen, the captains took on Madeira wine to sell at their destination, or failing that to bring back to England. In due course the ships reached the area of light winds close to the equator, known as the doldrums, where ships under sail were often becalmed for weeks at a time. The wine in the hold would gradually get hot, and would reach a temperature over 38°C (100°F). Then over the rest of the voyage, it would cool down again. It would also be jolted about, and it may seem surprising that when the wine was broached in Australia, it was still good, and even better than when it was shipped, for it had taken on a special flavour. Scientists who have looked at this phenomenon in the present century concluded that the gradual heating and cooling of the wine not only gave Madeira its special flavour, but rendered it proof against practically every malady that can affect wine. A glass of Madeira can be left open to the air for a long time without losing its flavour. This cannot be said of any other wine.

Fortification with Brandy

Under EEC rules, fortification with the local cane spirit is no longer permitted, and brandy is purchased from the Junta on the mainland. Madeiras are fortified after fermentation, but some grapes have so much sugar that the wine still remains sweet. Ordinary Madeiras are fortified after estufado, and blended (some using the solera system) quite early in the maturation period, but the finest, which are usually fortified before estufado, are watched very carefully and only

1 How long is Vintage Port (a) kept in cask; (b) matured in bottle.
2 (a) What categories of Port bear a date? (b) Where may they be bottled?
3 In what two ways may a tawny Port be produced?
4 Is white Port produced from lengthy maturation of tawny port or from white grapes?

blended when it appears that they are not going to attain the fineness required of a vintage. The wine of a single year must mature for twenty years before being declared a vintage, and may not be declared until thirty or more have passed; there is still some left of the 1792 vintage – as supplied to Napoleon in St Helena – in perfect condition.

Of course the people of Madeira were not slow to appreciate this great bonus, and so they made their wine in such a way as to imitate the conditions in the sailing ships. The *estufa* system came into being. The wine, having been made and racked, is placed in large tanks which are heated to a temperature of 50°C (122°F) and kept at that temperature for not less than 90 days. Seals are placed on the taps to ensure that no wine is added or removed, and the recording thermometer is also sealed to ensure that the temperature is maintained for the required time.

Styles of Madeira

Sercial, the driest Madeira, was popular in this country at the end of the last century, as 'elevenses'. In Victorian times a visit to the family solicitor or bank manager would often end with a glass of Madeira, usually with a slice of plain cake (later to be called Madeira cake). Verdelho is not so well known in this country, but has a pleasant fruitiness which may come from employing the port method of fortification. Bual and Malmsey are very popular as after-dinner drinks, which many prefer to Port. Madeira is also extremely useful in the kitchen and can be used to add flavour to sauces and soups. Stewed kidneys and oxtail, particularly, will be heartened by a spoonful of Malmsey.

Marsala

Another fortified wine having great value in the kitchen is Marsala. It comes from Marsala, at the tip of Sicily, off the toe of Italy. The wine is used for the famous sweet dish Zabaglione and for Escalope de Veau Marsala. But, strangely this may be said to be a truly British wine. Two British merchants, Mr. Smith and Mr. Woodhouse, who visited Marsala towards the end of the eighteenth century, were responsible for its development. They thought that the wine had

1 (a) 2-3 years; (b) at least 10 years.
2 (a) Vintage, Late-bottled Vintage, and Port with Date of Harvest. (b) In Portugal only.
3 By ageing a ruby wine in the wood, or by blending a ruby and a white Port.
4 From white grapes.

great possibilities, but could not be traded in its natural form. They fortified it and added sweetening. This they obtained by boiling down pure grape must, which they called *vino cotto*, 'cooked wine', not to be confused with the cooked wine from Madeira. This blend became very popular, and when in 1800 Nelson visited the island, he tasted the wine of Marsala, found it good and placed an order for the fleet. Fig. 17 shows Nelson's instructions added in his own handwriting; he had recently lost his right arm and was learning to write with his left hand.

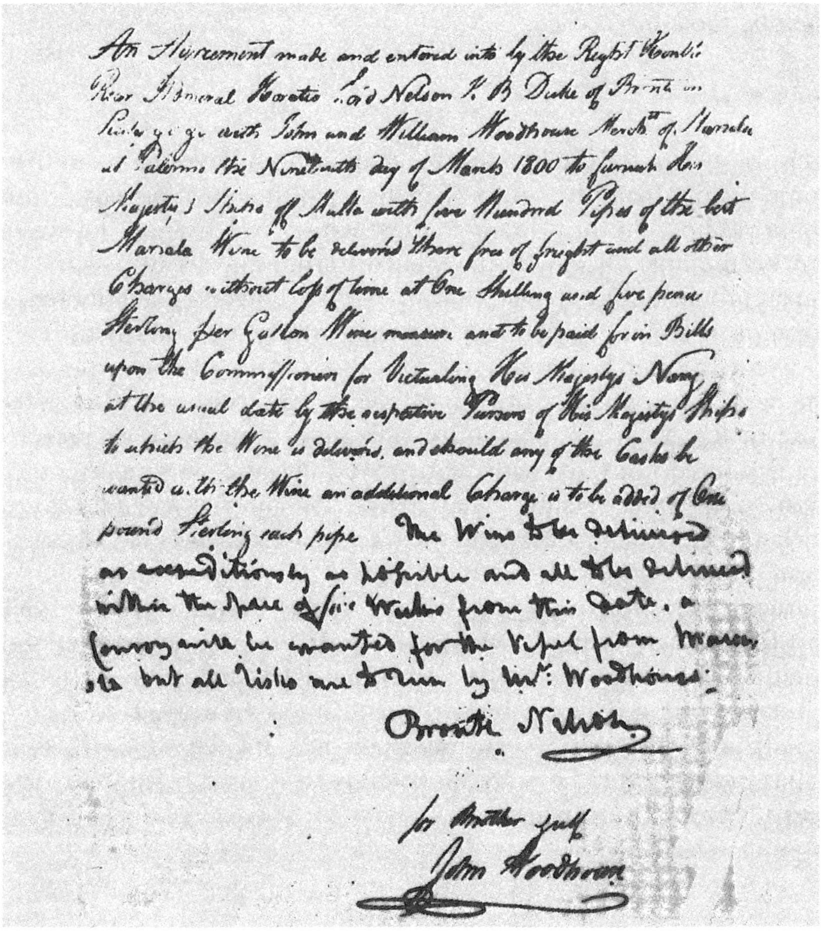

Fig. 17   Nelson's order for Marsala

1 How does the soil of Madeira vineyards differ from that of the Upper Douro and of Jerez?
2 What process is special to Madeira, and what does it consist of?
3 What spirit is now used for Madeira fortification, and where must it be bought?

LESSER-KNOWN FORTIFIED WINES

Other fortified wines include Malaga from the south of Spain, formerly known under the name of 'Mountain', which may yet become fashionable again; and the strong, sweet wine of Tarragona from the northeast corner of Spain, so popular in Lancashire. In France there are fortified wines called Vins Doux Naturels, natural sweet wines. These are well named, their sweetness coming from the original grape, preserved by the addition of alcohol before fermentation is complete – much as in the case of Port. The Muscatel grape is the one most often used.

VERMOUTHS

Vermouths are fortified wines which have been flavoured, and they come mainly from the south of France and the north of Italy. Both countries now produce a range of dry white, sweet white and sweet red Vermouths. Originally the French Vermouth was all sweet. The apparently paradoxical 'dry Martini' cocktail, first made with French Vermouth was in fact named after the barman who invented it.

The name Vermouth derives from the German *Wermut*, meaning the herb wormwood (*artimesia absinthia*). The flowers of this bitter herb have certain curative and exhilarating properties. Vermouths are flavoured not only with wormwood but also with many other herbs and alpine plants. They make an appetizing addition to cocktails and are most useful in the kitchen as a *bouquet garni* in liquid form.

Many countries, including Britain, make Vermouths and other fortified wines. Where claims of special tonic, restorative and curative properties are made for them, these are required to be substantiated on the label by the laws of most countries.

Fortified wines fill a very important need in the wine-drinking habits of the world. They are more likely to be used before and after meals, than with them.

1 Madeira is volcanic; Upper Douro is slaty; Jerez is chalky.
2 Estufado, heat treatment of the wine.
3 Brandy; from the Junta on the Portuguese mainland.

7

Spirits

HISTORICAL BACKGROUND

Many references to spirits have already been made, as for example when explaining how fortified wines are prepared. But when it comes to defining what a spirit is, either in legal or scientific terms, there are difficulties. The Customs and Excise Act of 1952 says that spirits means spirits of any description, including liquors mixed with spirits, and mixtures, compounds or preparations made with spirits, but excepting methylated spirits. This definition is not, however, very enlightening. Add to this the fact that spirits can be made in any part of the world and from practically any fermentable base, and

1 In the estufa process (a) how long is Madeira kept and (b) at what temperature?
2 Name four styles of Madeira in increasing order of sweetness.
3 From what part of what country does Marsala wine come?

definition may seem even further away. Indeed, little help comes from the fact that the process of distillation, carried on long enough, will produce a completely colourless, odourless, tasteless liquid – distinguishable only as pure ethyl alcohol – whatever base material was used to start the process. But, *for the purposes of the spirits trade*, the fermentable base materials of spirits, other than fruit spirits and rum, are restricted to grape and grain; and from there a definition starts to formulate. To the trade, a spirit is a liquid of high alcoholic content which is obtained by distillation from such fermentable materials. It must be distilled only to a point where it is purified, yet still retains sufficient by-products to impart the particular characteristics of the original base material. It is only necessary to add that distillation means the separation of alcohol from other substances in a liquid, by the application of heat.

STRENGTH OF ALCOHOLIC DRINKS

Strengths of alcoholic drinks are expressed as a percentage by volume of alcohol: the *Organisation Internationale de Métrologie Légale* (OIML) system measures this by hydrometer at 20°c; the Gay-Lussac system also expresses this as % vol but measures it by hydrometer at 15°c giving a reading slightly higher than the OIML; these have replaced the old proof system expressed in degrees Sikes.

Wines are of fairly low alcoholic strength: about 10% vol. Fortified wines are stronger: about 20% vol and they can only be made at that strength because they have been fortified with spirits.

Fig. 18 shows the various strengths of beers and ciders, wines, fortified wines, and spirits in % volume, with one or two reference points to Sikes, which may persist for some time. The difference between OIML, the new international system, and Gay-Lussac is negligible for the purposes of most readers: it is only when calculating duty charged by percentage per hl that this difference becomes significant. US proof is expressed in degrees, which are equal to twice the % vol or GL.

Fig. 18 is shown in the form of a hydrometer, and indications are made of the various UK duty bands: below 1.14% vol. (2° Sikes) – no duty; below 8.5% vol – beer and cider; above 8.5% all light

1 (a) Not less than 90 days; (b) at 50°C (122°F).
2 Sercial, Verdelho, Bual, Malmsey.
3 Sicily, in Italy.

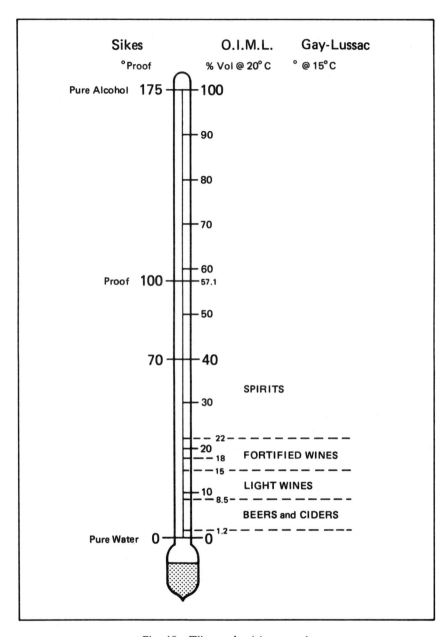

Fig. 18 Wine and spirit strengths

1 From what part of what country does Tarragona come?
2 What do the initials VDN stand for?
3 How did Vermouth get its name?

wines, to a maximum of 15%, with a special duty band for British wines up to 10%. Fortified wines are taxed, like those of weaker strength, on a flat-rate basis; they are taxed in two bands 15%–18% and 18%–22%. Above 22%, liquors are taxed per degree alcohol; these include spirits and nearly all liqueurs (a few are weaker in strength).

The normal strength at which spirits are sold in the UK is 40% vol. How can such strengths be attained, when the normal maximum strength obtained by fermentation is only 18% vol? Wine may be considered as a comparatively weak mixture of alcohol and water, with some flavouring elements. To get a higher degree of concentration of the alcohol, these two liquids must be separated; but, unlike a mixture of oil and water, where the oil floats on top of the water and can easily be separated by running off, the alcohol-water mixture is completely integrated. The molecules of each substance stick together closely at all levels of the mixture, much as burrs collected on a country walk attach themselves to the clothes.

THE SEPARATION OF ALCOHOL

However, alcohol and water, although both colourless and odourless liquids, have different physical characteristics, one being that they have different volatalities. Water freezes at 0°C(32°F) and boils at 100°C(212°F), whereas ethyl alcohol freezes at −133°C(−207°F) and boils at 78°C(172°F). So there are apparently two ways in which they could be seperated, by cooling to below 0°C(31°F), ort heating to above 78°C(172°F). The former method, called 'congelation', is sometimes used in Canadian homes to make 'applejack'. Cider is put out to freeze on a winter night. In the morning the ice which has formed is thrown away, and the remaining liquid is put out again the next night; after three or four nights the strength of the residue has increased somewhat. This method is illegal, not because it evades duty, but because it has great dangers, in retaining all the poisonous higher alcohols (fusel-oils). This part of the mixture must be got rid of; although it was present in the original cider, it was then diluted to a safe degree.

1 Northeast Spain
2 Vin Doux Naturel (natural sweet wine).
3 From Wermut, the German name for *Artemisia absinthia,* whose flowers are used to flavour it.

DISTILLATION

Congelation being dangerous – and rather ineffective, as the molecules tend to stick more closely together under cold conditions – distillation must be the answer. Distillation is separation by vaporization, not by boiling. Merely raising the temperature of a 'wash' to 78°C(172°F) will not vaporize all the alcohol and leave all the water in a liquid state, because water will vaporize at any temperature, even as ice. Our lungs depend on water vapour to keep them lubricated. By the slow heating of the alcoholic wash, a mixture of alcohol and water in liquid form is changed into a similar mixture in vapour form; but, when the liquid has held a temperature of 78°C(172°F) for some time and the temperature then starts to rise again, *all* the alcohol will have changed to the vapour state, but only part of the water and less volatile fusel-oils will have done so.

PRINCIPLES OF DISTILLATION: THE POT STILL

Fig. 19 on page 122 shows the principles of distillation. A boiler of alcoholic wash is heated by the fire beneath; the boiler leads into a pipe at the top, retaining the vapour. At the further end of the pipe, the vapour is condensed by a cooling bath, in which the pipe is coiled like a worm. This method, with refinements which will be explained, is known as the 'pot still' method.

Several spirits are produced by this particular method of distillation: Cognac brandy, Scotch malt whisky, Irish whiskey, Bourbon whiskey, rum, and some other spirits. The details of the still vary slightly, but the manner of carrying out the distillation is the same. The distillation is usually done in two stages, but sometimes, and for some spirits, it is done in three or even four stages. In the first stage, the wash is heated until all the alcohol has vaporized, and all the vapour is condensed in the worm and collected in a receiving vessel. The liquid thus collected amounts to about one-third of the original volume of wash. After the boiler has been emptied out and refilled, the process is repeated with a new charge of wash, twice, after which enough distillate has been collected to fill the boiler.

1 Define a spirit in general terms.
2 On 1st January 1980, the UK changed its system of measuring alcohol. What is the new system?

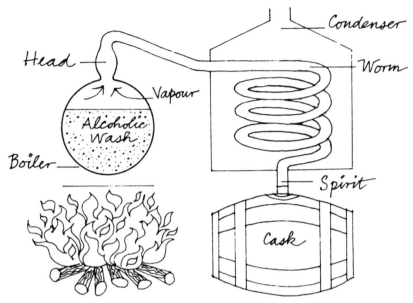

Fig. 19   Principles of distillation

SEPARATING POISONOUS 'HEADS' AND 'TAILS'

This *brouillis*, as it is called in Cognac, or 'low wines', as it is called in
Scotland, which has an alcoholic strength of about 35% vol, is then
redistilled. The first vapours coming off contain a high proportion of
volatile poisons, particularly acetaldehyde, which has a boiling-point
of 28°C(82°F). Passing from the domed head at the top of the boiler,
they condense in the worm and are collected in a special receiver.
Some of the less-volatile substances fall back into the boiler, to be
revaporized: the molecules of the different substances shake loose
from each other. The volatile poisons are lighter than alcohol, having
a lower specific gravity, and can be detected by using a hydrometer.
When the hydrometer readings, and the stillman's nose, indicate that
purer alcohol is coming over, the stillman will switch the stream of
water-white liquid coming from the worm into another receiver. As
the distillation progresses, a rank smell and a rising hydrometer

---

1 Liquid of high alcoholic content, obtained by distillation of alcoholic wash.
2 Percentage by volume of alcohol at 20°C, OIML (*Organisation Internationale de Metrologie
Legale*).

reading will indicate that the poisonous fusel-oils are starting to come over in greater concentration; so the stillman again switches the stream back to the first receiver. He has, during this second distillation, separated the poisonous 'heads' and 'tails', called respectively 'foreshots' and 'feints' in Scotland, from the good 'heart'.

It can be seen that this method is laborious, requiring the still to be emptied and refilled four times; and that the separation is somewhat arbitrary, leaving some of the volatile and non-volatile poisons in the 'heart', and some of the alcohol in the heads and tails. The alcohol in the heads and tails can be extracted by putting them back for redistillation with the next batch of brouillis or low wines. The poisons can be extracted from the hearts by further redistillation, as in Irish whiskey, or by long maturation in wood as with Cognac brandy and Scotch malt whisky.

FLAVOUR AND AROMA OF SPIRITS

The spirit which goes into the casks is water-white in colour, and has a strength of about 70% vol; after the normal maturation period of three years, its fieriness has abated, it has taken on a golden colour, and its aroma is pleasant and gentle. During this time, the various constituents of the spirit have reacted with each other, producing compounds to build up the flavour and aroma; there has also been a gradual evaporation of the liquids through the pores of the wood. The wood, in turn, has added tannin and colour; as much as three pounds in weight of oak products may be assimilated by the spirit in a new cask of Cognac brandy in one year. The microclimate of the maturing sheds or cellars will also determine the character of the spirit. Spirit matured in a warm, dry, atmosphere will lose bulk but keep its strength; while spirit matured in a colder, damper, climate – as in England – will lose strength but keep its bulk. Whichever condition applies, a large amount of alcohol will escape into the atmosphere. In Scotland, as much alcohol escapes as is drunk in the whole United Kingdom; in Cognac, as much as is consumed in the whole of France – there they call it 'the angels' share'.

1 What is the duty band for French light wines?
2 What is the strength at which spirits are usually sold in the UK?
3 What is the boiling point of: (a) water; (b) ethyl alcohol?
4 What is distillation?
5 If liquid containing alcohol has been heated in a still, what has happened to it when the temperature rises above 78°C (172°F)?

The Coffey or Continuous Still

The pot still, with its slow and laborious filling and emptying of the boiler, remained the only method of distillation until 1830, when an Irish Customs Officer named Aeneas Coffey invented a patent still. His design is still in use today, and is illustrated in Fig. 20. Basically, the apparatus consists of two tall columns, each about sixty feet in height, called the 'analyser' and the 'rectifier'. The wash is broken down into its constituent vapours, or analysed, in the analyser, and the vapours are selectively condensed, or rectified, in the rectifier.

The Analyser and Rectifier

Wash which has been heated in the rectifier is pumped into the top of the analyser, and trickles down the column through a tortuous passage of plates and bubble caps; steam is injected into the bottom of the column, and rises, bubbling through the wash as it goes. In so doing, it heats the wash above the boiling point of alcohol, and cools itself in the same process by heat exchange. The condensed steam, together with the unvaporized part of the wash, runs down to the bottom of the column and out; this liquid is equivalent to the spent wash left in the boiler of the pot still at the end of the first distillation.

The vapours rise, and pass out of the analyser through a pipe at the top, whence they are led to enter the bottom of the rectifier. The rectifier has cooling pipes running down through it; these are the pipes into which cold wash is pumped at the top. Again by heat exchange, the wash is heated by the hot vapours, and the hot vapours are cooled by the cold wash, the net result being that the rectifier is hot at the bottom and cold at the top. As the vapours rise, therefore, they cool, and fairly near the bottom of the rectifier the less volatile fusel-oils condense; a wire grid is stretched across the column to help them to do so, much as dew will condense on the gossamer webs of lawn-spiders in autumn. Being condensed, the liquid falls to the bottom of the rectifier, where it is heated and revaporized: it then rises again, and is condensed again, and so on, with each revaporization shaking loose more individual molecules from each other.

This process continues all the way up the column, the temperature steadily falling until a point is reached where the temperature is about

1 Between 8.5% vol. and 15% vol.
2 40% vol.
3 (a) 100°C (212°F); (b) 78°C (172°F).
4 Separation of two liquids with different boiling points, by vaporization and condensation.
5 All the alcohol has vaporized.

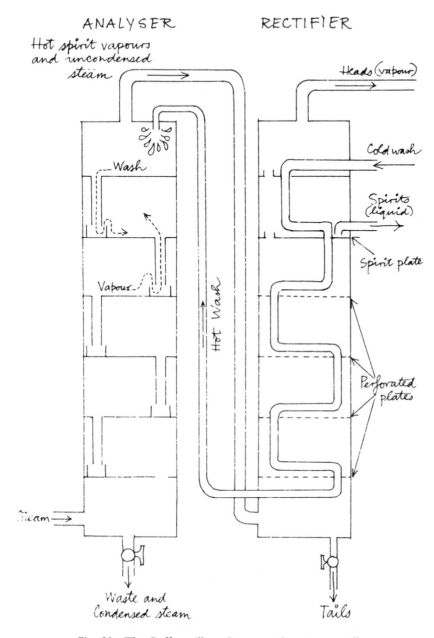

Fig. 20   The Coffey still, or Patent or Continuous still

1 If a distilled alcoholic liquid is put through the still again, how would the second
  distillation compare with the first?
2 How is the producer able to eliminate undesirable impurities from his spirit?
3 At what strength is Cognac brandy after the second distillation?
4 **Name** three developments of Cognac which take place in the cask, while maturing.

78°C(172°F). At this point, instead of a grid, a solid plate is stretched across the column, in order to collect the condensing vapours which will by this time be fairly pure alcohol. At a slightly higher level, another plate is placed to prevent the more volatile impurities from condensing and falling back to contaminate the alcohol. Most of the heads pass out of the top of the rectifier and are condensed in a worm; the less volatile impurities eventually fall to the bottom of the rectifier and are collected with the heads. In case there are any remaining traces of alcohol in them, they are fed back into the wash pipe to go through the still again.

As long as cold wash is pumped into the top of the rectifier, and at the same time steam is pumped into the bottom of the analyser, the still will continue to operate; for this reason, it is often called the continuous still. There are many other designs of continuous still, but the Coffey still illustrated reveals the basic principles of all of them.

The Pungency of Congeners

The spirit coming from a patent or continuous still is not completely pure. It still contains sufficient impurities to require a period of maturation. But the spirit is not nearly so pungent as that from a pot still, because it contains less of the 'congeners', as the impurities are sometimes called. It is therefore possible to tell the difference between a pot-still and a patent-still spirit on the nose, by the pungency of the former.

TYPES OF SPIRIT

Having established the two methods of distillation, the next step is to consider the various types of spirit and what they are made from. In general terms, alcohol can be produced from the fermentation of any sugar; so wash, and therefore spirit, can be produced from any sugar solution, or from honey, or from the natural sugar of fruit. Fig. 21 shows some of the various spirits and their origins. Brandy is made from grapes, but brandy is by no means the only fruit spirit. Plums,

---

1 The proportion of alcohol would be higher.
2 By separating the volatile 'heads' and the less volatile 'tails' from the good 'heart' spirit.
3 Not greater than 70°GL.
4 Chemical changes take place, the spirit takes on colouring from the wood and the alcohol content diminishes.

Pip fruits	GRAPES	COGNAC, ARMAGNAC, Brandies
	APPLES, PEARS	CALVADOS, Poire
Stone fruits	CHERRIES	Kirsch
	PLUMS	Slivovitz, Mirabelle, etc.
	DATES	Arrack
Soft fruits		Framboise, Fraise, etc.
Grains		WHISKY-EY, Gin*, Vodka
Other Vegetable	SUGAR CANE	RUM, Gin*, Vodka
	SUGAR BEET	Vodka*
	POTATO	Vodka*, Schnapps*
	CACTUS	Tequila
	and many others	
*Flavoured spirits		

Fig. 21   Origins of Spirits

apples, pears, cherries, strawberries and raspberries all contain natural sugar which can be fermented to give an alcoholic product for distillation. Sugar-cane also contains fermentable sugar, used to make rum. But there is another category of carbohydrates contained in some of the other spirits shown – starch – a very large, tough molecule, containing thousands of atoms, on which the ordinary enzymes of yeast are unable to work. However, there are enzymes which will turn it into fermentable sugar, and these occur in any living plant which itself needs sugar to feed on.

BARLEY AND THE ENZYME DIASTASE

If barley is steeped in water for a period and then exposed to gentle warmth, this simulates the action of rain and sun, and the barley will start to sprout. At this time the germ of the grain gives forth an enzyme called diastase, which turns the starch of the grain into a

1 In the Coffey still, what happens in the analyser?
2 What happens in the rectifier?
3 In the OIML system, to what do the figures of strength refer?

sugar called maltose; this sugar can be fermented by yeast to produce an alcholic wash. This is the basis of malt whisky. (This enzyme, diastase, is so powerful that it will also convert the starch of unmalted grains, such as wheat, rye or maize, to maltose, when mashed together with their ground or cooked grains and hot water.) The growth of the barley, as it converts its starch to sugar, must be stopped, lest the barley sprout should feed on the sugar as it would in nature, and consume it. It is stopped by heating in a kiln. In the case of malt whisky, the fire that heats the kiln is of peat.

MALT WHISKY

Malt whisky is, because of the peat smoke, and because of its distillation by the pot-still method, a very pungent spirit. Different areas of Scotland give different aromas and degrees of pungency to the final blend of 'Scotch'. The Lowlands produce a malt whisky that is soft and subtly flavoured, while the Highlands, particularly in the valley of the River Spey, produce a whisky redolent of peat and heather. The water of this district, running off granite and filtered through peat, has much to do with this. The Western Isles, especially Islay, produce the most pungent whiskies of all; and it is not too fanciful to imagine that the sea-wrack can be tasted in them.

These whiskies were originally too pungent to appeal to any but the hardy Scots, and until the arrival of the Coffey still were little sold outside Scotland; but when the pungency of the malt whiskies was softened by grain whisky produced in the Coffey still, a Scotch was born that would captivate the world.

GRAIN WHISKY

The grains used in grain whisky are maize (which has to be ground and pressure-cooked before it is amenable), and sometimes wheat, millet, and unmalted barley, together with malted barley, which alone provides the diastase necessary to turn the whole starchy mass into maltose.

1 The wash is broken down into its constituent vapours.
2 The vapours are selectively condensed.
3 Alcohol content by volume at a temperature of 20°C.

Scotch whiskies are blended, after their compulsory three-year maturation period, to suit the market. Certain countries will swear by one brand, others by another. Diligent market research has determined the choice of blend. A blend may consist of as many as fifty different malt whiskies, amounting to perhaps 35% of the bulk, the remainder being grain whisky from a single distillery. There are about 100 malt distilleries in Scotland, and ten grain distilleries producing much more spirit. The grain distilleries also export spirit from Scotland, after redistillation, for making into gin and vodka; but spirit for Scotch Whisky must be produced and matured in Scotland, and nowhere else.

Although the compulsory maturation period is three years, many bottles will be labelled '8-year old', '10-year old', or '15-year old'. These are generally known as 'deluxe' whiskies, being blends of older whiskies. *Every* constituent in whisky of such a blend must be at least as old as the age stated on the label: for a whisky labelled '15-year old' even the grain spirit must have been aged in wood fifteen years, although its flavour will not improve beyond three years.

BRANDY - COGNAC

Brandy can be, and is, produced wherever wine is produced from grapes; but two brandies stand out for their quality, and for the fact that their production is strictly controlled by law – in each case French law, for the brandies are Cognac and Armagnac. The Cognac region lies on the Atlantic coast of France, just north of Bordeaux, and consists of a central chalky district surrounded concentrically by districts of coarser soils. The grape of this region, the Ugni Blanc, locally known as the St. Émilion, produces a thin, acid wine; but from this wine can be distilled the finest spirit in the whole world. The method used is the pot still, and the shape of the still and its size are laid down by law. The spirit must mature in the region for not less than one year, and all but the least spirits are matured for three or four.

The finest brandies come from the three innermost districts, Grande Champagne, Petite Champagne and Borderies, each of

1 Of the Coffey and pot stills, which is continuous in operation?
2 Which produces spirit with greater pungency?
3 Where does the enzyme essential to the conversion of starch to sugar originate?

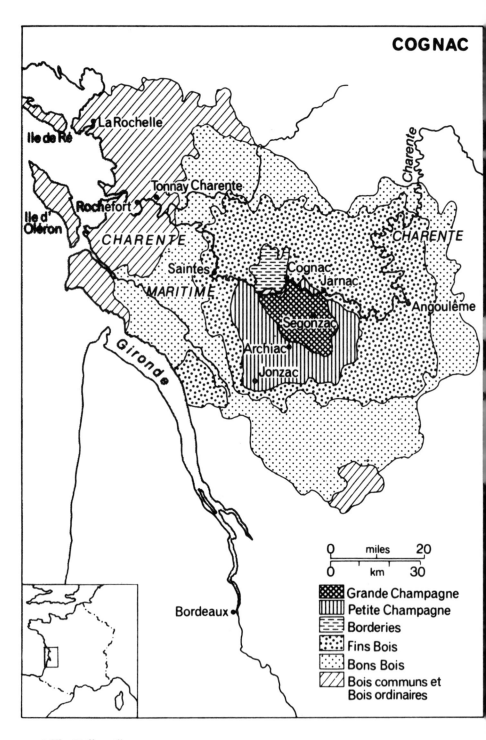

COGNAC

La Rochelle

Ile de Ré

Charente

Rochefort

Tonnay Charente

Ile d'Oléron

CHARENTE

CHARENTE

Saintes

Cognac

Jarnac

MARITIME

Angoulême

Ségonzac

Archiac

Gironde

Jonzac

	miles	20
0	km	30

Bordeaux

Grande Champagne
Petite Champagne
Borderies
Fins Bois
Bons Bois
Bois communs et
Bois ordinaires

1 The Coffey still.
2 The pot still.
3 In the germ of the barley.

which has its own Appellation; a further Appellation, that of Fine Champagne, signifies a Cognac blended only from Grande Champagne and Petite Champagne with not less than 50% of Grande Champagne in the blend. The Appellation Cognac may be embellished by other marks:*** is commonly used to denote the export blend, which is usually about five years old, taking the average of the ages of the brandies in the blend. VSOP is another mark which is often seen, denoting a brandy of superior quality; this must be more than four years old, and is likely to be about seven years old. The initials stood for 'Very Special Old Pale', a distinction from the days in the last century when 'Brown Brandy' was the popular drink.

Napoléon and other Brandies

The name of Napoléon has been taken in vain for too long, particularly in connection with Cognac: there is no evidence that Buonaparte ever drank it (although he almost certainly drank Champagne, as he used to stay with Moët et Chandon at Épernay on his way to and from Russia), and it would not now be any better than present-day cognac if it had been made in his day; for brandies will mature and improve in wood for no more than 35–45 years, after which they will taste more of oak than brandy. Before this period ends, the spirit must be put in glass carboys. After removal from wood brandies will not change further; but brandies from different years and different districts will retain their individuality, and will be required (in minute quantities) to give balance to blends. The store where such venerable Cognacs are placed is appropriately called 'Paradise'. As for 'Napoléon' Cognac, the French government has now decreed that the name should only be used to denote a cognac 'of twice the normal age'. This could be variously construed as two, six, or eight years, but is generally taken as six unless the initials VSOP are shown, when it must be at least eight years old.

Old brandies (blends with an average of not less than fifteen years) are sometimes termed 'liqueur' brandies. This does not mean that they are sweet, as are liqueurs, but merely that they serve as an elegant digestive, as liqueurs are intended to do.

1 What is the enzyme which converts barley starch to fermentable sugar?
2 Why is it necessary to heat the malt in a kiln?
3 Which grains are used to produce grain whisky?
4 What is the minimum age of the grain whisky component of a fifteen-year-old de luxe Scotch blend?

BRANDY - ARMAGNAC

The next most famous spirit of France is Armagnac, a brandy distilled in the Département of Gers, south of Bordeaux in the foothills of the Pyrénées – the land of d'Artagnan and the Three Musketeers. Here, not only the Ugni Blanc, but also the Picpoul and even a hybrid grape variety are grown, and their wine is distilled in the special Armagnac still; this still is something between the pot still and the continuous still in design. In it, the wine is processed only once and produces spirit at no greater strength than 63% vol, compared with the 72% vol of Cognac. The differences between the two brandies do not stop here; Cognac brandy must be matured in casks made from oaks of the forests of Limousin and the Tronçais (northeast of Cognac), while Armagnac brandy is matured in the sappier, black oakwood of the Pyrenees. The spirits themselves differ, and each has its devotees.

CALVADOS

Applejack has been mentioned as being distilled from cider; such a spirit is made in the Calvados region of France under strictly controlled conditions. This region lies along the coast of Normandy from Cherbourg to Dieppe, and for 50–80 km (30–50 miles) inland; within it there are districts, ranging from the Pays d'Auge where the finest apple brandies are made in Cognac stills, through lesser districts where the Armagnac still may be used, to the ordinary 'cider spirit' made in continuous stills. All are good. It is perhaps strange that in England, a land famed for its cider, nothing is heard of an apple brandy being made; the answer may be related to the fact that the best brandies, like Cognac, are made from wines that are thin and poor – Normandy cider, green as grass, certainly fits this description.

EAUX-DE-VIE

This chapter would not be complete if it did not deal with the universal spirit, variously known as marc (properly eau-de-vie-de-

---

1 Diastase.
2 To prevent the growing shoot from consuming the sugar.
3 Malted barley, and unmalted barley, maize and millet.
4 Fifteen years, as with *all* other components.

marc), grappa, bagaçeira, and other names applicable to every other country where wine is produced. The mass of dry skins, pips and stalks left over after the last drop of must or wine has been extracted, still contains sugar which can be fermented to make a rough alcoholic wash, which in turn can be distilled to produce spirit. These spirits can vary considerably in quality, the best being the marcs of Champagne and of Burgundy; there are other good ones, but they need knowing. The poorer ones can damage the liver if taken often, and it is alleged that the Frenchman does not swear 'Ma foi' (meaning 'my faith!'), so much as 'Mon foie' (meaning 'my liver!').

Spirits from the grape and the apple have been mentioned, but there are many other fruits containing fermentable sugars, and hence there are many other 'fruit spirits'. Pears give Poire Williams; plums, Slivovitz, Quetsch or Mirabelle; cherries, Kirsch; raspberries, Framboise or Himbeergeist; strawberries, Fraise; and there are spirits made from holly, blackberries, loganberries, and cloudberries which certainly give their flavour to liqueurs.

GRAIN SPIRITS

Grain spirits, in the form of Scotch whisky, have also been considered; but the chart also shows whiskey (note the difference in spelling: only the Scotch variety is spelled *whisky* or *whiskies*; all the others are *whiskeys*). Bourbon, traditionally coming from Bourbon County in Kentucky, is made from a sour mash of grains, and contains not less than 51% of maize, with added rye and with malted barley to give the diastase. Irish whiskey is made from malt, with unmalted rye and wheat; Canadian rye whiskey is made from maize, rye and malted barley. Of the various types of whiskey, Straight Bourbon and Irish whiskey are made by the pot still method, and both have the typical pungency of this method of distillation. Canadian whiskey, however, is made in a patent still, and consequently has lighter characteristics.

1 Name the six districts of the Cognac region.
2 What is Fine Champagne Cognac?
3 Does Cognac continue to improve after removal from cask?
4 What is (a) the minimum and (b) the maximum age of a VSOP 'Napoléon' cognac?

RUM

Rum is a spirit made by distilling fermented sugar-cane products, usually molasses. It can be light- or full-flavoured, according to the distillation method, and light or dark in colour, depending on the amount of caramel added. It must be manufactured in sugar-cane-producing countries, but is matured in more temperate climates. Under present British law, the minimum period of maturation is two years. There are many sugar-cane-producing countries in the world, but the word rum immediately turns the mind to the West Indies: to Jamaica, where the rum is full-flavoured and pungent, although light in colour, indicating that a pot still has been used. There are also Trinidad rums, Barbados rums, and the French rums of Martinique. As Martinique is part of metropolitan France, its rums count as produce of the EEC, with tariff advantages. Nearby, in Guyana, Demerera sugar, and hence Demerera rum, a blend of patent and pot still rum, is produced.

SPIRITS FROM ROOT VEGETABLES

Several of the spirits shown in Fig. 21 are marked thus*, denoting that they are flavoured. Grains do not provide the only starch that can be turned into sugar and fermented, although they provide the best; root vegetables such as potatoes and sugar-beet (which provides sugar direct) can be used as bases for spirits. Nevertheless, these root vegetables often give a rank flavour to the spirit, and this must be disguised. Many years ago, the Dutch found that they could distil a spirit from rye, but in those days they lacked the means of purifying it sufficiently to be palatable; they therefore flavoured it with juniper berries, which they called *genever*, or *gin* for short. The quality of the spirit has improved, but the flavour remains, though many further additives such as coriander, orris root, angelica root, liquorice and cardamom are now added to particular brands.

1 Grand Champagne, Petite Champagne, Borderies, Fins Bois, Bons Bois, and Bois Communs and Ordinaires.
2 A blend of not less than 50% Grand Champagne Cognac with Petite Champagne Cognac only.
3 No.
4 (a) 8 years, (b) as nature allows – usually no more than 45 years.

Schnapps and Vodka

Several spirits are derived from root vegetables. The Schnapps, or Snaps, so beloved by Scandinavians, is produced from maize flour or potatoes, and flavoured with caraway seed, or cumin. Vodka, which in Russian means 'little water', was traditionally made in the Baltic states from whatever crop happened to be surplus and, depending on the crop, was appropriately flavoured. Nowadays in England most vodka is produced from triple-distilled spirit (made in a continuous still), which has been further purified by filtration through activated charcoal until it is completely odourless and tasteless. The spirit may be obtained from grain or from imported molasses. In the latter case the spirit is known as cane spirit.

'Monk' Maladies and their Remedies

Flavouring of spirits, even in the sixteenth century when the Dutch made their gin, was not a new art. The monks, who were the pharmacists of the Middle Ages, knew the ability of alcohol to dissolve the medicinal element of herbs, and used it to compound their remedies. They knew three maladies: being of poor appetite, being surfeited by food, and being unwell the next morning. And for these they produced three remedies: the *apéritif,* the *digestif* and the *correctif.* In present times the first has remained as a Vermouth or flavoured wine, the second as a spirit or flavoured liqueur, and the third as bitters, now mostly known by trade names.

1 What is the other famous brandy of France, apart from Cognac?
2 What is eau-de-vie-de-marc?
3 From which fruits do the following spirits originate: (a) Calvados; (b) Slivovitz; (c) brandy; (d) Kirsch.
4 Is the pot or continuous still used in the production of: (a) Straight Bourbon Whiskey; (b) Canadian Rye Whiskey; (c) Irish Whiskey; (d) Rum; (e) Calvados; and (f) Grain Whiskey.

8
Liqueurs and How They are Made

PURPOSE AND DEFINITION OF LIQUEURS

Liqueurs, the sweet and sometimes brightly-coloured drinks that are offered at the end of many social occasions, were originally made in monasteries. The word itself derives from the Latin *liquefacere* – to make liquid or to dissolve. Not only should the essential elements of a liqueur be dissolved and intimately blended together, but, taken after meals, they should help to dissolve and blend the foods already eaten. One famous liqueur was first used to revive monks who had wilted at their work, and, before finally being commercialized, the same liqueur was used to protect peasants and fishermen from

1 Armagnac.
2 Spirit obtained by distilling the fermented wash from grape pomace.
3 (a) Apples; (b) plums; (c) grapes; (d) cherries.
4 (a) Pot; (b) continuous; (c) pot; (d) both; (e) pot (Cognac); (f) continuous.

malaria. The fundamental idea that a liqueur was first and foremost a medicine has persisted, and as recently as 1847 François Vincent Raspail – the forerunner of Pasteur – invented a liqueur which, he claimed, destroyed 'the parasites held to be the cause of most human sickness'.

KÜMMEL

Kümmel, which means literally 'caraway', is an excellent example of the adaptation of a known digestive to the liqueur medium. A child no more than a week old may be given gripe water to drink; this is flavoured with caraway. The caraway seed is often used in cakes for children. And in Europe caraway seeds are often served in small dishes with the cheese course, so that the seeds can be taken in a small spoon and sprinkled on the cheese. Kümmel is a caraway liqueur, and the combination of caraway and alcohol is a fine aid to digestion.

A liqueur is nothing but a spirit which has been sweetened and flavoured; this is its essential definition. The strength – in alcoholic terms – varies considerably between different types and brands, and the spirit may be any spirit. Malt whisky is used as the base spirit of some Scottish liqueurs; brandy is often used in French liqueurs, and rum in West Indian liqueurs; but many European liqueurs are based on plain spirits from a number of source materials, such as potato, sugar-beet, grain or molasses.

SWEETENING AND FLAVOURING AGENTS

The sweetening agent may be honey, or sugar in various other forms, but the individuality of each liqueur comes neither from the spirit nor from the sweetening agent, but from the selection of flavouring agents, of which there is an immense variety. One well-known liqueur has as many as 130 different peels, roots, herbs, spices and other constituents contributing to its flavour. It is still held that to be a genuine digestive liqueur, a purifying or curative ingredient, or a combination of several or many of them, must be incorporated. Perhaps this derives from the writings of Hippocrates,

1 Where is rum made?
2 How does gin get its name?
3 How is vodka made completely odourless and tasteless?
4 Name the remedies for maladies of the Monks.

the 'Father of Medicine', who in or about 460 BC claimed that the ancients practised the distillation of aromatic plants for medicinal purposes.

Flavouring agents form the most individual group of ingredients in liqueurs, and impart an air of excitement and mystery attractive to the consumer. Some aromas are water-soluble, and some are oil- or spirit-soluble. Some are not harmed by heating, others are. The choice of flavouring agent therefore determines to a large extent the method of extraction of the aroma from the base material.

METHODS OF EXTRACTING FLAVOURS

The three important methods are cold maceration (over a long time), hot infusion (over a short time), or distillation to produce 'elixirs' for blending. Maceration consists of soaking the flavouring material in alcohol or water to extract the flavour. This process may take from twenty-four hours up to a year. It is the only method that can be used in the case of aromatic plants, where not only the full freshness and fragrance of the aroma, but also the retention of their natural colour, is desired, or where the flavour would be destroyed by heating.

Hot infusion, or percolation, is an intensive variation of the maceration process, involving the circulation of hot solvent through a filter of the pulverized flavouring agent. The solvent is cycled on a closed circuit to extract essential oils. The hot infusion method is only suitable for flavouring agents stable to heat, but is a much faster process than cold maceration.

The distillation method consists of passing alcohol vapour through a filter of pulverized flavouring materials, or of distilling the materials dissolved in alcohol or water. This method is reasonably quick and safe for the treatment of quite delicate agents, as it is possible to lower the temperature of distillation under vacuum. The elimination of 'heads' and 'tails' during distillation is common practice, as only the middle fraction or 'heart' has the purity and strength necessary for the product. The distillates are almost water-white, strong and dry, and it is only necessary to add colouring and sweetening materials to balance the product as a saleable liqueur.

1 In sugar cane-producing countries.
2 From the Dutch Genever, meaning juniper, whose berries flavour it.
3 By distilling three times in patent stills, followed by filtration through activated charcoal.
4 The *aperitif*, *digestif* and *correctif*.

OTHER METHODS OF FLAVOUR EXTRACTION

It is also possible to extract flavour from certain types of ingredient, as for example the peel of citrus fruits, by mechanical pressure. Other ingredients are suitable for treatment with non-volatile compounds, such as fats, which can hold a bouquet for later extraction by alcohol.

The choice of flavours and ingredients which produce the distinguishing features of the great liqueurs are secret, and in most cases the actual recipes have never been written, but have been handed down from generation to generation by word of mouth. Certain of the ingredients are known to be used in some cases, but the permutations are too great for analysis to reveal all the truth. These ingredients fall into four main categories which identify the liqueurs themselves. So there are fruit liqueurs, citrus liqueurs, herb liqueurs (subdivided into those with a predominant flavour of one herb and those characteristic of mixed herbs), and bean and kernel liqueurs.

FRUIT LIQUEURS

It is a common mistake to confuse fruit liqueurs with fruit spirits, although they may be consumed on similar occasions and both are used in the preparation of sweet dishes. However, they are quite different. Liqueurs are made by adding flavouring and sweetening agents to spirit. A fruit spirit, however, is an unsweetened spirit in which the sugar of a fruit has been used for the original fermentation to produce a wash which has then been distilled, and this is the definition of eau-de-vie. Hence Calvados, Kirsch, Slivovitz and other fruit 'brandies' have been included in the chapter dealing with spirits. It does not matter that fruits used in the production of fruit liqueurs have a sugar content: they have spirit added. This may be done by a straightforward compounding of the fruit and spirit, or it may be by maceration or distillation.

Cherry Brandy, Apricot Brandy and Peach Brandy are all sweet liqueurs. Although they are all called brandies, they are not eaux-de-vie: they are liqueurs, and are produced in a number of countries,

1 Define a liqueur.
2 For what property is caraway renowned, and which liqueur does it flavour?
3 How many flavouring agents may be incorporated in a liqueur?

including England. Other famous fruit liqueurs include Maraschino from Italy, made from sour maraschino cherries and their crushed kernels, sometimes with sugar and flower-blossom perfumes added; Crème de Cassis, from the Dijon area, made from blackcurrants and grape brandy; the American Southern Comfort, very widely appreciated in the USA, having peach and orange flavours added to a base of Bourbon whiskey; Crème de Banane, favoured in Australia, having a deep banana bouquet emerging from pure spirit; and Suomuurain, usually called Lakka, a bittersweet liqueur culled from cloudberries in Finland in clement years.

CITRUS LIQUEURS

Some of the best-known liqueurs are among those made from citrus fruits, and the single word curaçao means a liqueur made with fruit from Curaçao in the West Indies. But the term has become generic, and now is used to describe a range of liqueurs in which the predominant flavour derives from the peel of the orange. Curaçaos are water-white liqueurs to which colouring is added, so that they may be found in several colours – orange, blue, and white. The highly rectified white *'triple-sec'* curaçao has a strength of 45% vol alcohol: Cointreau is among the more popular of these triple-sec curaçaos; Grand Marnier, another well-known curaçao, is made in the Bordeaux region with a Fine Champagne Cognac base. It is blended to sell as Cordon Rouge, the higher strength, and Cordon Jaune of lower strength and based on plain spirit.

An interesting variation on the curaçaos is Van der Hum – a South African liqueur made from nartjies, a native orange variant, and other flavouring ingredients. It was produced first by Dutch settlers in imitation of their beloved curaçao, but for some reason – could it have been their love of the liqueur? – they forgot who discovered it, and hence its name Van der Hum 'Mister What's-his-name'.

The Americans, with their eternal gift for epitome, christened one of their earliest liqueurs Forbidden Fruit, because it was as good as nectar. Made from shaddock, a type of grapefruit grown in the USA, Forbidden Fruit has a bittersweet flavour of citrus, and is

1 A spirit which has been sweetened and flavoured.
2 Digestive properties: Kümmel.
3 There is no limit; one mixed liqueur reputedly incorporates 130 flavouring agents.

marketed in an elaborate orb-shaped bottle. Rock and Rye, another American liqueur based on rye whiskey, deriving its name from the original label picturing crystallized rock candy, is also flavoured with citrus fruits.

Many other countries have their citrus liqueurs, and among those that have attracted an export market are: Aurum from Italy, Filfar from Cyprus, Kitron from Greece, Mersin from Turkey, Sabra from Israel, and Bergamot and Citroneneis Likör from Germany.

MIXED AND SINGLE HERB LIQUEURS

Herb liqueurs have a particular attraction for the palate, because of their subtlety of flavour, which in some cases derives from a number of mixed herbs, and in others from only one. Two Scotch whisky liqueurs, one old and one not so old, have mixed herb flavouring. Drambuie, the older and better known, can be quoted for its popularity and its history, but not for its herbal ingredients. The recipe was handed by Bonnie Prince Charlie to Mackinnon of Strathaird when Mackinnon gave shelter to the Prince after the unsuccessful rebellion of 1745; and the Mackinnons produce and market Drambuie by a secret formula to this day. Glen Mist, the second-oldest whisky liqueur, though young by comparison with Drambuie, has had a chequered career. A substitute was made in Eire for nearly twenty years from 1945, when sugar and Scotch whisky were in short supply. It is flavoured with a blend of herbs, spices and honey, and is claimed to be the driest of Scotch whisky liqueurs.

Bénédictine

Bénédictine is a name to conjure with among liqueurs. At the beginning of the sixteenth century, the monk Dom Bernardo Vincelli invented the recipe at the Abbey in Fécamp. It revived the tired monks, and was successful in combating malaria in the surrounding countryside. King Francis I of France visited the Abbey in 1534 to investigate 'Bénédictine ad majorem Dei gloriam'. The

1 Name three methods of extracting aroma from flavouring agents.
2 What does maceration consist of?
3 How does Kirsch differ from Cherry brandy?

Procureur Fiscal of the Abbey saved the recipe when the Abbey was destroyed in the French Revolution. The recipe passed into the hands of a wine-merchant, Monsieur Alexandre le Grand, who developed Bénédictine commercially, with a special label bearing the initials DOM, for Deo Optimo Maximo – 'To God, most good and great' – on every bottle.

CHARTREUSE, TRAPPISTINE AND LE VIEILLE CURE

Near Grenoble in the French Alps is Chartreuse, where the ancient Carthusian Order was founded by St. Bruno. Here in 1848, a group of army officers billeted at the monastery were offered a *digestif*. How long the monks had kept their secret is not known, but so intrigued were the officers that the fame of Chartreuse spread rapidly, and in 1860 a distillery was built at Fourvoirie to meet a rapidly growing commercial demand for the liqueur, which is marketed green at 55% vol and yellow at 43% vol.

Two other liqueurs from French monasteries are Trappistine and La Vieille Cure. Trappistine, from the monks of the Abbey of Grace-Dieu, comes from the herbs of the Jura mountains. It is distilled with Armagnac, and is green-yellow in colour. La Vieille Cure, from the Abbey of Cenon in the Gironde, is made from fifty root and aromatic plants steeped in Armagnac and Cognac. The recipes are well-preserved secrets surviving from medieval times.

OTHER MIXED HERB LIQUEURS

Every country which produces a spirit produces liqueurs, and there are thousands of them. It follows that Drambuie, Glen Mist, Bénédictine, and Chartreuse are by no means the only liqueurs made from mixed herbs – there are hundreds of them, and generally their recipes are closely-guarded secrets. Liqueurs with the flavour of single herbs predominating can be described more objectively however, and an excellent example is Absinthe. The original product marketed by Henri Louis Pernod was made from aromatic herbs from the Jura mountains, including aniseed, coriander, fennel,

1 Hot or cold maceration, hot infusion, and distillation.
2 Soaking the flavouring agent in alcohol or water to extract the flavour.
3 Kirsch is the spirit from fermented cherries; Cherry brandy is brandy flavoured with cherries and sweetened.

hyssop, liquorice and wormwood stalk. It was of high strength, and wormwood stalks (unlike the flowers) were harmful; consequently it was banned by France and Switzerland before 1914. A substitute, from which wormwood stalk was eliminated, was marketed as Pernod, and this dry liqueur is still consumed in the same way as Absinthe – with water and ice which turns it milky. Ladies of the Edwardian era found Absinthe so bitter that it was poured through a lump of sugar on a special spoon placed over the glass.

Pernod is perhaps the best-known of the aniseed liqueurs, but many others are produced, and Anisette, first made by Marie Brizard of Bordeaux in the eighteenth century, is an important example. With her nephew Jean-Baptiste Roger, she compounded Anisette and other liqueurs, and the firm of Brizard today is acknowledged as a founder of the French liqueur industry. Ouzo, a drier aniseed liqueur, is produced in Greece and Cyprus and is drunk 'on the rocks', when it turns slowly milky.

CARAWAY, ANISEED, AND MINT

Caraway is undoubtedly the flavouring agent which, with aniseed and mint, predominates among the single-herb liqueurs. The properties of caraway, already mentioned, have been known for centuries, and the Dutch cultivated the caraway plant extensively in the Middle Ages. Lucas Bols was the first to make Kümmel in Amsterdam in 1575, and Bols-kümmel is famous still. The taste for Kümmel was carried east towards Russia and the Baltic following a visit of Peter the Great of Russia to Amsterdam in 1699. The Riga Kümmels of the Wolfschmidt family have subsequently found their way to a considerable market in England.

Danziger Goldwasser is an interesting liqueur made in Danzig by Der Lachs since 1598. The liqueur, water-white, is flavoured with aniseed and caraway, and gold flakes have been added from the days when it was believed that gold had properties for treating certain diseases. Since the destruction of Der Lachs' distilleries in Danzig during the World Wars, Danziger Goldwasser (and Danziger Silberwasser also, with silver flakes instead of gold) is produced in West Berlin.

1 In what category is each of the following liqueurs: (a) Crème de Cassis; (b) Curaçao; (c) Maraschino; (d) Grand Marnier.
2 Is colour significant in grouping liqueurs?
3 Name two mixed herb liqueurs from Scotland.

Finally, among those single-flavoured, are the mint liqueurs, produced by practically every liqueur manufacturer. Mint in the form of Crème de Menthe is renowned as a digestif.

BEAN AND KERNEL LIQUEURS

Bean and kernel liqueurs, the final identifiable group among the digestive spirits, are made variously from cocoa beans, fruit kernels, coffee beans, nuts and vanilla beans. Best known are Crème de Cacao, made by maceration or infusion of the Venezuelan cocoa beans, and marketed as a colourless or brown liqueur; Tia Maria, flavoured with Blue Mountain coffee extracts in Jamaican cane spirit; Kahlua, a Mexican coffee liqueur, very popular in the USA; Créme de Vanille, from vanilla beans; Crème de Noisettes, made from hazelnuts; and Crème de Noyau, from peach and cherry kernels.

CREAM LIQUEURS

Advocaat, a thick custard-like liqueur, made from yolk of egg and grape brandy, originally had its own Customs category, having a strength of only 17% vol/alcohol. Today, however, a number of new liqueurs containing stabilized dairy products are finding their place in the market: they include Brandy, Grand Marnier, Scottish, Irish, Jersey, and Peppermint Creams. The Dutch advocaats remain the best known among advocaats from several European countries.

CLASSIFICATION OF FRENCH LIQUEURS

The French are meticulous in the classification of their wines, and the principle has been extended to include their liqueurs. A simple liqueur is a sweetened spirit which must contain 20 kg of sugar per 100 litres of liqueur. The *demi-fines* must have a standard strength of 23° GL, with 20-25 kg of sugar per 100 litres of liqueur. *Fines* and

---

1 (a) Fruit; (b) citrus peel; (c) fruit; (d) citrus peel.
2 No – Curaçaos, for instance, can be coloured orange, blue, red, or white.
3 Drambuie and Glen Mist.

surfines must have standard strengths of 28° and 30° GL respectively, the former with 40–45 kg and the latter 45–50 kg sugar per 100 litres.

'Double liqueurs', though theoretically containing 100% increase in flavouring agents, more usually contain only a 50% increase. This is because certain oils, if present in greater proportions, tend to cloud the liqueurs when water is added.

Other Liqueur Definitions: Triple-sec, a misleading term applied loosely to curaçaos which have been doubly rectified; *ratafias,* originally liqueurs drunk at the ratification of treaties or agreements, but latterly meaning liqueurs based on wine spirits; *Eis-liköre,* for German liqueurs intended for drinking 'on the rocks'; and *Kristal-liköre,* and *millefiori,* for German and Italian liqueurs containing sugar crystals.

LIQUEURS IN THE KITCHEN

Liqueurs play their part in the kitchen, but because of their natural sweetness, are used mainly for embellishing sweet courses. The more famous recipes include Triple Sec for Crêpes Suzettes, Grand Marnier for soufflés, Maraschino for Compôte des Fruits, and Crème de Noisettes for hazelnut meringues. Liqueurs do, however, find their way into fish dishes and entrées. Homard Flambé, cooked with Trappistine and flamed and basted with a mixture of Trappistine and brandy, is a delectable dish. And kebabs or fish for grilling over an open fire, brushed with a mixture of oil and Pernod before cooking, and basted with the resultant marinade, impart a delicate bouquet of fennel.

To do justice to the story of liqueurs in a single chapter is impossible, for the romance behind a hundred of the world's most famous liqueurs would fill a hundred books. It is enough to say the liqueur's *raison d'être* lies in its digestive qualities, and there can be no more elegant coda to a good dinner.

---

1 The label of Bénédictine bears the initials 'DOM'. Give the original Latin and its English translation. Why is it there?
2 In what category are the following liqueurs: (a) Drambuie; (b) Kümmel; (c) Bénédictine; (d) Danziger Goldwasser; (e) Pernod?
3 Name three other French liqueurs deriving from monasteries.

9

Beers and Brewing

EARLY HISTORY

Whatever the Romans came to England for, it was not the beer.
They were apparently somewhat surprised to find the natives
drinking a fermented liquor made from barley and wheat, and that
the practice was by then long established. Barley was cropped by the
Britons some 3,000 years earlier; their grains had come from Egypt,
whence the Britons had also learned the art of brewing.

The Romans do not appear to have cared for the raw drink of the
Britons, and certainly ignored it in their chronicles. Ale, mead from
honey, and cider from apples were all established as beverages,

1 Deo Optimo Maximo – 'To God most good and great'. In gratitude, by the wine
merchant who was given the formula when the Abbey in Fecamp was destroyed.
2 They are all herb liqueurs.
3 Chartreuse, Trappistine and Le Veille Cure (from Cenon in the Gironde).

though ale may only have been available in the southern half of England, where climate and soil were more suitable for growing barley. As with wine, it was the church which established the brewery in the layout of the monasteries, and slowly, as ecclesiastical and moot law was written, ales came to take their position in the developing civilization.

By the end of the seventh century AD there were three different ales: clear ale, mild ale, and Welsh ale, the last being a form of *bragawd* in which honey, cinnamon and cloves were among the ingredients. Whether these beverages were available at the earliest inns set up for travellers is not known, but ale-houses and taverns certainly came into the picture during the eighth and ninth centuries, and were sited not only in the cities but also along the old Roman roads. Most were no more than very primitive huts beside the house of the brewer.

First Steps towards Law and Order

In the tenth century, King Edgar's Archbishop, Dunstan, decreed that these ale-houses be limited to one per village, thereby giving status to those surviving. It was Dunstan who in 959 proclaimed 'There shall be one system of measurement, and one standard of weights such as is in use in London and Winchester.' Whether the law was fully effective is doubtful, for it was revised in Magna Carta, but it dates the probable beginnings of capacity measurement.

By the eleventh century the Britons had settled down to an administrative system of law and order. The country was subdivided and ruled by King, church and squire, who together were to fashion the English way of life. And much of that has evolved round the most famous English drink of all – beer. At the end of the twelfth century, under King Henry II, ale was taxed for the first time, and at about the same time, the Common Council of the Corporation of London decreed at Guildhall that ale-houses in the City be licensed and be built of stone, against the risk of fire.

1 Name three Bean and Kernel liqueurs.
2 What is the minimum strength for a liqueur described as *Fine*?
3 What liqueur would you use in making crêpes suzettes?
4 What dishes might be improved by Pernod?

AMALGAMATION IN THE MODERN INDUSTRY

In 1986, over 1,000 million hl of beer were consumed throughout the world every week. In order of consumption per head, Britain came tenth, with a consumption of two litres per week by every person entitled to drink. The picture changes, however, when it comes to world production; for here Britain (with 8%) came third after the USA (23%) and West Germany (12%). The importance of the industry and of the product must therefore not be underrated. The proprietorship of the independent brewers throughout the country has steadily fallen into the hands of national combines during the twentieth century; in the ten years to 1973 the number of independents fell from just under two hundred to about eighty, at which figure it has remained. All the other independents – and at the beginning of the twentieth century there were 6,000 of them – are now in the hands of some half-dozen national groups. This evolution has naturally revolutionized production methods and equipment, for beer is now mass-produced and marketed in cans as well as bottles and kegs. But the fundamental process of producing beers remains the same.

Definition of Beers

Beers, by definition, are fermented drinks deriving their alcoholic content from the conversion of malt sugars into alcohol by brewer's yeast. Basically beers are made from barley, yeast, hops and water. Sugar and cereals may be added, and in recent years it has been possible to adjust the very important mineral content of the water, which originally determined the siting of breweries, as for example in Burton-on-Trent and Dublin.

Beers are produced in three main categories. The first is Ales, which may be Pale, Dark or Strong; the second, Stouts, which may be Sweet or Bitter; and the third is Lagers. The barman may be forgiven his confusion when asked merely for 'a beer', as so often happens. All of these beers share the same early treatment in their manufacture, and their alcoholic content is very much the same, except for those specifically described as strong. Draught bitter, light

1 From: Crème de Cacao, Tia Maria, Crème de Vanille, Crème de Noisettes, and Crème de Noyau.
2 28°GL.
3 Triple-sec.
4 Kebabs and grilled fish.

ale, stout and lager all average 3.5%–4% vol of alcohol, although in different brands they may vary below or above these figures. Pale ales, however, can have as much as 6.5% alcohol, strong lager 8% and strong ale as much as 10%.

MANUFACTURE

The manufacture of beer starts with the malting of barley. The industry today is so vast that malting is ideally done at centralized maltings where it is automated in drums or saladin boxes and continually monitored by biochemists. However, it is best understood by following the original art of the maltster, which is still practised by some small independent producers. Barley is the best cereal for the purpose for several reasons, foremost being that it produces malt of the best flavour. Secondly, barley husks form a filter bed during the mashing stage of the malting process, and neither wheat nor maize have this husk. Wheat is also unfavourable as an alternative because the wheat germ breaks easily and will tend to form moulds in the mash. Whatever other cereals are used, barley is supreme.

MALTING

The malting process requires considerable skill. It is carried out in 'maltings', special premises attached to breweries or situated in barley-growing areas. The maltster soaks the barley in water for about sixty hours, following which the barley is spread on the floor of the maltings to germinate. This part of the process is called 'flooring', and what is actually happening during germination is the conversion of the insoluble starch in the barley into soluble sugar. The temperature must be controlled very carefully during the ten days of flooring and the maltster will rake the barley continuously for this purpose. At the end of this period, the germination will have converted most of the starch into sugar, and should be stopped from going further. The green malt is 'screened' to clean off the culm

1 Is beer a recent invention?
2 When was ale first taxed in England?

(small roots that have grown during the flooring) and is then loaded into a kiln to stop the germination and cure the malt. In this drying process the characteristic half-nutty, half-biscuit aroma of the malt develops. According to the type of beer to be made, the malt is kilned to a greater or lesser degree producing malts of different colours and flavours. The main types, in increasing intensity of colour, are white, crystal, amber and chocolate malt. The last gives colour to stouts.

This in its simplest terms is the process of malting. Brewers rate the quality of malt so produced above that of the malt extracts which save the brewer the time, space and labour involved in the malting process.

MASHING OF GRIST

The malt is next crushed by mills which have been minutely adjusted, so that the barley grains are crushed without being ground down to flour; at this stage the malt assumes the name 'grist' and goes on a conveyor belt to the grist case to await mashing.

The grist is now mashed with hot liquor in a mash tun. The liquor is water of correct mineral balance. In the mash tun the diastase in the malt converts the starch remaining in the grist to sugar, together with that of unmalted cereals such as flaked maize. At the same time the sugar dissolves in the hot liquor. After a period of one and a half to two hours, the sugary liquid, known as 'wort' (pronounced 'wert'), is drained off through slotted plates at the bottom of the mash tun. These slotted plates retain the solid remains of the grist, which still contain some sugar; this sugar is recovered by 'sparging' – spraying the grains with hotter liquor. This further wort is drawn off to join the first, and the spent 'brewer's grains' are sold as cattle food.

ADDING HOPS TO THE WORT

The wort passes on to the copper, which is a circular vessel of copper or stainless steel, where hops and any sugar that may be required are added. Hops are added to give flavour to the beer, and the tannin in

1 No. It was made 3000 years ago.
2 At the end of the twelfth century, under King Henry II.

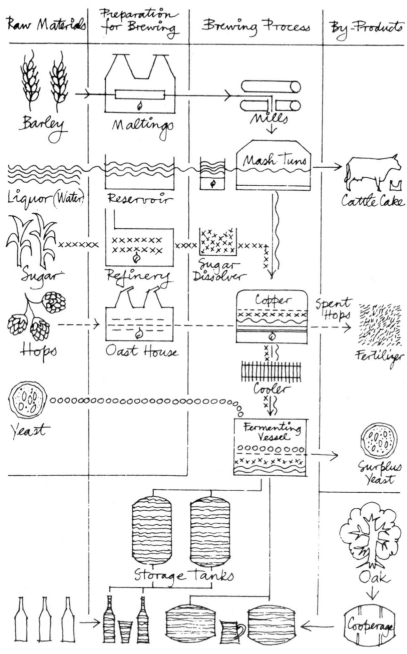

Fig. 22 The brewing process

1 About what percentage of the world's beer is produced in Britain?
2 What are the three main categories of beers, and how may they be subdivided?

them helps to preserve it. They contain no sugar and are nothing to do with the production of alcohol.

The hop is one of a family of perennial plants belonging to the genus *humulus*, which also includes the nettle. The part of the hop used in brewing is the cone, which fruits from the female flower and which is 5–10cm long with overlapping scales, pale green in colour. The hop fields, called hop gardens in southeast England and hop yards in the west Midlands, need careful husbanding from early spring until late August, when picking begins. As soon as the hops are picked they must be carefully dried with hot air. This takes place in 'oasthouses', and many original ones may still be seen lending charm to the English countryside. The tapering roof of the traditional oasthouse was capped by a pivoting wooden cowl which was designed to stop the back-draught in windy weather. The hops are spread on the porous oasthouse floors, through which hot air rises; after twelve hours they are dry and are then packed in 'pockets', long sacks in which they will be delivered to the brewer. Nowadays they may be delivered in the form of concentrated pellets. The selection of the right variety of hop is important to the brewer. It will affect the aroma, flavour and resin content of the beer. There are a number of English hops, the more important being the Fuggle and Golding varieties. The bitterness of the hop comes from the resin and aromatic oils of the *lupulin* – the golden dust found at the base of the hop flower petals.

FROM COPPER TO COOLER

The hops are then introduced to the brewing process in the copper. The wort has been run from the mash tun through a tank called the 'underback' or 'wort safe', and on into the copper. The wort and hops are boiled together for about two hours, to extract the resin and oils from the hops, and to sterilize the wort. The enzyme diastase, no longer required, is destroyed. Furthermore, the specific gravity of the wort is controlled by the boiling time, during which water will evaporate. Also, during this process unwanted impurities are precipitated or evaporated. In the giant breweries there are coppers with capacities up to 400 hl (250 barrels), heated by steam coil.

1 About 8%.
2 (a) Ales – pale, dark, or strong; (b) Stout – sweet or bitter; (c) Lagers.

The wort is run off from the copper into a 'hop back', where the spent hops and impurities sink to the bottom. When the hop back is drained, these residual materials are retained on a false bottom, and are sold as fertilizers. The wort next passes to the 'cooler' which, as a heat–exchanger, also preheats the liquor for the next charge of the mash tun. In the cooler, the wort is brought down to a temperature of about 16°c(61°F) in preparation for the essential yeast activity in the next stage. As the wort goes into the fermentation vessel, the Government becomes interested in excise duty, and each charge must have its volume and specific gravity, 'the Original Gravity', recorded in the Excise Charge Book.

FERMENTATION AND BREWERS' YEASTS

Fermentation in brewing has precisely the same object as in wine and spirit manufacture: to convert sugars into alcohol and carbon dioxide. Brewer's yeast, used for the fermentation, is a cultivated version of *saccharomyces cerevisiae*. It is mixed and added soon after the wort starts running into the fermenting vessels. As fermentation progresses the gravity reduces, and the temperature rises. Cooling coils are fitted in the fermenting vessels to keep the ferment at the correct temperature. This may be done equally effectively by running cold water over the external walls of the vessel, which also makes cleaning easier. Fermentation of beers and stouts takes three to four days, during which gravities and temperature are constantly measured by the brewer. During the process of producing these non–lager beers, a frothy head starts to form inside the fermenting vessel. This is composed of flocculating yeast cells. The head undergoes visual changes which enable the brewer to check the progress of fermentation. When the yeast head is fully formed it is skimmed off and pressed to produce a valuable by-product. The yeast has been multiplying during fermentation, and the quantity of yeast removed in this way will amount to up to five times the quantity put in. The pick of the yeast crops are carefully set aside in cold storage, ready to ferment subsequent brews. This yeast used for

1 What are the four main types of malt? Which is used for stouts?
2 What is 'liquor' (in the context of brewing)?

production of ales and stouts is known as 'top yeast', because it rises to the top of the fermenting vessel.

LAGER PRODUCTION

In lager production a different yeast, *saccharomyces carlsbergensis*, is used. This is known as 'bottom yeast', because it sinks to the bottom of the fermenting vessel rather than rising to the top. Fermentation of lager takes place at a much lower temperature, therefore, taking much longer; after primary fermentation, the beer is run into lagering vessels at a temperature of 2–3°C(36–37°F) or even lower. Lagers remain in tank for conditioning and 'chill-proofing' for two to six months – whence the name comes, 'lager' meaning 'store'. According to marketing policy, lagers may be carbonated. They are best served chilled, too.

CELLARING

Ales and stouts coming from the fermenting vessel are allowed to settle for a day or two in racking tanks before filling into casks or cellar tanks. Draught beer is perishable, but bottled, canned, and container beers are stabilized. Cellar treatments of beer include 'fining', 'priming', 'conditioning' and 'dry hopping'. The clarifying process of fining is done by the addition of isinglass fining solution. Priming is the addition of sugar solution to sweeten the finished beer, and conditioning is carbonation to increase liveliness. Dry hopping is the addition of a small quantity of choice hops to the cask of finished beer in order to increase its delicate hop flavour and aroma.

The modern process of brewing follows all the development stages of the original: malting, mashing, sparging, boiling with hops, and fermenting with yeast. Equipment has been introduced to check and control the physical conditions throughout the process, and also to make the process a continuous one, with raw materials being fed in at appropriate stages, and beer flowing continuously from the fermentation vessels into racking tanks.

1 White, crystal, amber and chocolate. Chocolate.
2 Water of correct mineral balance.

CONTAINERS FOR DRAUGHT AND BOTTLED BEERS

Beers for sale in bulk are put up in hygienic containers known always as casks. Today the traditional oak casks have virtually disappeared and stainless steel and aluminium casks have taken their place. They are of varying sizes, their capacities ranging from the 'butt' of 500 litres (108 gallons) down to the 'firkin' of 40 litres (9 gallons) and the 'pin' of 20 litres (4.5 gallons). Draught beers reach the public house and other points of sale by tanker or cask. Latterly, sufficient supplies of keg beers, which are chilled and filtered to keep stable, are kept at depots close to the point of sale.

Bottled beers may be matured before or after bottling. A bottle of beer contains about double its own volume of carbon dioxide gas in solution; its fresh, sparkling appearance and its traditional head in the glass are all due to this gas. Maturation is a continuous process and thus there is a right time to drink beer after bottling.

Bottling plants are highly geared to deal with millions of bottles daily, and yet reject any that are imperfect or unclean. So-called 'bottled' beers are distributed in returnable bottles, non-returnable bottles or cans. These vary in size from the 'nip' of 20 cl (almost 7 fluid oz) to the seven-pint or gallon cans for parties. The service given by the brewer to the public is both compact and complete.

1 What is a 'Fuggle'?
2 What is a hop back?

10

Cider and Perry

HISTORY

Cider and perry have been known in England for many years, but were probably only made extensively after the Norman conquest. Normandy is famed for its cider and to this day some Normandy apples and apple juice are imported to supplement home supplies when necessary.

Cider (or Cyder) has had the reputation of being a bucolic drink of great power, and until recently was not readily obtainable outside the

1 A variety of English hop.
2 A vessel in which the resin and oils of the hops are extracted.

traditional areas of production. Until the end of the last century, commercial production was in the hands of many small producers, who sold only locally, and most farmers would make their own cider for their family and workers: some still do, without penalty of licensing and taxation, but private cider presses are becoming harder to find.

In the present century, particularly during the last fifty years, UK commercial production has been concentrated into the hands of only two or three large groups, who alone are able to provide sufficient capital for orchards, mass production, and marketing. While it is sad that small businesses cannot survive in this field, additional finance for research allows improvement of the product for the consumers' benefit. Probably the leading research establishment in the world for cider and perry is that at Long Ashton, the horticulture department of the University of Bristol. Perhaps this is logical, for England is not commercially a wine-producing country and its cider production takes precedence over wine. Other countries producing wine commercially apply wine regulations to cider production.

DEFINITIONS OF CIDER AND PERRY

Cider is the alcoholic beverage obtained by fermentation of apple juice or a mixture of apple juice and up to 25% pear juice. Perry is similarly obtained from pear juice, with up to 25% of apple juice. Basically perry is made in a similar way to cider, and will only be mentioned specifically where differences occur.

Besides England and Normandy, cider is made in Italy, Spain, Germany, Switzerland, Canada, USA, Australia, and New Zealand. All these countries also sell non-alcoholic apple juice as 'apple juice' except the USA where it is sold as cider; there, alcoholic cider is known as 'hard cider'.

1 What is 'conditioning' of beer?
2 Why are further hops added to beer during cellaring? What is this called?
3 Why is there a right time to drink beer after bottling?

TYPE	CONTRIBUTION	VARIETY
Sweet	Sugar	Sweet Coppin Court Royal
Bitter Sweet	Sugar Tannin	Yarlington Mill Dabinett
Sharp	Acid Sugar	Tom Putt Brown's Apple Bramley Seedling (culinary) Cox's Orange Pippin (dessert)
Bitter Sharp	Acid Tannin	Kingston Black Stokes Red

Fig. 23   Cider apples

Areas of Production: The English areas of production are the counties of Devon, Somerset, Gloucester, Hereford, Kent, and Norfolk, where the best cider orchards are found. In general, the cider orchard regions of the world overlap the wine regions (extending a little further towards the Poles), but although cider and wine are both alcoholic beverages obtained from fermentation of fruit juices, their production requirements differ greatly. To apply cider techniques to wine-making in the UK would not improve English wine; that English cider is better than French may be due to France's imposing wine regulations on its manufacture.

1 Carbonation to increase its liveliness.
2 To give flavour, and help to preserve it. Dry hopping.
3 Because maturation is a continuous process.

VARIETY OF APPLES USED

Cider is obtained by fermentation of the juice of the apple, *Malus pomona* of the order *Rosaceae*. We know generally of dessert apples and culinary apples, but cider apples are different. Dessert apples give sweetness, and culinary apples acid – but cider also requires the bitterness of tannin to balance the flavour and to help preserve it. Cider apples therefore are divided into four categories, of which examples of varieties are given in Fig. 23.

Unlike culinary and dessert apples, cider apples are harvested from the ground after they have dropped, perfectly ripe, from the tree; the trees are shaken to release them. Another reason why small cider orchards and companies have not flourished is the difficulty of getting labour to do the back-breaking job of gathering apples off the ground; this job is now done by expensive and complicated harvesting machinery. In April or May the apple and pear will flower, and good weather without gales or rain is needed for a good fertilization and set of fruit. Like the vine, most varieties are self-pollinating. In June the fruit sets, and at the end of this month surplus fruitlets drop, leaving as many as the tree can bring to fruition. The harvest is from October to mid-November, about 150 days after flowering; the apple takes longer than the 100 days for the grape.

After the harvest, fruit is taken to the press houses where it is washed to get rid of grass and leaves picked up by the harvesters. Apples are then floated in water through large pipes to bins to await processing. If necessary, they can be stored under a blanket of inert gas for some time. If culinary apples such as Bramley Seedlings or dessert apples are used, these will be either windfalls or fruit that has been bruised in transit. Immediately before pressing, the apples are pounded, grated, or sliced in a mill, so that juice can be easily released in the press. Enzymes may be added to the pulp to break down pectins, making release of juice more complete. The consistency of the pulp has to be right – if it is too much like porridge, it becomes difficult to press: if it is too coarse, not enough juice will be released.

1 Are cider and perry recent additions to our repertoire of drinks?
2 Where is the leading research establishment for cider and perry?
3 Name three countries, other than England and France, in which cider is made.

PRODUCTION AND STYLES OF CIDER

The traditional method of pressing is to make packets of pulp by wrapping them in cloth, and to pile these 'cheeses', interspersed with wooden boards, in a vertical press operated by screw or hydraulic pressure. Now, pulp is pressed in batches in large automatic horizontal presses such as the Swiss Bücher-Guyer, or continuously in screw or belt presses. If it is to be fermented immediately, the juice is analysed to find its composition and treated with sulphur dioxide to kill wild yeasts; its acidity is increased if necessary with citric acid, and it may be enriched by increasing its sugar content with sugar or concentrated juice. Blending of juices from different fruit may also take place at this stage. Cultured yeasts known to produce cider with good flavour characteristics and good yield of alcohol are added, and fermentation is carried out in wood or stainless steel open vats. Unlike grape must, there is no initial violent fermentation; the fermentation takes place at a temperature of $18°$-$24°$c($65°$-$75°$F) – not in any case exceeding $27°$c($80°$F) – and continues for four to six weeks until fermentation is complete, leaving a completely dry cider.

Three main types of cider are marketed: draught, keg, and bottled. Draught cider is unfiltered and, while not cloudy, is not 'starbright'. It may have had a little sugar and yeast added in the cask to give it 'condition', that is to say a slight sparkle from dissolved carbon dioxide. Draught cider can be completely dry – often known as 'scrumpy' – or it may be sweetened with sugar. Draught cider is rarely seen outside its own area of production as, in its oak casks or plastic containers, it has a limited life and is more liable to infection.

The chief disorder of cider, as of wine, is acetic fermentation by acetobacter. Other bacteria which can cause marked cloudiness and a smell of bananas ('cider-sickness') are rarely found nowadays, but contamination by lactic acid bacilli, which will only occur if cider is not properly looked after, can cause 'ropiness', a condition in which the flavour is not affected, but the cider becomes unpleasantly mucous in consistency. Such maladies are unknown to manufacturers who guard carefully against them, but customers may find them in cider left on ullage in pubs or restaurants.

1 No, they have been known for many years, even before the Norman Conquest.
2 In England – the horticulture department of the University of Bristol.
3 From Italy, Spain, Germany, Switzerland, Canada, USA, Australia and New Zealand.

Unlike draft ciders, keg and bottle ciders are pasteurized or sterile-filtered to render them 'starbright', which at the same time destroys or removes all potentially infective micro-organisms. At this stage, ciders may be blended, and the following other treatments may be carried out.

They may undergo a second fermentation (usually in tank) to render them sparkling; their acid balance may be adjusted; they will almost certainly be sweetened; and their strength may be adjusted. Finally, they will usually be carbonated by the injection of carbon dioxide gas. The specific treatments are all approved by the Ministry of Agriculture, Fisheries and Food, although several of them could not, under EEC laws, be applied to wine.

Typical characteristics of the most popular keg and bottle ciders are as follows:

Medium Sweet (carbonated)	4% vol alcohol
Medium Dry (carbonated)	6% vol alcohol
Special (some carbonated)	8.3% vol alcohol

Some Special ciders undergo a second fermentation to make them sparkling, and these, among others, may be bottled in sparkling wine bottles.

PERRY PRODUCTION AND STYLES

Perries, which generally follow the cider production method, are often made more sparkling and come into the Special range. They may be carbonated; or their sparkle may come from a second fermentation in sealed tanks. The perry is filtered under pressure; blending, sweetening, and other treatments are also carried out under pressure.

1 What are the four categories into which cider apples are divided?
2 Into which cider apple categories do (a) Tom Putt; (b) Yarlington Mill; (c) Court Royal; (d) Stokes Red, fall?
3 What are the principal areas of production of cider in England?
4 What three qualities are required of apples to give good cider?
5 How are cider apples harvested?

CIDER AND PERRY WITH FOOD

Cider and perry are not only healthy, refreshing drinks on their own, but are an excellent accompaniment to dishes of all sorts. A sparkling drink with a difference makes a good start to a celebration: in each glass place a lump of sugar, and put two or three drops of bitters – lemon, orange, or Angostura – on it; cover with Calvados, and fill up with dry sparkling cider or perry. Top up with sparkling cider or perry alone, as otherwise guests may not be able to appreciate the dinner prepared for them!

Fish can be poached in cider, and it is surprising what it will do for cod. As pork needs apple sauce, so all pigmeats (including sausages) are improved by marinating or cooking in cider or cider vinegar, ham particularly. Cider vinegar gives a gentle piquancy to salad dressings, and for wine-lovers dry cider can be an improvement on lemon juice in a vinegar-free dressing. Such a dressing complements perfectly orange salad served with duck. Desserts and sweets in plenty benefit from cider.

And, if the party goes on to dancing, a cider cup with orange juice and lemonade satisfies the thirst and puts back the energy; should the party be in winter, cider mulled with spices, ginger wine, and a dash of Calvados warms the heart and body.

TAXATION

Below a strength of 2° proof (1.14% vol alcohol), fermented apple juice is not cider; over 8.5% vol, it becomes 'apple wine' and is taxed as British Wine. Cider below this strength was taxed, for the first time since 1923, in 1977 under a Labour Government.

LEVELS OF CONSUMPTION

This short chapter reiterates the fact that, far from being bucolic drinks of great power, cider and perry are very moderate beverages that can be enjoyed by everyone. This is being recognized more and more, for the total consumption in Britain, which in 1960 amounted

1 Sweet, bitter-sweet, sharp, and bitter-sharp.
2 (a) Sharp; (b) bitter-sweet; (c) sweet; (d) bitter-sharp.
3 The counties of Devon, Somerset, Gloucester, Hereford, Kent, and Norfolk.
4 Sweetness, acid, and bitterness – to produce a balanced cider.
5 By shaking the trees and gathering the fruit from the ground.

to only 810,000 hl (18 million gallons) rose by 1970 to 1,480,000 hl (35 million gallons); by 1977, this had increased to 2,150,000 hl (47 million gallons), and it is expected that this increase will continue.

1 When do the apple and pear flower? When are they harvested?
2 How is the juice extracted from apples for making cider?
3 What are the three main types of cider on the market? What is 'scrumpy'?
4 Give the percentage vol. alcohol of: (a) Medium Sweet; (b) Medium Dry; (c) Special ciders. Are they all carbonated?

11
Anatomy of the Trade

To the consumer, this is perhaps the most important chapter of all in the story of the preparation of wines, spirits, liqueurs and beers. For it tells of the massive investment, the implicit crafts and skills, the infinite care and patience, and the deep sense of responsibility of the world industries involved in the process of bringing these products to the market-place. Together they represent the guarantees of quality and description of the contents of the bottle offered for sale.

1 In April or May; from early October to mid-November.
2 The apples are pounded, sliced, or grated, and the pulp is then pressed.
3 Draught, keg, and bottled. Completely dry draught cider.
4 (a) 4%; (b) 6%; (c) 8.3%. Special ciders are not always carbonated: the others always are.

MARKETING

The marketing operation is an international one, and involves not only the producers but many allied industries, such as bottle and cork manufacturers, coopers, land and sea transport operators, insurance brokers and operators of warehouse services, lawyers and accountants. There are also those who act as wholesalers and retailers selling direct to the consumer. The trade is international, and the journey from producer to consumer may be long or short.

THE SHORT AND LONG JOURNEY

The short journey is made where a large wine merchant owns vineyards, bottles in his own cellars and sells the wine through his own retail outlets: in much the same way, large brewing groups sell their own beer in their tied public houses. The long journey is made where a small proprietor sells his wine, either in bottle or in cask, through a broker, to a *négociant,* from whom a shipper in England buys the wine and imports it, selling it to his customers. These customers may be the wine divisions of large brewing groups, small off-licence traders, hotels and restaurants, or favoured individuals. There can be a short journey from the small proprietor too, for many a Frenchman buys a cask of wine from a little vineyard that he knows, and bottles it himself at home. Of course, it may not be so well bottled, but it will have cost him less.

Within the trade, the existence of organizations created by those sharing mutual interests goes back and is lost in time. In England, six of the ancient Livery Companies of the City of London received their charters from the Crown for watching over different aspects of the industry – the Vintners, Brewers, Innholders, Coopers, Distillers, and Carmen: in France, the 'Courtiers Picquet en Vin', the ancient and honourable body of wine-brokers, received their charter from Philippe le Bon in the fourteenth century. These traditional organizations still have a role to play in the modern operation.

---

1 Which foods are improved by cooking in cider?
2 Is.it right to describe cider and perry as 'bucolic drinks of great power'?

Measures and Methods of Sale

A measure often used in the sale of wine from the larger vineyards, in Bordeaux particularly, is the tonneau. This is a measure amounting to four barriques or hogsheads each of 225 litres. The wine sold in this fashion is not necessarily sold in bulk, but frequently in bottle, the tonneau being 96 dozen bottles. Some of the most famous owners of the Médoc test the market by offering a portion of their production (a *tranche*) at a fixed price per tonneau – which will be a high one. Depending on the response to his offer, the great owner will offer further tranches at a higher or lower price. Meanwhile, of course, all the other growers who employ this method will have had to guess the success of his offer, and offer their own wines at appropriate prices, bearing in mind their status in relation to the first. It is rather like horse-racing, and doubtless just as exciting.

But there are many owners who bottle at domaine or château and sell to négociants, who appear at different levels in the marketing strata, and indeed many vineyards are owned by négociants who may bottle at château or in their cellars in the towns. Other vineyards may be owned by hotels or trading groups; for instance Château Loudenne in the Médoc, which has been in the hands of one owner (Gilbey SA) longer than any other property in Bordeaux, except that of Mouton-Rothschild. In much the same way, the production and sale of spirits varies from the giant international distilling groups to the small grower in Cognac, who keeps a few casks of his own distillation at home until funds are needed for a family wedding or funeral (such Cognac is highly valued by the great Cognac Houses).

The Broker and Négociant

Few of the basic producers of wine and spirits dispose of their merchandise without the services of a broker, whose job it is to assess the produce where it is made, and to introduce it to the négociant. In France, this is still the role of the courtier. The broker takes his commission on the actual sale of the wine or spirit, and may not deal on his own behalf. Usually it is the négociant who buys: his

1 Fish and pork.
2 No. They are pleasant and moderate drinks, which can be enjoyed by everyone and used in cooking to enhance ordinary dishes.

full title is *négociant-éleveur*, for he is responsible not only for buying wines and spirits, but also for shipping or marketing them. Wines may come to his cellars in bulk containers, road and rail tankers and a variety of other containers. His main task is looking after young wines until they are ready to be bottled – raising them like children – and this is just what *éleveur* means: teacher.

Some of the wines bought by the négociant will be unable to stand in the market on their own, and will need to be blended. Blending is a great art, demanding a critical and well-trained palate. The aim of the blender is to make two or more insufficient wines balance their faults and virtues to produce a better wine, meaning one that sells. The négociant will finally sell his wines at home, or export them in bulk, or both.

SHIPPERS AND FORWARDING AGENTS

The representatives of the shippers from the importing countries will pay frequent visits to the négociants, whose agents they are, to taste the wines, discuss prices, and arrange details of shipment. Or, if their agency agreements allow, they may look around to find wines which will be good value for their customers. Such men need to have a good knowledge of markets, costing practice, and shipping and customs procedures, as well as a discerning and objective palate. The importer, called a shipper, will use the services of UK shipping and forwarding agents, whose particular expertise in shipping, documentation, and the entry, clearance, and insurance of such parcels, represents a considerable saving of manpower in the modern economy.

TRAVEL SICKNESS IN WINES

Having received the wine into his bonded warehouse, and after satisfying himself that the wine is acceptable, the shipper will have to decide if it needs any treatment. Wine does not like being jerked about in travel or subjected to sudden changes in temperature, and will require time to rest after its journey. Moreover, it may have

1 Many industries worldwide have made a massive investment in servicing the wine, spirits, liqueur and beer industries. What does this represent to the consumer?
2 How is the transport industry connected with the Wine and Spirit Trade?
3 Which Livery Companies of the City of London watch over the wine and spirits industries?

contracted some sickness on its travels: a cask may have had a faulty stave, which would give the wine a 'woody' taste: or the lining of a Safrap container may have been damaged, allowing the wine to come in contact with iron, resulting in a greyish haze and possibly a smell of bad eggs. These faults can be cured, but their cure requires a diagnosis and treatment just as skilled as a doctor's in treating his human patients.

Once the wine is rested and cured of any sickness, it is ready for the next stage. If it arrived in bottle it can be sent out to the wholesaler or retailer, after checking samples for quality; if samples of a wine bottled at source, abroad, show signs of secondary fermentation in bottle, the whole consignment will have to be disgorged, filtered, and rebottled in sterile bottles. The British trade has always been renowned for its skill in bottling, and attempts of foreign agencies to enforce bottling at source have always been resisted. If the wine is ordinary wine in bulk, it may require blending. Just as people in unison can produce something greater than any one of them on his own, so can individual, perhaps even nondescript, wines be blended into something better: the shipper's skill lies here, in his vision of the final product when purchasing its components. Having decided on his blend, the shipper makes it.

DISTRIBUTION AND LICENSING IN THE UK

The next link in the chain is the wholesaler, who may in fact be the shipper himself. Now, having the United Kingdom particularly in mind, licences should be mentioned. The wholesaler needs no licence for selling quantities over 9 litres (2 gal) or one dozen bottles of wine (for beer and cider the equivalents are 20 litres (4.5 gal) and two dozen bottles). In the UK, retailers selling lesser quantities for consumption OFF the premises require a Justices' licence. Establishments which sell wines, spirits and beers direct to the public ON the premises also require a Justices' licence; but in the UK they are subject to special controls, imposed for social reasons. The hours

1 Guarantees of the quality and description of the contents of the bottle offered for sale.
2 In transporting the goods, or in selling them to passengers.
3 Vintners, Brewers, Innholders, Coopers, Distillers and Carmen.

when alcohol may be consumed are laid down, and so are the persons to whom it may be sold: no person under eighteen may buy or consume alcohol in a bar, nor may he serve in one. The licensee must be of good character, and must not allow his premises to be used as a resort of criminals or prostitutes. Drunkenness observed on the premises can cost him his licence. He may obtain an extension of hours to his licence on special occasions: an occasional licence may be obtained (not necessarily by a licensee) to cover a dance, or 'wine and cheese party' in another location where alcohol is to be sold. But every occasion when alcoholic beverages are sold for consumption requires a licence. There are variants of the full on-licence, such as the club licence, the restaurant licence, and the residential licence for guests at hotels and boarding houses, each restricting service to a particular class of customer. On-licences also specify the exact premises, down to the room in a house, where alcohol may be consumed. And even this does not end the list of licences required for different purposes. In the UK, distillers must have an excise licence (for no matter what quantity or distillate), and brewers require a brewers' licence.

THE CROWN LOCK AND SPIRIT SAFE

As soon as the sugary wort or must starts to ferment and becomes alcoholic, further processing must, by law, be continued under Crown lock – on warehouse, washback, still or spirit safe. The home brewer or wine-maker in the UK is exempt from licence, provided he produces only for the use of his own household.

We have seen that there can be a long chain between the producer and the customer. Some large groups of companies have been formed in the trade to encompass this vertically: they are, at the same time, vineyard owners, négoçiants-éleveurs, shippers, wholesalers and retailers. On a smaller scale, the shipper can be found who runs a chain of off-licences and also restaurants. Firms also integrate horizontally, in handling wines of several négoçiants and countries, together with spirits and liqueurs of various sorts.

1 What is a tonneau?
2 Does the representative of an importer need to know much about wines?
3 Should wine, imported in bulk, be bottled for immediate sale?

TRADE ASSOCIATIONS

A number of international, national, and regional associations exist to protect the trade and the good name of their products. In some cases they also promote sales. INAO, for example, sponsored by the French Government, protects the reputation of French wines; Consorzi, Juntas, and Consejos do the same for other countries and individual regions. The receiving countries also find the need to form associations of particular interests.

UK ASSOCIATIONS FOR TRADE PROTECTION

In the UK, there are associations or committees of Champagne shippers, of brandy shippers, of Sherry shippers, of Cyprus wine shippers, of gin distillers and rectifiers, and of rum importers, to name but a few. Their members come together for mutual assistance and protection. Similarly, there are regional associations of wine merchants who resolve local matters between themselves besides presenting the views of local trade and consumer interests to the Wine and Spirit Association of Great Britain and Northern Ireland. This Association represents the views of the British trade at large to the Government, especially in the fields of taxation and customs procedures, and has daily contact with Government departments and with Parliament on these and any other matters affecting the trade: it passes on the results of its investigations and representations to its subscribing members. Subscriptions are required because this work costs money, and the individual firms who benefit must pay for the service. The service is so valuable that no firm of any worth would consider not belonging. It is not the only national association in the field of wines and spirits: there are the Scotch Whisky Association, the Brewers' Society, the National Federation of Off-Licensees, and others which reflect particular interests. All of these keep in close contact with one another and coordinate their efforts as far as possible, so that uniform opinion may be presented to the Government.

1 A tonneau is a selling measure of 900 litres (200 gallons).
2 Yes, because he must find wines which will be good value for his customers.
3 No. It needs time to rest after its journey.

UK SERVICE ASSOCIATIONS

Three service organizations in the UK should be mentioned here: the Wine Development Board, which promotes public interest in wines and spirits and educates the consumer; the Wine and Spirit Education Trust, set up by the Vintners' Company and the Wine and Spirit Association to improve the knowledge of people engaged in the wine and spirit and associated trades; and the Wine Standards Board, set up by the Vintners' Company with government approval, to control the proper documentation of imported wine.

International Associations: On the international scale, there are more associations. With new entries into the European Economic Community during the 1980s, half the member states are wine-producing countries, so an EEC wine-importing countries group has been formed. There is also an EFTA wine-merchants group. On the global scale, there is an International Federation of Wine and Spirit Merchants (FIVS), which annually holds a Congress in some important world centre to discuss such matters as international labelling regulations, the substances which should be permitted to be added to wines and spirits, and professional education of the wine and spirit merchant.

GOVERNMENTAL CONTROL

Perhaps it is through the eyes of the Government inspector that a review of some wine and spirit standards and controls can best be observed. Firstly, he will know the Government departments who share the responsibility of administering the law. The most important ministry today to the Trade is the Ministry of Agriculture, Fisheries and Food, but other ministries such as the Department of Health and the Home Office are concerned in the administration of certain Acts.

1 How would a supermarket obtain a licence to sell wines?
2 If you invite people to your house for a wine and cheese party, and charge 50p per glass of wine, do you need a licence?

Customs and Trading Standards Officers

Labelling requirements are affected by the Customs and Excise Management Act, the Food and Drugs Act and the Labelling of Food Orders made under it, the Weights and Measures Act, the Trade Descriptions Act, the Anglo-Portuguese Trade Treaties Acts, and a wealth of case law.

Labels now constantly need to conform with new international agreements, binding EEC, EFTA, and other grouped countries. The Customs officer will need to know and to be able to recognize on sight the different containers for wines and spirits, and know their capacities. Particular attention will be given by him and the Trading Standards Officer to the alcoholic strengths in relation to taxation and to the claims made on the label.

Wines in Bond

Reference has been made to the activities of wine-makers, brokers, négociants, shippers, importers, wholesalers and retailers, and in the context of these references, two things have not been mentioned. Both are very important. Firstly, the wine which is the subject of a series of deals along the line is rarely, if ever, bought, sold and passed on immediately. Sometimes years elapse before a consignment of wine passes from one stage to the next. There are wines which have been lying in bond in the London docks for over fifty years. Secondly, before any deal is made, the wine is tasted. The method of tasting will bear careful examination and is most interesting. A large volume of wine changes hands at wine sales, where professional tasting is the key to the bidding. While there is room for the talented amateur on such occasions, the uninitiated buyers who do not know how to taste objectively and value a wine can get their fingers burnt.

WINE TASTING

Everyone should know how to taste, in order to gain the maximum benefit from each mouthful. Wines and spirits are expensive, and it is

---

1 By application to the local Justices.
2 Yes, because alcoholic beverages are being sold for consumption.

a pity to pour them down the throat without fully appreciating them, and the work of all those who have brought them from vineyard or distillery. The grower tastes, as he makes his wine, to see that it is progressing favourably and is not getting sick. The broker, négociant and importer will all taste the wine to see that it will suit their purposes. The shipper will also taste as he blends wines together, to see that they suit his market. The importer will taste a sample from each cask on arrival, to see that the quality is up to the sample that he tasted in the vineyard region. The wholesale or retail buyer tastes to select suitable wines for his customers.

Tasting, to the layman, might infer drinking, but this is not so. 'Testing' could be a better term. Tasting is used as a judgement of quality and soundness, but it does not only involve the sense of taste – wine also has to be seen, smelt and felt.

THE SENSES OF SIGHT AND SMELL

First then, sight. If a wine does not look bright – if it is hazy or has an unnatural colour – it is unlikely to taste good and the taster is unlikely to let it into his mouth, but will proceed with the utmost caution. Clarity tells that the wine is wholesome and colour can help to tell its age. Wine that is young looks fresh in colour, and white wines may turn gold from pale yellow, or possibly from almost white. Red wines start off their life looking a light or a dark purple, depending on where and how they were made. With age, these colours dull gradually, so that a very old red wine may look the colour of a fine old mahogany table, and an old white wine may look a deep golden colour. If a red wine looks a dirty shade of brown this will indicate that all is not well.

Next, smell the wine. If the wine fails to look bright it is unlikely to smell good, and if it does not smell clean then, once again, the taster is unlikely to let it into his mouth. Sound wines must look sound and smell sound. They should *not* smell of rotten eggs, cabbage, old socks or dirty drying-up cloths. A sick wine can smell of any of these, although the last smell may be just that – from a dirty glass. So the wine-taster will always be careful to see that his glass is well-washed and polished and free of taint.

1 What is the name of the national association representing the views of the British Wine and Spirit Trade?
2 How does this association learn of problems affecting provincial traders?
3 Which Ministry has prime responsibility for the Wine and Spirit Trade?

Fine wines smell strongly. They will have a good bouquet of fruit or spices, and will shout their quality from the roof tops: they smell beautiful. The lesser wines are very good to drink, but do not smell of very much, which is possibly one reason why their price is more reasonable. If wine has a chemical smell which catches the back of the nose, this may be cured by exposure to the air.

WINE ON THE TONGUE, GUMS AND PALATE

After sight and smell have contributed to the diagnosis, the next stop is to taste. The palate will normally confirm what the eyes and nose have already discovered. The taster will take a generous mouthful of wine and hold it in his mouth. He may also draw air through the wine in his mouth to bring out the aroma of the wine. The sense organs of his mouth are distributed between the tongue, the gums and the palate, and they may occur in different places for different people. A wine with a high degree of sweetness, but having a balancing acidity, might well taste too sharp on the tip of the tongue, yet too sweet down the back of the throat. The sides of the tongue and sides of the mouth detect the bitterness of tannin, particularly in red wines. The gums are quick to detect alcohol as a prickly sensation. Alcohol, like tannin, is a preservative, and the presence of both indicates that a wine is likely to last well. The 'feel' of the wine in the mouth is also experienced at this time.

While the taster has the wine in his mouth, he should be reaching a conclusion as to whether the wine is balanced, for this is what he is looking for. The wine should be neither too sweet nor too acid, neither too heavy in alcohol nor too light. It should not be flat, and its sweetness and alcohol should be balanced by acid. When his judgement is made, the professional wine-taster will spit out the wine. This he does primarily to remove the memory of the wine in readiness for the next, and a dry biscuit will help him to do this. Young tannic wines, were they swallowed during a tasting, could easily upset the stomach; also the cold sober judgement of the taster could be affected as the day wore on, if wines were swallowed rather than ejected from the mouth.

1 The Wine and Spirit Association of Great Britain and Northern Ireland.
2 Through representations from regional associations of wine-merchants.
3 The Ministry of Agriculture, Fisheries and Food.

The Meaning of 'Finish'

But there is one quality of a wine which may not be immediately apparent – the quality known as 'finish'. This is the very *character* of the wine, and it is difficult to put into words. If, however, the taster asks himself 'How long can I remember the wine?' he is talking about finish. The memory of a great wine will stay vividly on the palate, possibly for a period of twenty-four hours or more, and will do so in spite of other wines and foods consumed during this time.

Some Dont's for Wine Tasters

These tests come to the merchant's aid when a shipment of wine, or even a single bottle, is unlabelled. The labels may have been washed off, or they may never have existed and the invoice may have been mislaid. Then the taster must ascribe an origin and value to the wine, in order to sell it. In the trade, very few people have to do this, and very few people can. It is an art based on long experience and a phenomenal memory. The reader may be fortunate enough to be invited to one of the tastings held by firms in the trade. Smoking is not permitted: this is not to say that smoking destroys the palate – about half the Masters of Wine are smokers – but non-smokers could not detect anything in a wine if someone were smoking in their presence. For the same reason, ladies invited to trade tastings will not use perfume, nor will gentlemen have used strong aftershave lotion. Men may note that vodka makes a good odourless aftershave lotion!

Wine Tasters' Notes

One problem confronting the taster is how to record his sensations: memory is a fickle thing, and the senses of smell and taste, though very evocative, are fleeting. It is wise, then, to take notes, at the time if possible, but if not, as soon as possible afterwards. In the notes should be recorded the name of the wine, its vintage, the name of the shipper, and the price. Then, impressions of the appearance of the wine, to the eye, to the nose, and to the palate should be noted,

1 Is duty paid immediately on wines placed into bond?
2 Is a cloudy wine likely to smell good?

ending with a general assessment. The language in which all these things are recorded should be restrained: 'A well-travelled little wine appearing rather above its station' does nothing to describe the wine, but much to describe the author of the remark.

The eye will record clarity, haziness and deposit; it will note the colour of white wines, ranging from white through straw or green, to deep or old gold; and will record the colours of red wines from purple through garnet, to mahogany. As at a presentation of wines all should be starbright, only the rare exception will call for a remark on clarity.

The nose will record bouquet – of fruit or flower, of spices, of fragrance, and the peppery or baked smell of wines made in hot countries. But the nose must be alert for the sickly sweetness of a wine turning to vinegar, or the acetic smell of one that already has; and for the musty smell of a cask with a faulty stave.

The palate will record alcoholic strength from the pricking on the gums, acid, sweetness, and tannin from the tongue. These sensations may be described as body, acidity, sweetness, lusciousness or heaviness (of alcohol); and, at this stage, the taster will make up his mind if the wine is balanced, or too acidic or too flat; if the sweetness is counterbalanced by acidity and fruitiness, or the general impression is cloying or nondescript. The tannin content of red wines comes into the computation also: red wines may be hard, with much tannin, or soft, with little.

Pricing Wine before Bidding

The finish, which is perhaps determined shortly after tasting, sets the seal on the whole operation: fine wines not only shout their qualities aloud but also stay long in the memory, which is one reason why they are so expensive. And from all this information, the taster must try to price the wine; if at an auction, he must know whether to bid, and to what level; if at an off-licence he must consult his memory and decide whether to buy at the price offered; or if at a restaurant, he must again consult his memory and decide which wine gives the best value for his money.

1 No. Many years may elapse before it is required for sale or consumption.
2 No. Cloudiness in wines indicates sickness.

WORLD OUTPUT

Every year the world output of wine alone amounts to the equivalent of over 43,000 million bottles; with the addition of spirits and beers, the alcoholic drinks industry has a weekly turnover measured in hundreds of millions of pounds. The weight of money and labour involved in the mammoth task of the manufacture and distribution of this great volume of consumable merchandise is enormous, and this short chapter provides a brief sketch of the structure of the trade which manages it.

1 When appreciating wine, why should it not be swallowed straight away?
2 Irrespective of value, what quality should the taster look for in wine?

12

Wines, Spirits, and the Consumer

SENSIBLE USE OF ALCOHOLIC DRINKS

The reader will by now have learned much of the variety of wines and spirits, and have been tantalized by the immense range available. He may, by this time, be thirsty, and eager to test his newly-gained knowledge in practice. In this story of the origin and manufacture of wines and spirits, drinking habits have been shown to change with fashion and necessity. But underlying the preferences and constraints of each succeeding generation, there are unchanging reasons for drinking in the first place. Certainly everyone needs a regular liquid intake merely to live, and for that, pure water will do nicely.

1 It should be held in the mouth to give all the senses a chance of evaluating it.
2 A proper balance between alcohol, sweetness and acidity.

However, it is the stimulus of alcohol that appeals to the human being. In tiredness he is revived; in trouble, consoled; in despair, encouraged; in perplexity, inspired; in solitude, befriended; in happiness, uplifted; and in company he is at home.

There will always be a sound reason for enjoying a drink. Dean Aldrich of Christ Church, Oxford, some two hundred and fifty years ago, had it thus:

> If all be true that I do think
> There are five reasons we should drink:
> Good wine – a friend – or being dry,
> Or lest we should be by and by,
> Or any other reason why.

The Dean may have had his tongue in his cheek, but the gentle scholar nevertheless had the right idea. Wines and spirits are always enjoyable in company, and need no justification. Such drinking transforms an occurrence into an occasion, and the intangible power of alcohol which helps people rise to this occasion is perhaps the most telling of its qualities.

Thanks to a helpful, efficient and informed off-licence trade, wines and spirits can be enjoyed in the home as well as in the restaurant, hotel, club or pub. This has become particularly true in recent years, when there are so many chain stores and supermarkets selling wines and spirits; wines can be, and are, picked up with the groceries, and there is no longer any prejudice about the housewife buying them. They are now, in Britain, commonplace items of everyday life – which is not to say that they should be mishandled, misused or unappreciated.

SOCIAL ASPECTS OF ALCOHOL

This is perhaps an opportune moment to bring in the subject of the social aspects of alcohol, a subject which demands serious consideration by every wine-merchant, consumer, and citizen. There has

1 Under what headings would a taster record his notes?
2 In terms of tasting, what is the difference between lusciousness and flabbiness?
3 In the long run, what decides the price of wine?
4 What senses are used in tasting?

always been a vociferous lobby of those who decry alcohol as a curse, and on those grounds would deny it to all. The number of these people is very small, but their voice should be heeded for, to some unfortunates, alcohol *is* a curse: they are the ones who become addicted, become unfit to work, and suffer personality changes which make them a burden to their families and lose them their friends. They, their firms, their families, their friends, blame alcohol as the cause, yet no one knows why one person should succumb, while another does not. Those who do succumb need all the skilled help they can be given, for they are not wrongdoers, but unfortunate casualties, who may be afflicted progressively with liver or brain damage. *Skilled* help is emphasized, for the first and hardest part is to persuade the patient that he or she is in need of help.

The 300,000 chronic alcoholics in the United Kingdom are only a small minority of the whole population, but there are many more who, while not addicted, sometimes forget that alcohol should only be taken in moderation – and that does not mean taking a moderate man's weekly portion in one evening! Such extreme behaviour makes people unpleasant to their companions and the community, and quite possibly dangerous to themselves and others, certainly if they are driving. Immoderation can be a failing of youth; few have not at some time overindulged, but most have grown out of it. Because sensible drinking requires a mature personality and outlook, licensing laws restrict alcohol consumption generally to those who have attained their majority. Business efficiency suffers when moderation is exceeded, and management must watch for it – usually, all that is required is a quiet reminder.

WHAT IS MODERATION?

The mature consumer may well ask 'What is moderation?', and be told, 'That which is good for the health'. But, how much is good for the health? This varies considerably between individuals, but Pasteur averred that up to a bottle of wine taken during the course of a day could be beneficial to the health. The official records for 1986 show that British people, on average, drank the equivalent of no more than

---

1 Label details, price; appearance to the eye, to the nose, to the palate; followed by conclusions.
2 Lusciousness denotes a sweet, yet firm and well-balanced wine; flabbiness, a cloying or nondescript wine.
3 The willingness of the buyer to buy.
4 Sight, smell, taste, 'feel'.

two glasses of wine (one third of a bottle) per day – most of it as beer, and very little as spirits.

Obviously, some drink more than others, and some not at all, which affects the figures (a recent NOP survey indicated that nine per cent of the population were teetotallers); on the other hand, some, regrettably, drink too much. But for the main body of the population, recent growth in total consumption is due more to increase in the number of people who drink moderately than to greater consumption by a few.

The question, 'Why do some people drink too much?' demands an answer. The answer which springs to the lips of the abolitionists is that alcohol is too readily available; it is readily available, but this is too facile an answer. Alcohol itself is not the problem, only the abuse of it, and it was always available to those who would abuse it. The answer lies in the increased pressures of everyday life, in the loneliness of single people in large cities, and, regrettably, in the lessening of control over the young at home and at school, coupled with a general reduction in the standards of social behaviour.

THE DISCIPLINES OF CORRECTION

Correction of the abuse of alcohol, therefore, does not lie in reduction of the total consumption level, but in improvement of social attitudes towards alcohol and approval of, and respect for, moderation. However, it is not enough for members of the Trade or consumers to satisfy themselves that they are moderate. Alcoholism exists, and must be conquered. It can be conquered, if parents bring up their children to respect alcohol and are supported by teachers; and if responsible persons in business control drinking habits in their firms (which does not mean banning alcohol) and are alert for signs of potential alcoholism, thereafter giving positive help to those affected. This help will chiefly lie in the detection and removal of stress, so that neither workers nor managers will ever feel the need to drink to escape from their problems.

1 Name three groups of people who must (and generally do) give serious consideration to the social aspects of alcohol.

SELECTION OF DRINKS

To enjoy wines and spirits to the full, it is necessary to choose the most suitable drink, not only for the occasion, but also for the company. Before meals, for 'a drink before lunch' (meaning that the guest is *not* expected to stay for lunch), or for cocktails, either sherry or mixed drinks are usual. The host can serve gin and tonic, if possible with ice and a slice of lemon, or whisky, remembering to ask if the guest likes soda, water, or ice, and refusing to be shocked if he likes cola with it. It is also well to know the names of some of the more fashionable cocktails, and what goes in them (a short list is given in Appendix 3); the impression that a Martini consisted of equal quantities of gin and brandy has proved to be not only expensive but socially disastrous. Non-alcoholic drinks should always be offered.

The 'Drink before Lunch'

Often it is better to serve wine, particularly if there are large numbers. Sherry has been mentioned, but this can cloy the palate if more than a couple of glasses are taken. Dry white port, with its fruity flavour, can make a lovely apéritif served well chilled. But light wines can also suit this sort of occasion perfectly, and there are many to choose from: the white wines of Germany, Austria, Yugoslavia, Hungary, and The Cape are all good. France also produces wines light enough for such parties, and the best one is Champagne, the wine of kings, and the king of wines. But not all our readers are kings, nor as rich as sultans, and Champagne is deservedly expensive, as has been mentioned in an earlier chapter. There are other sparkling wines which may take its place, to please without undue expense – Vouvray or Saumur from the Loire, Bourgogne Crémant, Asti Spumante from Italy and branded wines from France and Spain – speaking for the western hemisphere. Here is a recipe, from Germany originally, for a summer drink.

The night before a lunchtime party, take $\frac{1}{2}$ kg (1 lb) of strawberries, fresh cherries, or sliced peaches and lay them in a bowl. Cover them with caster sugar. In the morning, add one bottle of dry white

---

1 Wine-merchants, consumers and citizens.

wine and $\frac{1}{3}$ bottle of brandy. When the guests arrive, add two more bottles of dry white wine, a bottle of sparkling wine, and a large bottle of soda-water. Stir and serve. This will give about thirty glasses.

SELECTION OF WINES TO COMPLEMENT FOOD

With meals, there is a whole panorama of wines to choose from, which may be indeed embarrassingly large for the uninitiated. Generally speaking, the rule is to drink what one likes, or what one knows one's guests like, which may not be the same thing. But there are a few tips which may be helpful about wines that do not go well with certain foods. With savoury dishes, sweet white wines can be very cloying. Fish makes a tannic red wine taste metallic. Because of the sulphur in eggs, they rarely go well with red wine. And cream cheeses, such as Camembert or Brie, can make some white wines, particularly those from the Rhineland, taste very nasty indeed. Apart from these warnings, some generally-accepted suggestions can be made for matching wines with food, and these will be useful either when choosing wines for guests or when recommending wines for customers whose particular tastes are unknown. The light dry wines suitable as apéritifs will also complement shellfish and the lighter white fish; but for heavier or oilier fish, such as salmon, sole or halibut, a more full-bodied dry white wine will stand up to the food better. These wines will also complement veal, pork or chicken dishes. Light dry white wines tend to be paler in colour than the full-bodied ones, which is a rough guide when buying ordinary 'table wines'. The following are a few selected quality wines of the EEC which fall into these two categories:

Light Dry White Wines

FRANCE: Chablis, from Burgundy; Muscadet, Sancerre or Pouilly Blanc Fumé, from the Loire; Brut Champagne.
GERMANY: Mosel wines.
ITALY: Verdicchio, from Marche; Frascati from Lazio.

1 Why is there such a vociferous anti-alcohol lobby?
2 Is alcohol harmful?
3 To the majority, how much alcohol in a day could be taken without harm?
4 Consumption of alcohol in the UK is increasing. Why?
5 How can abuse of alcohol best be corrected?

Full-Bodied White Wines

FRANCE: Meursault or other Côte de Beaune, from Burgundy; White Graves or Entre-deux-Mers, from Bordeaux; Alsace wines; Condrieu or Hermitage, from the Rhône valley.
GERMANY: Rheingau, Rheinhessen or Nahe.
ITALY: Soave, from Veneto; Orvieto Secco, from Umbria.

Also in the full-bodied white category are the wines of Austria, the wines of Lutomer in Yugoslavia and Balaton in Hungary, the white Riojas of Spain and many more, too numerous to detail, from all parts of the world. Australia, The Cape, Argentina, Chile and California all produce fine white wines, both light and full-bodied.

Light Red and Rosé Wines

The lighter meats may also be complemented by the lighter red wines. Examples are young Chianti from Italy, young Beaujolais from Southern Burgundy, and the rare red wines of Chinon and Bourgueil in the Loire valley. And, not far removed from the lighter red wines, are rosé wines, although these vary considerably in sweetness and body. The rosé of Tavel in the Southern Rhône valley and the rosés of Cataluña and Southern Portugal will be good with white meats. The rosés of Anjou and the semi-sparkling rosés of Northern Portugal are sweeter and for some palates might clash with savoury dishes. Well chilled, however, they are perfect for picnics.

Full-Bodied Red Wines

Roast beef and game, and game birds, are full in flavour, and would make the light red wines and all but the biggest and most full-bodied white wines taste insipid. These meats therefore need a heavier red wine, just as red wines, with their extra tannin content, need robust foods to complement them. Although all red wines are normally put up in coloured bottles, to avoid their colour being affected by light, it is usually possible to assess the density of the colour by holding the bottle up against the light. Generally speaking, the denser the colour, the heavier and more tannic the wine will be. These wines can be hard when young; that is to say, some of the tannin gives a harsh

1 Because, although most people use alcohol sensibly, a number misuse it.
2 Doctors deny it to sufferers from certain medical conditions where it may be harmful. To the healthy majority there is no harm in alcohol, only in its misuse.
3 Up to a bottle of light wine (*or* eight single measures of spirits *or* three pints of beer) taken during the course of a day.
4 Because more people are drinking, not because few are drinking more.
5 By improvement of social attitudes towards drinking and by early detection and helping of potential alcoholic casualties.

texture to the wine in the mouth. This can often be alleviated by exposing the wine to air for a short time, by decanting. As wine ages, the excess tannin is precipitated as a deposit, which lies at the bottom of the bottle.

There are many fine red wines to choose from in Europe. Among the more expensive are the château-bottled clarets of Bordeaux, the fine Burgundies from the Côte d'Or, Châteauneuf-du-Pape from the southern Rhône, the fine red Riojas of Spain and the Barolos and Barbarescos of Italy. In the middle price range are the ordinary Bordeaux, Burgundy, and Rhône wines, and a number of wines with unfamiliar names from the Midi region of southern France. The labels of some of these wines may bear the letters AC or VDQS as a mark of quality. From Italy, Valpolicella and Bardolino are in the same price range as the older Chianti, which is made to lay down as well as to drink when young. Such Italian wines would be labelled DOC. Red wines are particularly suited to accompany cheeses, especially English cheeses. The French usually take cheese before the sweet course so that they can first enjoy what remains of their robust red wine, which will not taste the same after sweet food.

Sweet Wines for Sweet Courses

There is another range of wines to draw from for sweet courses – the sweet white wines, particularly those that have been made from 'noble rot' grapes. For very special occasions there are the expensive Sauternes from Bordeaux, the Beerenausleses and Trockenbeere-nausleses from Germany, Ausbruch wines from Austria and Tokay from Hungary. For lesser celebrations, the white Italian wines marked abboccato from Orvieto, wines from Penedés in Spain (until recently possibly called 'Spanish Sauternes'), or a sweet white Graves from Bordeaux, are all excellent; those with sweeter preferences could happily drink any of them throughout a meal.

And so to Nuts – and Port!

With nuts, or as in England with the cheese at the end of the meal, the great dessert wines come into their own. Port – truly the Englishman's wine – and Bual and Malmsey Madeiras are wines for

1 How should a 'gin and tonic' be served?
2 Which wine would be most suitable as a lunchtime aperitif for a party of ladies?

drinking great toasts with, and for sipping gently through some-times interminable speeches. It is customary at this stage to place the decanters on the table, leaving each diner to help himself. Tradi-tionally the decanters are passed to the left, after the host has helped himself; one way only, so that the decanters don't all get stuck at one end, and to the left, because most people are right-handed and the glasses are always placed to the diner's right. Pity the poor left-hander who has to reach across – and pity also the principal guest on the host's right hand: a good host will pour wine for this guest before he passes the decanter.

At Lloyd's in London there is a collection of Nelson relics, including a coaster in the shape of a jolly boat given by Nelson to the Master of the 'Victory'. There is a story that when the port in this silver coaster got stuck at one end of the mess table the officers would cry 'Push out the boat' to get it under way again: the origin of a happy expression.

LABELLING REGULATIONS

What should one look for when buying wines? First, a good supplier – one who knows his wines and his customers, and who can therefore make sound suggestions for their enjoyment. If he is right, they will return to buy again. But if the customer finds himself in a strange town, he is left to his own devices. His choice will be narrowed by knowing what sort of wine he wants, but even then there may be a confusingly large range on offer. That is why wines and spirits are labelled. And, to protect the consumer, they have to be, by law.

THE 'APPROPRIATE DESCRIPTION'

First of all, the label must contain an 'appropriate description': 'Whisky,' 'Gin', 'Rum', 'Vermouth', and 'Sherry' are all 'appropriate descriptions'. So are the names of wines, and if those names are the names of EEC quality wines, such as Nuits St. Georges, Côtes-du-

1 With ice and a slice of lemon.
2 A light white wine, such as Moselle.

Rhône, or Bordeaux, they must *be* those wines, and have the letters AC or AOC, meaning Appellation Contrôlée, or VDQS, meaning superior wines from a legally delimited area, on the label. In Italy, quality wines are labelled DOC or DOCG [Denominazione d'Origine Controllata (e Garantita)], while in Germany they would be labelled Qualitätswein, or Qualitätswein mit Prädikat. Nor can any other wines be labelled similarly, with intent to deceive. 'Spanish Sauternes' is not now a permitted labelling, nor would 'Shablee' be acceptable.

Shippers' or Bottlers' Name and Address

The next item that must appear on the label is the name and address of the shipper or bottler, for if there is any fault with the wine or spirit, it must lie at his door and, if it has caused any sickness, he is liable to pay damages. Should anything be found in the bottle which should not be there, on analysis by the Trading Standards Officer, the bottler is liable for prosecution on account of the harmful substance. But on the credit side, his is the name to look for, because the name of a reputable shipper is a guarantee that the wine or spirit will be good value for money, particularly when the name of the wine is a brand name unfamiliar to the customer. In the past, any overproduction in the quality wine areas could be sold in the UK under the same name as the limited quantity entitled to the name in its country of origin, but without the letters AC. This is now no longer legal; the producer must either destroy the surplus, or sell the total production as Table Wine. The customer who trusts his shipper, and knows his brand names, can get a wonderful bargain.

Country of Origin

Another item which must appear on the label is the country or countries of origin of the wine or spirit, for this enables a faulty product to be traced back to its source. So the customer may find that his latest bottle of branded wine bears the words 'Produce of Italy' while the last bottle of the same brand bore the words 'Produce

---

1 Why do game birds and game need full-bodied red wines?
2 Give examples of full-bodied red wines from countries other than France.
3 Which wines are particularly suited to accompany cheeses?
4 Is it likely that Bordeaux Rouge would go well with lobster?
5 At a restaurant, your guests order a variety of foods ranging through lobster, veal, pork, chicken, and Camembert. What wine could you choose to go with all of these?

of Austria, Hungary and Yugoslavia'. Does this matter? Not at all, for it means that the shipper who blended the wine has found that he can make his standard blend better, at that time, from the wines of Italy than he could from the wines of the other countries. Having regard to the element of luck in every year, this is not surprising, and the customer should merely be grateful for the skill of the blender.

CONTROL OF CLASSIFICATION

One important matter to be remembered in connection with blended wines is that the label of a blend of quality wines may not show any classification higher than the common name to which all constituents of the blend would be entitled. Thus, a blend of Gevrey-Chambertin and Chambolle-Musigny could not be entitled to any name higher than Bourgogne Rouge. A blend of Médoc and St. Émilion could only be called Bordeaux, or Bordeaux Supérieur if its alcoholic strength exceeded 10.5° GL. Recent legislation requires the statement of average contents (within close limits) to be stated on all labels; the statement must be expressed in litres or centilitres and, if the capacity is of an approved size, the letter 'e' may also appear on the label or bottle.

If wines from different EEC countries are blended, the label must bear the words 'Blend of wines from different countries of the European Community'; or if a wine is made in one EEC country from grapes grown in another, this also must be stated. In both cases, the words 'Table Wine' must also appear on the label and these statements must be in the language of the Member State in which the wine is to be sold.

STRENGTH OF TONIC AND SPECIAL WINES

Until now, the strength of ordinary wines in the UK did not have to appear on the label; but this information has had to appear on the labels of spirits and liqueurs or of wines for which special tonic or other properties are claimed. This also applied to 'wines' made from fruit other than grapes, or from a mixture of fruits. On the continent

---

1 Because they are full in flavour and would make other wines taste insipid.
2 Red Riojas from Spain, or Barolo or Barbaresco from Piedmont in Italy.
3 Red wines.
4 No. The lobster would make the Bordeaux taste metallic.
5 Alsace wine, or Chablis for some and Beaujolais for others (for example).

strength is shown in degrees Gay-Lussac, equivalent to percentages of alcohol by volume: in the UK, the strength is shown in % OIML. As previously stated, this differs from GL by a minute amount, due to the fact that OIML measurements are taken at 20°C and GL at 15°C; but such differences do become significant with large quantities and high excise duties. See Fig. 18 on p. 119.

CHOOSING FROM A WINE LIST

The label gives the consumer a great deal of information, but it will not usually tell him what the liquid inside the bottle is going to look or taste like: only experience, or the advice of the seller, can do that. Much has been said about buying wines from the off-licence, store or supermarket; but most customers will gain their experience in a restaurant to begin with. The wine list can be just as confusing as the array of bottles in a store; but the wine waiter, particularly if he is a graduate of the Academy of Wine Service, can give as good advice as the manager of an off-licence.

THE HOST'S DILEMMA IN ORDERING FOR GUESTS

What has been said about wines with food may have given some guidance on what part of the wine list to examine. But what should the host do if all his party have ordered different foods – some fish, some steaks, some game? There are several ways of tackling the problem. The normal bottle contains six glasses, and a half-bottle, three: and with a reasonably-sized meal, a half-bottle of light wine is not excessive for one person. So, if there are two diners, and one orders sole and the other steak, why not have a half-bottle of red wine and a half-bottle of white? The same solution applies if both have fish followed by meat, but then the sommelier should be told when to serve the wines. Another solution is to choose a wine that can be drunk all through the meal, one which will go with anything. The white wines of Alsace are an excellent example, as they will

1 Why should port decanters be passed to the left?
2 What do the letters VDQS convey?

complement every food, even strong creamy cheeses, and the same applies to the white wines of Germany, Austria, Hungary and Yugoslavia if the stronger cheeses are avoided. Young Beaujolais or Chianti, being very light on the palate, can be all-purpose wines except for shellfish or sweets. And for those who can afford it, Champagne has always been the wine for every occasion and every food. With oysters, with duck, or with Brie, Champagne tastes delicious.

What the Sommelier should know

When the wine has been ordered, the sommelier should bring the bottle without opening it, and show the label to the host so that he may confirm that it is the wine selected. Perhaps 'Chianti Classico – DOCG was ordered; but on inspection, the label includes the words 'Chianti – Denominazione d'Origine Controllata', and not the word 'Classico', or the words 'e Garantita', which denotes an inner district of higher-quality wines, at an appreciably higher price. Having pointed out to the sommelier that this is not the wine ordered, he will immediately change it for the right one: it is an easy mistake to make, as the difference on the label is so small.

Having agreed the bottle, the sommelier will then remove the foil from the top of the neck, draw the cork, and serve a small portion to the host, so that he can tell that it is sound by its appearance and smell. At this stage, and for this purpose, it is seldom necessary actually to taste the wine. It is fortunately very rare to find a bottle in poor condition – 'corky' wine may be discovered only once in a lifetime, and will probably never reach the customer, because the sommelier will already have smelled the cork and withdrawn the bottle without serving it. However, when first opened, a fine old wine may smell a little musty, but this 'bottle stink' caused by its long imprisonment in the bottle, will soon evaporate with exposure to air. If in doubt, the sample of wine may be poured from one glass to another: if the bad smell fades, all will be well – as previously mentioned, the glass itself may be at fault.

---

1 Because most people are right-handed, and the glasses are always on the diner's right.
2 Superior wine from a legally delimited area of France.

STORING WINE IN THE HOME

The host who wants to give his guests wine at home will do well to keep a small store. Although the off-licence may be just around the corner, it may be shut when the unexpected guest calls. Also, it is often cheaper: most wine-merchants will give a small discount on orders of a dozen bottles or more. Moreover, it is annoying, when another bottle of a particularly enjoyable vintage is wanted, to find that it has all been sold or that it has increased in price or that it is early-closing day.

WINE MERCHANTS WILL HELP NON-EXPERTS

Price increases are neither unusual nor wrong, because as wines, especially red wines, mature in bottle, they increase in quality and value. Also, each vintage has an effect on the price of its predecessors. For instance, 1971 was a good vintage for red Burgundies, while 1972 was only average, and 1973 and 1974 were poor. So, the 1971 Burgundies increased in value and price. This is not, by the way, to say that *all* Burgundies were good in 1971 and bad in the other two years; there is always some good wine from poor years, just as there is always some poor wine from good years. It is better to trust the judgement of a reputable wine-merchant than to go by the across-the-board statements of the vintage charts, although the best of these are useful as a rough guide. Some details of recent vintages are given in Appendix 2, but they are couched in only very general terms, and relate only to vintages that are well worth drinking, and likely to be encountered at a wine-merchant, restaurant, or auction.

WHERE BEST TO KEEP WINE

Having bought the wine, where and how should one store it? In a private house, the ideal place to keep any wines is in an unheated cellar, below ground level. Such a cellar will keep an even temperature around $9°C-14°C(48°F-57°F)$ and will also be free from vibra-

---

1 What labelling rule applies to all blended quality wines?
2 What qualification will assure the customer of the knowledge and efficiency of his wine waiter?

tion and light; the actual temperature, if even, is the least important of these conditions. For those who do not have a cellar, the cupboard under the stairs may be the next best place. The loft is not usually a good place for storage, because it is too hot in summer and too cold in winter.

Spirits should always be stored standing up, while wines should always be stored on their sides; keeping them on their sides will keep the corks damp, for these will lose their elasticity and ability to seal the bottle if they dry out. It is best to lay the bottles in racks, which can be obtained quite cheaply, even to fit the triangular under-stair cupboard. But, if no rack is available, the divided case in which the bottles were delivered will do as a temporary measure. The bottles should be stored with their labels uppermost, for then these can be read without undue disturbance, and also it will be known that any deposit (as in the case of older red wines) is lying on the other side of the bottle. The deposit is bitter to taste, and care should be taken when pouring to see that none gets into the glass. This can be avoided by decanting the wine from the bottle into a flask or decanter.

SERVING WINE

If sufficient notice has been given, it is best to take the bottle from storage to stand upright for a day before decanting, so that the sediment will fall to the bottom of the bottle. The lead or plastic capsule should be cut $\frac{1}{2}$ cm below the lip of the bottle to ensure that it does not contaminate the wine during pouring. The bottle should not be disturbed when drawing the cork. The shoulders, as well as the neck of the bottle, should first be wiped so that the wine coming from the bottle can be observed. To make this easier, a light should be placed behind the bottle before decanting, so that the sediment can be seen approaching the neck. The bottle should be held label-side up, and the wine poured gently into the decanter in one steady movement, stopping when the sediment starts climbing into the neck. The half-glass of wine left in the bottle is not worth drinking, but it is a valuable asset to the cook for making sauces.

1 They may not show any classification higher than the common name to which *all* constituents of the blend would be entitled.
2 Graduation in the Academy of Wine Service.

SPARKLING WINE HANDLING

Sparkling wines should be opened with care, and the cork should never be allowed to leave the hand, lest it should hurt someone: with a pressure of up to four atmospheres, and a cork the exact size of a human eyeball, accidents could happen. The following procedure will ensure that the bottle is safely opened and that none of the precious wine is lost. Keeping the left thumb pressed firmly on the top of the bottle, release the wire muzzle which holds the cork down (the gold foil has already been removed) and lift it away. Hold the bottle at about thirty degrees from the vertical, by the base, in the right hand, protecting the hand with a napkin against the unlikely event of the bottle bursting. Still holding the cork in place firmly with the left hand, gently turn the bottle with the right. As the cork is eased out, restrained by the left hand, any surplus pressure can escape gently, allowing the wine to be poured out without loss. A discreet 'pop' may be permissible.

Obviously, the colder the sparkling wine is when opened, the lower will be the pressure and the risk of losing any wine. But although sparkling wines should be served chilled, this does *not* mean iced. Iced sparkling wine, descending into a warm stomach, explodes like a bomb, creating discomfort and embarrassment.

TEMPERATURES FOR SERVING WINE

What are the best temperatures at which to serve wines? Fig. 24 shows the ideal temperature ranges. Sweet wines, with the notable exception of Vintage ports and Madeiras, should be chilled: the sweeter, the cooler. Old Tawny port gains from being slightly chilled. So also do light white wines. The fuller-bodied white wines, the rosés, and the lighter red wines, are best served at cellar temperatures, while the full-bodied red wines (that is to say, the general run of red wines) taste better if served at room temperature.

When bringing white wines from cellar temperature to chilled temperature, care should be taken that the change is done gradually. A few minutes in the bottom of the refrigerator (*never* a freezer), or an hour in a wine-cooler, should suffice to bring a wine to the right

1 Why should price increases, of red wines particularly, be acceptable as they grow older?
2 When ordering Italian wines, is the word 'Classico' important?

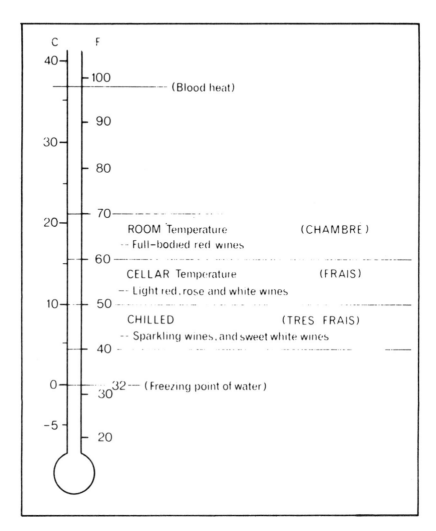

Fig. 24 Wine service temperature

degree of chill. The wine-cooler is often called an ice-bucket, and is sometimes misused by placing the bottle on a bed of ice which freezes the bottom of the bottle, and does not cool the wine. The wine-cooler should be deep enough to contain the whole length of the bottle, and should be half-filled with cold water: some pieces of ice should be placed in the water to keep it cool. To bring red wines from cellar up to room temperature, they should be placed in the

1 Because they mature in bottle and improve in quality.
2 Yes, it denotes the wine of an inner area, of higher quality.

room for several hours. Restaurants often have a 'dispense' in the dining-room, where a small supply of the more popular red wines are kept. But, if a bottle has to be brought directly from the cellar, it should *never* be placed in the oven or in hot water: such treatment would harm the bouquet. The only artificial method that might be acceptable is to decant the wine into a warmed (not hot) decanter, but it is really better to tell the guests that the wine should be warmed in the glass with the hand, and to serve a lesser quantity in the glass until the wine has had time to come to room temperature.

STANDARD WINE GLASS SHAPES

Particularly if this method of warming the wine is necessary, the glass should be thin; it should also be large enough to contain a reasonable amount of wine when filled two-thirds full – the proper level. It should be of clear glass, so that the consumer can see the colour of the wine, and it should be tulip-shaped, to conserve the aroma for the nose. Glasses for white wine should have a long stem, so that the hand does not warm the wine, nor the wine chill the hand. Fig. 25 shows five shapes of glass generally encountered. Note that the saucer-shaped glass is unsuitable for sparkling wines, as it lets the bubbles escape too quickly.

Another type of glass, the waisted 'schooner' or 'Elgin', is often used on licensed premises for the service of fortified wines, e.g. Sherry. It is not very suitable as the nose cannot be buried in the glass to capture the aroma, and wine spills easily from it.

SERVING MEASURES

A line is often drawn on wine glasses (which are themselves of different sizes) to indicate the filling level; but to 1988 there has been no uniformity in the size of measure served for wines, whether light, fortified, or sparkling. Although there is no legal definition of 'a glass of wine', this is in direct contrast to the licensed service of ciders, beers, and spirits, which must be sold in legally specified quantities or in sealed containers. In 1988 the quantities for ciders and

1 Why should a sommelier, opening a bottle of wine, cut the lead foil *below* the lip of the bottle?
2 Why should a light be placed behind a bottle while decanting?
3 Why should sparkling wine not be chilled to freezing point?

Champagne Flute   Champagne Saucer   German Wines

Sherry Sampler   Table Wines   Brandy

Fig. 25   Shapes of glass

beers were the Imperial pint and half pint. A single measure of rum, gin, vodka, or whisky is one-quarter, one-fifth, or one-sixth of a gill as is specified by a legal notice in the establishment. In England the measure is nearly always one-sixth of a gill; in Scotland one-fifth. An unofficial measure in Ireland can be deduced from their reference to a standard (75 cl) bottle as a 'ten-glass bottle' and to a 40-oz 112 cl bottle as 'a fifteen-glass bottle!'

This elementary study of alcoholic drinks and their industries is intended to provide an introduction for the uninitiated, and it is hoped that two things have been achieved. Firstly, that it will have encouraged the reader to learn more (Appendix 4 lists a few of the many books available). And secondly, that it will have brought a greater appreciation of wines, spirits and beers, and through that, a greater enjoyment of them.

1 Because the wine might react with the lead foil to produce minute quantities of lead poisoning in the glass.
2 So that the sediment in the bottle can be seen approaching the neck, and decanting then stopped.
3 Because it would be unpalatable, and cause discomfort when the bubbles erupted in the stomach.

13

Cigars

EARLY HISTORY

Natives were seen smoking cigars by Christopher Columbus when
he landed in America in 1492, and Pane recorded the taking of snuff
as early as 1494. A few years later tobacco chewing, apparently an
ancient tribal custom, was also observed in America. The leaf was
first brought to Europe for King Philip II in 1592 by Francisco
Fernandes; three years later tobacco seeds were sent to Catherine de
Medici, wife of Henry II of France, by the ambassador to Portugal,
Jean Nicot (hence 'nicotine'); Queen Catherine became one of the
first European users of snuff. Originally the American Indians

1 What is a reasonable and proper level to which a wine glass should be filled?
2 Is the shape of the glass related to the temperature at which the wine should be
  consumed?

inhaled their tobacco smoke through a pipe called a *tobago*, and Columbus gave one of the West Indian islands this name because it resembled the tobago in shape. Smoking gained rapidly in popularity in Europe, but not until the nineteenth century did cigar smoking enjoy a vogue, dating from the Napoleonic wars.

MODERN TOBACCO HABITS

Although the main consumption of tobacco now sways between pipes and cigarettes, there has always been a sizeable minority of cigar smokers; while the cigars of Cuba (Havana) have always been preferred, they are expensive. In recent years smaller panatella cigars have found an extensive market in the U.K. and, since 1945, cigars of Dutch and Swiss manufacture from tobacco of Indonesian origin have been introduced to the British market and have gained considerable popularity.

THE TOBACCO PLANT

The tobacco plant, *Nicotiana tabacum*, a native of South America, requires rich soil and plenty of sunlight in a sub-tropical or warm temperate climate. After harvesting, the leaf is dried or cured by one of four methods, sun, air, fire, or flue, of which each produces different colours and flavours in the tobacco; it is then fermented, before being sent to the manufacturers for blending and conversion. The old-established regions of production are Cuba, North and South America, Jamaica, Sumatra, Borneo, Java, and West Africa, but a fair amount of tobacco is now grown in Europe for its domestic markets.

The plant is subject to attack from caterpillars, particularly those of the Sphinx moth, which lays its eggs on the leaf; an undetected egg can live through the tobacco-producing processes to emerge as a weevil that will bore its way through made-up cigars, leaving a tunnel with the diameter of a small knitting needle behind it. One weevil could ruin every cigar in a box.

1 Two-thirds full.
2 Yes, to utilize the warmth of the hands for red wines, and to avoid that warmth for white wines.

STRAIGHT AND TORPEDO CIGARS

To appreciate fully the qualities of a cigar it is necessary to trace the origin and development of cigars of standard size and acknowledged quality. Two distinct shapes of cigars have been made from the earliest days of smoking – the straight, firmly-packed Corona, tending to be square-shaped in a cross-section, and the rounder torpedo which is tapered to a point at each end. The torpedo has recently waned in popularity to a marked extent. Coronas are made in five standard descriptions and sizes: Corona Grandes, the largest, 6 inches in length, known also as 'Churchills' or 'Lonsdales'; Coronas, $5\frac{1}{2}$ in.; Petit Coronas, 5 in.; Tres Petit Coronas, $4\frac{1}{2}$ in; and Half Coronas, $3\frac{1}{2}$ in. All are (or can be) of equal quality, but a longer cigar gives a cooler smoke, and allows the fragrance to be better appreciated.

'FILLER', 'BUNCH', AND 'WRAPPER'

The modern cigar can be made by machine as well as by hand; whichever process is used, the cigar itself is built up in three stages. At the centre of the cigar is the filler, a compressed mass of leaves, brown in colour, roughly assuming the shape of the final cigar. A binder is wrapped round the filler, to form a 'bunch'; and it is this bunch around which the finest green leaf, the wrapper, is then wound diagonally. The best wrapper leaf comes from Cuba, Sumatra, and Connecticut; other regions growing cigar tobacco plants cannot match these wrappers and have to import them. The wrapper is consequently an expensive component, accounting for over half the cost of a finished cigar. A skilled cigar-maker can make some 750 cigars by hand in the course of a week, the number varying to some extent according to size of cigar. The modern machine will turn out the same number of cigars in an hour, but whereas the filler of a hand-made cigar will usually be made of a better quality, longer leaf, the machine-made cigar will often have a chopped filler of short strands.

1 By what method is the measure of spirits sold by the glass legalized in the UK? What are the usual measures?

Spiral and Machine-wrapped Cigars

The binder in machine-made cigars, particularly those of Swiss, Dutch, or British manufacture, may be a sheet made after the fashion of paper from pulped tobacco leaves, rather than the natural leaf of a hand-made cigar. But the wrapper of a good machine-made cigar will be of natural leaf to give the degree of perfection sought after by the discerning cigar smoker. The wrapper for a single cigar is made either from a left-hand or right-hand half of a tobacco leaf after removal (stemming) of the midrib, and consequently the cigar may have either a clockwise or anti-clockwise spiral when manufactured. It is customary for all the cigars in one box to have the same spiral. Whichever way the spiral goes, the wrapper will end with a little circular cap to cover the end of the cigar, which must be cut or removed before the cigar can be smoked.

Colour of Cigars

Cigars vary considerably in colour; this is not an indication of strength or quality, but rather of taste or fashion. To achieve the light colour of the *Claro* wrapper, the plants are protected from the sun by muslin cloth. The colours favoured by the British market are (from light to dark) Claro, *Colorado Claro*, and *Colorado*, labelled CCC, CC and C respectively. The wrapper may have a greenish tinge, or may on occasion present a mottled appearance; this is not a sign of any fault, but is the result of localized burning of the leaf by the sun, whose rays are concentrated through droplets of rain or dew which act like lenses.

Cigar Boxes

Cedarwood is used almost universally for the packing of cigars, having proved to be the most suitable material. This wood seems to preserve the rich aroma and flavours of the cigar and contributes no taint to the tobacco. Even when cigars are packed individually in aluminium tubes or in glass jars of fifty, they are protected by cedarwood linings. Normal packaging units are 25 to the box, with

---

1 According to a notice displayed in the establishment. In England the legal measure is nearly always one-sixth of a gill and in Scotland one-fifth.

thirteen cigars on the top layer and twelve beneath, rising to bundles of 50 or 100, and to cabinets holding up to 1000 cigars.

'Green Cigars' and the Humidor

A freshly-made cigar is known as a 'green cigar' even though this has nothing to do with its colour, which may or may not be green. Green cigars contain some moisture, and are immature; some connoisseurs like to smoke them in this state (just as some people prefer the flavour of green walnuts to that of the ordinary variety). For this purpose they must be kept in sealed glass humidor jars. But normally cigars are left to mature and are warehoused – almost always in bond because the duty is so high – for up to eighteen months before being sold. Cigar importers are experts in the storage and maturation of cigars. Catering and hotel establishments customarily purchase cigars on an annual basis and leave them in bond in the custody of the importer until required. Under correct storage conditions cigars will keep for many years, and even those becoming too dry may be restored to prime condition in a humidor.

In the restaurant, cigars should be left in their boxes at an even temperature of 17°C(62°F), well away from the kitchen – from which they might assimilate undesirable odours.

Cutting and Lighting Cigars

Most cigars carry a band. This should *not* be removed – whatever society decrees – unless this can be done without risk of damaging the delicate wrapper: to make a hole in the side of the wrapper would render the cigar unsmokable. Some cigars are cut at both ends, but most cigars of quality will have one end sealed, and this seal or cap must be removed. The best instrument is the guillotine cutter, and the next best that which makes a V-shaped cut across the tip; those who know the construction of a cigar can remove the little cap with their thumbnail or teeth. If at all possible the cigar should not be pierced, although this is probably the most common habit; piercing a cigar produces too small an orifice which leads to uneven burning and a hot smoke; it also concentrates the tar.

1 Christopher Columbus named a West Indian island connected with smoking: which and why?
2 What are the old-established regions of cigar production?
3 What are the five standard sizes of Corona, and what are their lengths?

Cigars are best lit from a gas flame; a wooden match is next best, provided that the sulphur head has been allowed to burn away entirely. Petrol lighters can taint the cigar with their fumes.

Holding a cigar to the ear whilst rolling it in the fingers tells nothing and may damage the cigar. A gentle pressure of the thumb and forefinger on the side of a cigar – to see that it is resilient – should be enough to prove that the cigar has not dried out; and, if in a strange restaurant, the purchaser may wish to satisfy himself by sniffing to confirm that it has not been stored near the kitchen.

Disposing of 'finished' Cigars: Particularly in a private house, it is well to remember that a finished cigar will expire quickly if laid in the ashtray; it should not be stubbed out because this will produce an offensive stink that will impregnate hair, clothing, and curtains – for which the host or hostess will not be grateful.

1 Tobago. Because its shape resembled the tobago, or pipe used by the Indians.
2 Cuba, North and South America, Jamaica, Sumatra, Borneo, Java, and West Africa.
3 Coronas Grandes ('Churchills' or 'Lonsdales') (6 in); Coronas ($5\frac{1}{2}$ in); Petit Coronas (5 in); Tres Petit Coronas ($4\frac{1}{2}$ in); and Half Coronas ($3\frac{1}{2}$ in).

Official Classification of Bordeaux and Burgundy Wines

BORDEAUX

This classification has been widely disputed, and one change (Ch. Mouton-Rothschild) has already been made; it is usually more important for the reader to remember which growth a particular château falls into, than its exact position in the list. To facilitate reference, we have therefore departed from the original order (which may be found in most books on Bordeaux wines), and have arranged châteaux in alphabetical order for each growth; the alphabetical order for Premiers Crus (First Growths) *only* was decreed in 1973.

---

1 Name the three colours of cigars favoured in the British market, from light to dark, and give their respective labelling codes.
2 Should the band on a cigar be removed before smoking?
3 How should a capped cigar be prepared for smoking?

Most names in Bordeaux are prefixed by the term Château, but where a different term such as *Clos* is used, this is shown in italics.

The 1855 official classification of the wines of the Gironde

RED WINES

	Château	*Appellation Contrôlée*
Premiers Crus	Ch. Haut-Brion	Graves
	Ch. Lafite	Pauillac
	Ch. Latour	Pauillac
	Ch. Margaux	Margaux
	Ch. Mouton-Rothschild (elevated to Premier Cru by Presidential decree 1973)	Pauillac
Seconds Crus	Ch. Brane-Cantenac	Margaux
	Ch. Cos d'Estournel	Margaux
	Ch. Ducru-Beaucaillou	Margaux
	Ch. Durfort-Vivens	St. Estèphe
	Ch. Gruaud-Larose	St. Julien
	Ch. Lascombes	Margaux
	Ch. Léoville-Barton	St. Julien
	Ch. Léoville-Las-Cases	St. Julien
	Ch. Léoville-Poyferré	St. Julien
	Ch. Montrose	St. Estèphe
	Ch. Pichon-Longueville-Baron	Pauillac
	Ch. Pichon-Lalande	Pauillac
	Ch. Rauzan-Gassies	Margaux
	Ch. Rausan-Ségla	Margaux
Troisièmes Crus	Ch. Boyd-Cantenac	Margaux
	Ch. Calon-Ségur	St. Estèphe
	Ch. Cantenac-Brown	Margaux
	Ch. Desmirail	Margaux
	Ch. Ferrière	Margaux
	Ch. Giscours	Margaux

---

1 Claro (CCC), Colorado Claro (CC), and Colorado (C).
2 Only if it can safely be done without damaging the wrapper leaf.
3 By cutting the cap off with a sharp blade, *not* by piercing.

	Ch. d'Issan	Margaux
	Ch. Kirwan	Margaux
	Ch. Lagrange	St. Julien
	Ch. Langoa	St. Julien
	Ch. La Lagune	Haut-Médoc
	Ch. Malescot-St-Exupéry	Margaux
	Ch. Marquis-d'Alesme	Margaux
	Ch. Palmer	Margaux
Quatrièmes Crus	Ch. Beychevelle	St. Julien
	Ch. Branaire	St. Julien
	Ch. Duhart-Milon-Rothschild	Pauillac
	Ch. Lafon-Rochet	St. Estèphe
	Ch. La Tour-Carnet	Haut-Médoc
	Ch. Marquis-de-Terme	Margaux
	Ch. Pouget	Margaux
	Ch. Prieuré-Lichine	Margaux
	Ch. St-Pierre (formerly Chx. St-Pierre-Bontemps and St.Pierre-Sevaistre)	St. Julien
	Ch. Talbot	St. Julien
Cinquièmes Crus	Ch. Batailley	Pauillac
	Ch. Branaire	St. Julien
	Ch. Camensac	Haut-Médoc
	Ch. Cantemerle	Haut-Médoc
	Ch. Clerc-Milon	Pauillac
	Ch. Cos Labory	St. Estèphe
	Ch. Croizet-Bages	Pauillac
	Ch. Dauzac-Lynch	Margaux
	Ch. du Tertre	Margaux
	Ch. Grand-Puy-Ducasse	Pauillac
	Ch. Grand-Puy-Lacoste	Pauillac
	Ch. Haut-Bages-Libéral	Pauillac
	Ch. Haut-Batailley	Pauillac
	Ch. Lynch-Bages	Pauillac
	Ch. Lynch-Moussas	Pauillac
	Ch. Mouton-Baron-Philippe	Pauillac

1 How should you deal with a finished cigar?
2 If you do not know this book thoroughly, what should you do?

	Ch. Pédesclaux	Pauillac
	Ch. Pontet-Canet	Pauillac

WHITE WINES

Premier Grand Cru	Ch. d'Yquem	Sauternes
Premiers Crus	Ch. Climens	Barsac & Sauternes
	Ch. Coutet	Barsac & Sauternes
	Ch. de Rayne-Vigneau	Sauternes
	Ch. Guiraud	Sauternes
	Clos Haut-Peyraguey	Sauternes
	Ch. Lafaurie-Peyraguey	Sauternes
	Ch. La Tour-Blanche	Sauternes
	Ch. Rabaud-Promis	Sauternes
	Ch. Rieussec	Sauternes
	Ch. Sigalas-Rabaud	Sauternes
	Ch. Suduiraut	Sauternes
Seconds Crus	Ch. Broustet	Barsac & Sauternes
	Ch. Caillou	Barsac & Sauternes
	Ch. d'Arche	Sauternes
	Ch. de Malle	Sauternes
	Ch. Doisy-Daëne	Barsac & Sauternes
	Ch. Doisy-Védrines	Barsac & Sauternes
	Ch. Filhot	Sauternes
	Ch. Lamothe	Sauternes
	Ch. Myrat	Barsac & Sauternes
	Ch. Nairac	Barsac & Sauternes
	Ch. Romer	Sauternes
	Ch. Suau	Barsac & Sauternes

St. Émilion 1955 official classification

Appellation St. Émilion Premier Grand Cru Class´A Contrôlée	Ch. Ausone Ch. Cheval Blanc	

1 Let it expire in an ashtray. If stubbed out its stink will impregnate hair, clothing, and curtains.
2 Read it again!

Appellation St. Émilion
Premier Grand Cru
Classé B Contrôlée

Ch. Beauséjour-Bécot
Ch. Beauséjour-Duffau-Lagarrosse
Ch. Bel-Air
Ch. Canon
Ch. Figeac
Clos Fourtet
Ch. La Gaffelière
Ch. Magdelaine
Ch. Pavie
Ch. Trottevieille

Appellation St. Émilion
Grand Cru Classé
Contrôlée

Ch. l'Angélus
Ch. l'Arrosée
Ch. Baleau
Ch. Balestard-la-Tonnelle
Ch. Bellevue
Ch. Bergat
Ch. Cadet-Bon
Ch. Cadet-Piola
Ch. Canon-La Gaffelière
Ch. Cap-de-Mourlin
Ch. Chapelle-Madeleine
Ch. Chauvin
Ch. Coûtet
Ch. Couvent-des-Jacobins
Ch. Croque-Michotte
Ch. Curé Bon
Ch. Dassault
Ch. Faurie-de-Soutard
Ch. Fonplégade
Ch. Fonroque
Ch. Franc-Mayne
Ch. Grand-Barrail-Lamarzelle-Figeac
Ch. Grand-Corbin
Ch. Grand-Corbin Despagne
Ch. Grand-Mayne
Ch. Grand-Pontet
Ch. Grandes-Murailles

Ch. Guadet-St-Julien
Ch. Haut Corbin
Clos des Jacobins
Ch. Jean-Faure
Ch. La Carte
Ch. La Clotte
Ch. La Cluzière
Ch. La Couspaude
Ch. La Dominique
Clos La Madeleine
Ch. Lamarzelle
Ch. Lamiote
Ch. Larcis-Ducasse
Ch. Larmande
Ch. Laroze
Ch. Lasserre
Ch. La-Tour-Figeac
Ch. La-Tour-du-Pin-Figeac
Ch. Le Châtelet
Ch. Le Couvent
Ch. Le Prieuré
Ch. Matras
Ch. Mauvezin
Ch. Moulin-du-Cadet
Clos Moulin-du-Cadet
Clos de l'Oratoire
Ch. Pavie-Decesse
Ch. Pavie-Macquin
Ch. Pavillon-Cadet
Ch. Petit-Faurie-de-Souchard
Ch. Ripeau
Ch. St-Georges-Côte-Pavie
Clos St-Martin
Ch. Sansonnet
Ch. Soutard
Ch. Tertre-Daugay
Ch. Trimoulet
Ch. Trois Moulins

Ch. Troplong-Mondot
Ch. Villemaurine
Ch. Yon-Figeac

Graves 1959 official classification

RED WINES

Appellation Contrôlée	Graves	Ch. Bouscaut
		Ch. Carbonieux
		Domaine de Chevalier
		Ch. Fieuzal
		Ch. Haut-Bailly
		Ch. Haut-Brion
		Ch. La Mission-Haut-Brion
		Ch. La Tour-Haut-Brion
		Ch. La Tour-Martillac
		Ch. Malartic-Lagravière
		Ch. Olivier
		Ch. Pape-Clément
		Ch. Smith-Haut-Lafitte

WHITE WINES

Appellation Contrôlée	Graves	Ch. Bouscaut
		Ch. Carbonnieux
		Domaine de Chevalier
		Ch. Couhins
		Ch. La Tour-Martillac
		Ch. Laville-Haut-Brion
		Ch. Malartic-Lagravière
		Ch. Olivier
		Ch. Haut-Brion (added 1960)

BURGUNDY

Appellations Grands Crus Contrôlées

Côte de Nuits	*Gevrey-Chambertin (Commune)*
	Le Chambertin

Chambertin-Clos-de-Bèze
Chapelle-Chambertin
Charmes-Chambertin
Griotte-Chambertin
Latricières-Chambertin
Mazis-Chambertin
Mazoyères-Chambertin
Ruchottes-Chambertin
Morey-St-Denis
Bonnes-Mares (also in *Chambolle-Musigny*)
Clos-de-la-Roche
Clos-de-Tart (also in *Chambolle-Musigny*)
Clos-St-Denis
Chambolle-Musigny
Bonnes-Mares (also in *Morey-St-Denis*)
Clos-de-Tart (also in *Morey-St-Denis*)
Les Musigny (including a little white wine)
Vougeot
Clos-de-Vougeot
Vosne-Romanée
Échézeaux
Grands-Échézeaux
La Tâche
Richebourg
Romanée-Conti
Romanée-St-Vivant

Côte de Beaune

Aloxe-Corton
Charlemagne (white wines only, but no wine under this appellation has been marketed for some time)
Corton (red wine and some white wine)
Corton-Charlemagne (white wine only)
Puligny-Montrachet & Chassagne-Montrachet
(white wines only)

Bâtard-Montrachet
Bienvenues-Bâtard-Montrachet
Chevalier-Montrachet
Criots-Bâtard-Montrachet
Le Montrachet

Some Recent Vintages

Bold type indicates an outstanding vintage

Red Bordeaux

Poor	Average	Good
		1961
	1962	
1964		
1965		
		1966
	1967	
1968		
1969		
		1970
	1971	
1972		
	1973	
1974		
		1975
	1976	
1977		
		1978
		1979
	1980	
		1981
		1982
		1983
1984		
		1985

Sauternes

Poor	Average	Good
	1961	
		1962
1964		
1965		
	1966	
		1967
	1969	
		1970
		1971
1972		
1973		
1974		
		1975
		1976
1977		
1978		
	1979	
	1980	
	1981	
	1982	
		1983
1984		
1985		

Champagne – Generally declared vintages

1973	1976	1979	1981	1983
1975	1978	1980	1982	

Red Burgundy

Poor	Average	Good
		1945
		1959
		1964
		1969
	1970	
		1971
	1972	
	1973	
		1976
	1977	
		1978
	1979	
	1980	
1981		
	1982	
		1983
	1984	
		1985

White Burgundy

Poor	Average	Good
		1969
	1970	
		1971
	1972	
	1973	
		1974
	1975	
		1976
	1977	
		1978
1979		
1980		
	1981	
	1982	
		1983
	1984	
		1985

Rhine and Mosel

Poor	Average	Good
	1969	
		1971
	1973	
	1975	
		1976
	1978	
	1979	
1980		
	1981	
	1982	
		1983
	1984	
		1985

Port – Generally declared vintages

1945	1966	1972	1978	1983
1947	1967	1975	1980	**1985**
1955	1970	**1977**	1982	1986

Mixed Drinks

The mixing of drinks is an ancient art – the Greeks and Roman used to mix herbs and spices with their drinks at table. In these days, mixed drinks fall into several categories: punches, hot and cold; wine cups; apéritifs; cocktails; and pick-me-ups.

For punches and cups, the advice given by Colonel Peter Hawker in his *Hints to Young Shooters*, published in 1844, is still the best: 'Here is a recipe in the form of a rhyme which any shallow-headed boy may readily remember:

> One sour
> Two sweet
> Four strong
> Eight weak

But for cold punches, which may by their refreshing nature beguile the consumer, *twenty* weak should be substituted.'

Translation into a detailed recipe for hot punch, this would give:

One sour – the juice of one lemon

Two sweet – double the sour quantity of sugar or honey

Four strong – double the sweet quantity of spirit – say rum, whisky, whiskey or brandy

Eight weak – double the strong quantity of wine, beer, cider or even water. Heat all the ingredients *except the spirit* with spices (usually ginger, cinnamon, nutmeg or allspice as desired) to near boiling-point, but do not boil. Add the spirit and serve in heat-proof glasses. A rum punch is improved if a little brandy is included, and also if a small pat of butter is added to the hot mixture before the spirit.

There is a large permutation of ingredients which may be used, and the results are often given special names: for instance Bishop (Port and Burgundy), Pope (Port and brandy), Glühwein (hard red wine and brandy), and Wassail (Marsala and brandy with the addition of eggs).

For the occasion when a lot of cold, wet friends arrive on the doorstep, here is a recipe for a quick punch:

Heat three bottles of red wine with one bottle of ginger wine and the juice of two lemons, together with a stick of cinnamon. Add a quarter bottle of brandy and serve. (Five minutes, for thirty glasses.)

Cold punches and cups should always be well chilled. Claret or cider cup can be pre-mixed to serve a large number of people, but there are many other long drinks which are usually mixed individually. The following are some examples:

Planters' Punch: Fresh lime, rum and soda.

The Collins's: Fresh lemon or lime, gin and soda. 'John' uses Dutch or London gin; 'Tom' uses sweetened Old Tom gin.

Horses Neck: Gin or whiskey, and ginger ale.

Dog's Nose: Gin and ginger beer: this is a little dog; gin and light ale: this is a big dog. Which is taken may depend upon the size of the one encountered the night before.

Sangria: Sweetened orange juice and red wine.

Shandygaffs: Usually known as shandy. These consist of a half-and-half mixture of bitter beer and either ginger beer or lemonade. 'Lager and Lime' is a modern variation and consists of putting a small quantity of concentrated lime juice into lager.

Redeye: Half tomato juice, half bitter beer. An acquired taste, beloved by French Canadians.

Black Velvet: Half chilled Champagne, half Guinness.

Buck's Fizz: Half chilled Champagne, half orange juice, served in a large goblet with a dash of brandy.

Buck's Head: One part Spanish brandy to three parts fresh orange juice.

Champagne Cocktail: Put a lump of sugar in the bottom of a goblet and shake three drops of angostura bitters on to it; add a measure of brandy and a dash of curaçao. Fill with chilled Champagne. Replenish with straight Champagne.

This marks the division between the long drink, which may be taken at any time of day, and the apéritif or cocktail, taken to sharpen the appetite before a meal. There are thousands of different cocktail recipes; the following are a few of those most likely to be encountered:

Gin and French: Half gin, half dry French vermouth.

Martini: Two parts dry London gin to one part of dry French vermouth.

Dry Martini: Dry London gin with a dash of dry French vermouth.

Bronx: Two parts gin to one part each of sweet Italian vermouth and dry French vermouth, with a dash of orange bitters and a tablespoonful of orange juice.

White Lady: Two parts dry gin to one part each of Cointreau and fresh lemon juice.

Pink Gin: Put three or four drops of angostura bitters in a glass and swirl them round; some like the bitters left in, others like it shaken out. Add gin and water to taste.

Many cocktails are improved by a drop of angostura bitters, which serves to sharpen the flavour of the various ingredients. This is especially true of the Gimlet.

Gimlet: Half gin, half concentrated lime juice.

Screwdriver: Two parts of vodka to one part of orange juice with a half teaspoonful of caster sugar.

Bloody Mary: Three parts tomato juice to one part vodka, with a teaspoonful of Worcester sauce and the same quantity of lemon juice; add a shake of red pepper and celery salt.

Bullshot: Stir two ounces of vodka and a teaspoonful of Worcester sauce, with the juice of half a lemon and a dash of red pepper, into a can of chilled condensed consommé.

Bloodshot: Empty a can of condensed consommé into a jug; refill the can with tomato juice, and add it to the consommé; refill the can with vodka, and add it to the mixture. Add some celery salt, the juice of one lemon, and as many dashes of Tabasco sauce as the cold demands. It tastes much better than it looks and, as 'Golfers' Breakfast', it has despatched many early-morning fourballs happily down the first fairway.

Manhattan: Two parts rye or bourbon whiskey to one part each of dry French vermouth and sweet Italian vermouth. This is the whiskey counterpart of its New York neighbour, the Bronx.

Americano: Two parts of sweet Italian vermouth to one part of Campari.

Sidecar: Two parts brandy to one part each of Cointreau and fresh lemon juice. This is the brandy counterpart of the White Lady.

It cannot be too strongly emphasized that all these cocktails must be *very* well chilled.

Oldfashioned: Rub a lump of sugar on the rind of an orange. Place sugar in the bottom of a tumbler with a slice of orange, and crush the two together with a pestle. Fill the tumbler to the brim with crushed ice. Then fill up the gaps in the ice with bourbon whiskey.

Mint Julep: In a tall tumbler place alternate layers of *crushed* ice and shredded mint leaves until the tumbler is full. Fill up the gaps in the ice with bourbon whiskey.

The Oldfashioned and the Mint Julep are replenished by adding bourbon whiskey until the glass is full again, which means that the drink gets stronger and stronger as the nose gets colder. The Mint Julep is less of a cocktail than a way of life.

It is not usual to serve mixed drinks after dinner, but two deserve mention.

Irish Coffee: In a large goblet put two teaspoonfuls of brown sugar and fill threequarters full with black coffee; stir well. Add Irish whiskey, and immediately float thick cream over the back of a spoon on to the surface, covering the whole. Those mistaking this for Guinness will burn themselves. Variations using brandy or Scotch whisky are called by appropriate names.

Pousse-café: An old Victorian seduction trick which consisted of pouring coloured liqueurs of different specific gravities into a special-shaped glass and inviting the admiring young lady to drink the multicoloured result. This 'Pousse-café' is very pretty to look at, and rather alcoholic. The order is as follows: Crème de Cacao; Blue Curaçao, Yellow Chartreuse; Maraschino; Bénédictine; Green Chartreuse; Cognac.

On occasions when the 'morning after' is tiresome, the following recipes may help to redress the situation:

Prairie Oysters: These are for the really unwell, and here are two of several variations:

Oyster 1: One ounce of cognac and one teaspoonful each of wine vinegar and Worcester sauce; add a dash of red pepper. Pour this mixture over a whole raw egg and drink without breaking the yolk.

Oyster 2: To a can of tomato juice add four dashes of angostura bitters and a dash of Worcester sauce. Float a whole raw egg on top and help the afflicted to drink it, before it looks at him.

Port and Brandy: This has no name, but is very soothing to the stomach.

Enzian: A spirit, sold under this name, flavoured with the bitter root of the giant yellow gentian of the Jura mountains. Most effective, and definitely not habit-forming.

A Short Bibliography

Allen, H. Warner. *A History of Wine* (London: Faber & Faber, 1961).

Anderson, B. *Pocket Guide to Italian Wines* (London: Mitchell Beazley, 1987).

Baillie, Frank. *The Beer Drinker's Companion* (London: David and Charles, 1973).

Bezzant, Norman. *The Book of Wine* (London: Ward Lock, 1988).

Broadbent, J. M. *Wine Tasting* (London: Christies Wine Publications, 1977).

Burroughs, D. & Bezzant, N. *Wine Regions of the World* (London: Heinemann, 1988).

Clarke, J. *Table and Bar* (London: Edward Arnold, 1987).

Cossart, Noel. *Madeira, The Island Vineyard* (London: Christies' Wine Publications, 1984).

Foulkes, N. *The Illustrated Guide to Wine* (London: W. H. Smith exclusive, 1986).

Hallgarten, Peter. *Liqueurs* (London: Wine & Spirit Publications, 1967).

Jeffs, J. *Sherry* (London: Faber, 1961).

Johnson, Hugh. *Wine* (London: Thomas Nelson & Sons, 1973).

——. *World Atlas of Wine* (London: Maison Fondée/Mitchell Beazley, 1977).

Lichine, Alexis. *An Encyclopaedia of Wines and Spirits* (London: Cassell Ltd., 1987).

Miles, J. G., ed. *Innkeeping* (London: Barrie & Jenkins, 1972).

Ordish, George. *The Great Wine Blight* (London: J. M. Dent & Sons, 1972).

Robertson, G. *Port* (London: Faber 1978).

Protz, Roger *The Great British Beer Book* (London: Impact Books, 1987).

Robinson, Jancis. *The Demon Drink* (London: Mitchell Beazley, 1988).

Stevenson, T. *Champagne* (London: Sotheby's, 1986).

Glossary and Pronunciation Guide

Abboccato, *abokahtoh,* Italian term meaning sweet

Acetic, tasting of vinegar

Acetobacter, *asseetohbakter,* an aerobic bacterium containing enzymes which convert the ethyl alcohol of wine into acetic acid (vinegar)

Acid, a desirable constituent of wine to balance alcohol and sweetness. The amount is important: too little and the wine will be flat; too much and it will be tart like green apples

Advocaat, *advohkah*

Albariza, *albareethuh*

Aloxe-Corton, *aloss-kortaw*

Alsace, *alsass*

Alvarhão, *alvaruhn*

Alvarinho, *alvareenyoo*

Amontillado, *amonteeyahdoh*

Anãda, *anyahdah*

Anjou, *awnzhoo*

Aramon, *aramaw*

Armagnac, *armanyak*

Aroma, the taste of wine discovered in the mouth

Artisan Growths, grouped with Bourgeois Growths, they ranked in the 1855 classification of the Gironde between the Great Growths and the Exceptional Growths

Astringency, the dry feeling produced in the mouth, particularly at the sides of the tongue, caused by the high tannin content of young wines

Auslese, *owsslayzuh*

Ausone (Ch.), *ohzohn*

Bad Dürkheim, *bad* deerk*hime*

Bad Kreuznach, *bad* kroyts*nak*

Bagaçeira, *baga*sayra

Baked, an adjective applied to the bouquet and aroma of wines originating in hot countries, which taste cooked and earthy

Barbera, *bar*bair*uh*

Barrique, *bareek,* a Bordeaux hogshead, containing about

225 litres (48 gallons), yielding about 24 cases

Beaujolais, *bohzholay*

Beaune, Côte de, *koht de bohn*

Big, of a full-bodied, mouth-filling wine with plenty of alcohol and flavour

Bodega, *bodayguh*

Body, describing the mouth-filling qualities of a wine

Bottle sizes, One bottle contains 75 cl (Champagne 80 cl); one half bottle contains 37.5 cl (Champagne 40 cl). The Magnum equals two bottles, the Tappit-hen three bottles, the Jeroboam four bottles, the Rehoboam six bottles, and the Methuselah eight bottles. The Salmanezah (twelve bottles), Balthazar (sixteen bottles) and the Nebuchadnezzar (twenty bottles) are not now made

Bouquet, *bookay,* the smell of wine discovered by the nose

Bourgeois Growths, *boorz-hwah,* see Artisan Growths

Bourgeuil, *boorguh-ee*

Brouillis, *brooyee*

Brut, *broo*

Bual, *booal*

Butt, a Spanish cask (particularly of sherry) containing just under 500 litres (about 108 gallons), and yielding 51 to 53 cases

Cabernet Franc, *kaburnay fraw*

Cabernet-Sauvignon, *kaburnay-sohveenyaw*

Cacao, Crème de, *krem de kakow*

Calon-Ségur (Ch.), *kalawsay-goor*

Cambium, the extremely thin layer beneath the bark of a twig, branch or trunk, which must be joined between the stock and scion for a graft to succeed

Carignan, *kareenyaw*

Carton, Case, the standard selling unit of wines and spirits, containing 12 bottles, 24 half bottles or 6 magnums, amounting to 9 litres. A carton of Bordeaux bottles weighs 22kg (48lbs) and measures 26 × 39 × 33cm (10″ × 15″ × 13″)

Chablis, *shablee*

Chai, *shay*

Chambolle-Musigny, *shombol-moozeeny*

Chardonnay, *shardonay*

Chassagne-Montrachet, *shassine-mawnrashay*

Chasselas, *shasuhlah*

Château, *shatto,* literally *castle,* applied to a French mansion and to its vineyard. Abbreviated to 'Ch.' See also 'Domaine'

Châteauneuf-du-Pape,
shattohnuf-doo-pap
Chenin Blanc, *shenan blaw*
Chianti, *keeanti*
Chinon, *sheenaw*
Cinsault, *sansoh*
Classico, klas*seekoh*
Climens, (Ch.), *Kleemaw*
Coaster, a tray, sometimes on wheels, for holding a decanter or bottle, to be passed round a dining-table
Cognac, *konyak*
Cointreau, *kwahntroh*
Condrieu, *kondree-uh*
Corky, a rotten, persistent smell, caused by a cork that has gone bad
Côte d'Or, *koht dor*
Coutet (Ch.), *kootay*
Criadera, *kreeah*dairuh
Curaçao, *kyoorasoh*

Deidesheim, *die-des-hime*
Doisy-Daëne, *dwahzee-den*
Domaine, the Burgundian equivalent of a château
Dordogne, *dordoyn*
Doux, *doo*
Ducru-Beaucaillou   (Ch.), *dookroo-bohk-eye-yoo*
d'Yquem, (Ch.) *deekum*

Eau-de-vie-de-marc,
ohduhveeduhmah
Edelfäule, *adelfoyluh*

Eiswein, *icevine*
Entre-deux-Mers,
awntruh-duh-mair
Esters, compounds of alcohols and organic acids which give flavour to wines and spirits

Garganega, *gargan*ayga
Gay-Lussac, *gay-loossak,* a French scientist who defined the process of fermentation chemically. One metric system of describing alcohol strength (% by volume) is named after him
Genever, *henayver,* Holland's gin
Gevrey-Chambertin,
zhevrayshawmbertan
Gewürztraminer,
gevoorstraminer
Grand Marnier, *graw marneeay*
Graves, *grahv*
Grenache, *grenahsh*
Grolleau (Groslot), *grohloh*
Guyot Double, *geeoh doobluh*

Haut-Médoc, *oh-maydok*
Hermitage, *ermeetahzh*
Hogshead, a general term for a cask of about 225 litres (50 gallons), having different names and capacities in different regions. A hogshead of sherry equals half a butt, a hogshead of Port equals half a pipe, a

hogshead of brandy equals half a puncheon. See also 'Barrique' and 'Pièce'

Hospices de Baune, *ospeess de bohn*

Infusion, filtering hot or cold wine, spirit or water through a bed of flavouring herbs, as in making coffee

Jerez, *hereth*
Jura, *zhooruh*

Kiedrich, *keedrik*
Kirsch, *keersh*
Kümmel, *kimmel*

Lafite (Ch.), *lafeet*
Léoville-Barton (Ch.), *layohveel-bartaw*
Lees, sediment in the bottom of a cask, vat or bottle; eliminated by filtering, racking or decanting
Liebfraumilch, *leebfrowmilk*
Light, light in body, as opposed to full-bodied
Lynch-Bages (Ch.), *lansh-bahzh*

Maceration, soaking flavouring herbs in hot or cold wine, spirit or water, as in making tea
Mâconnais, *makonay*
Maderized, 'like the wines of Madeira'; this is a libel on the name of a fine wine. Both wines have a 'burnt' flavour and a brown colour, but the flavour and colour of maderized wines are not clean, being caused by oxidasic degeneration through excessive exposure to light and air

Malbec, *malbek*
Malmsey, *mahmsay*
Manzanilla, *manzaneeyuh*
Maraschino, *maraskeenoh*
Marc, *mah*
Margaux (Ch.), *margoh*
Médoc, *maydok*
Merlot, *mairloh*
Meursault, *muhsoh*
Midi, *meedee*
Mourvèdre, *moorvedruh*
Müller-Thurgau, *miller-toorgow*
Muscadet (Gamay Blanc), *mooskaday*
Muscat, *mooskah*

Nahe, *na-huh*
Niederhausen, *neederhowsen*
Nierstein, *neershtine*
Nuits, Côte de, *koht duh nwee*
Nuits St. George, *nwee san zhorzh*

Oestrich, *uhstrik*
Orvieto, *orveeaytoh*
Ouzo, *oozoh*
Oxidized, a burnt, raisiny smell and taste of wine that

has been exposed to the air, perhaps through faulty storage. See also 'Maderized'

Pauillac, *poyyak*

Pedro Ximenes, *paydroh himaynes*

Periquita, *perikeeta*

Pétillant, *payteeyaw,* slightly sparkling; less than 1.5 atmospheres pressure

Picpoul, *pikpool*

Pièce, *pee-ess,* a Burgundy or Champagne hogshead of about 225 litres (50 gallons)

Pinot, *peenoh*

Pinot Gris, *peenoh gree*

Pinot Noir, *peenoh nwar*

Pipe, a cask, longer and thinner than the Spanish butt, containing about 455 litres (100 gallons). A pipe of Port or Tarragona holds 522 litres (115 gallons); a pipe of Madeira or Marsala holds 420 litres (92 to 93 gallons)

Pommard, *pommar*

Portacask, a shipping container made of fibreglass, lined with stainless steel, holding 26.4 hl (580 gallons)

Pouilly-Fuissé, *pooyee-fweessay*

Pricked, acetic

Puligny-Montrachet, *pooleenyee-mawnrashay*

Puncheon, a cask. A puncheon of brandy holds 545 litres (120 gallons); a puncheon of rum is normally 422 litres (93 gallons), but varies considerably

Qualitätswein mit Prädikat, *kvalitaytsvine mit praydikat*

Quinta, *keentah*

Rayas, *ryeas*

Rheingau, *rinegow*

Riesling, *reessling* (the most frequently mispronounced wine word!)

Rioja, *reeohka*

Robust, full-bodied, rich in alcohol and/or tannin. Such wines can stand travel well, but may need ageing to become palatable

Saar, *zah*

Safrap, a steel container lined with plastic, holding 24.4 hl (535 gallons)

St. Émilion, *santaymeelyaw*

St. Julien, *sangzhoolyan*

Santenay, *sawntenay*

Saumur, *sohmoor*

Sauternes, *sohtern*

Schaumwein, *showmvine*

Schloss Böckelheim, *schloss buhrkelhime*

Sémillon, *saymeeyaw*

Sercial, *sershal*

Soave, *soh-ahvay*

Spätlese, *shpaytlayze*

Suduirant (Ch.), *sooderoh*

Syrah, *seerah*

Tailles, *tie*

Tannins, phenolic substances occurring in the stalk, skin and pips of the grape (and in many other plants, especially the wood from which casks are made). Tannins help to preserve the wine and to clear it, besides influencing colour

Tart, excessively acid

Tokay, *tokkoy*

Tonneau, *tonnoh,* a selling measure amounting to four hogsheads (900 litres), yielding about 96 cases. There is no cask or vat of this name

Ugni Blanc, *oonyee blaw*

Urzig, *oortsik*

Valpolicella, *valpolichella*

Verdelho, *vair*daylyo

Verdicchio, *verdeekyoh*

Vigneron, *veenyeraw*

Vin de Goutte, *van de goot*

Vin (Rouge, Blanc, Rosé), *van roozh, van blaw, van rohzay,* wines without any distinguishing appellation. These vins ordinaires can be excellent. Eighty per cent of all wines consumed are of this order. The 1914 soldier's pronunciation of 'vin blanc' originated the term 'plonk'

Vinhos Verdes, *veenyoosh vairdsh*

Vosne-Romanée, *vohn-rohmanay*

Vougeot, *voozhoh*

Voovray, *voovray*

Wehlen, *vaylen*

Winkel, *vingkel*

Worms, *voorms*

INDEX

Principal entries are numbered in **Bold type,** references to maps, charts, and diagrams in *Italic type,* and other entries in plain type.